THE RIGHT TO STRIKE IN INTERNATIONAL LAW

This monograph was originally developed as a direct response to the claim made by members of the 'Employers Group' at the 2012 International Labour Conference, namely that the right to strike is not protected in international law, and in particular by ILO Convention 87 on the right to freedom of association.

The group's apparent aim was to sow sufficient doubt as to the existence of an internationally protected right so that governments might seek to limit or prohibit the right to strike at the national level while still claiming compliance with their international obligations. In consequence, some governments have seized on the employers' arguments to justify new limitations on that right.

The Right to Strike in International Law not merely refutes this claim but is the only complete and exhaustive analysis on this subject. Based on deep legal research, it finds that there is simply no credible basis for the claim that the right to strike does not enjoy the protection of international law; indeed, the authors demonstrate that it has attained the status of customary international law.

The Right to Strike in International Law

Jeffrey Vogt
Janice Bellace
Lance Compa
KD Ewing
Lord Hendy QC
Klaus Lörcher
and
Tonia Novitz

·HART·
OXFORD · LONDON · NEW YORK · NEW DELHI · SYDNEY

HART PUBLISHING

Bloomsbury Publishing Plc

Kemp House, Chawley Park, Cumnor Hill, Oxford, OX2 9PH, UK

1385 Broadway, New York, NY 10018, USA

HART PUBLISHING, the Hart/Stag logo, BLOOMSBURY and the Diana logo are
trademarks of Bloomsbury Publishing Plc

First published in Great Britain 2020

A catalogue record for this book is available from the British Library.

Library of Congress Cataloging-in-Publication data

Names: Vogt, Jeffrey, author.

Title: The right to strike in international law / Jeffrey Vogt, Janice Bellace, Lance Compa,
KD Ewing, Lord Hendy QC, Klaus Lörcher, Tonia Novitz.

Description: Chicago : Hart Publishing, an imprint of Bloomsbury Publishing, 2020. |
Includes bibliographical references and index.

Identifiers: LCCN 2019050421 (print) | LCCN 2019050422 (ebook) |
ISBN 9781509933556 (hardback) | ISBN 9781509933570 (Epub)

Subjects: LCSH: Right to strike. | Strikes and lockouts—Law and legislation. |
Labor laws and legislation, International.

Classification: LCC K1744 .R54 2020 (print) | LCC K1744 (ebook) | DDC 344.01/892—dc23

LC record available at https://lccn.loc.gov/2019050421

LC ebook record available at https://lccn.loc.gov/2019050422

ISBN: HB: 978-1-50993-355-6
        ePDF: 978-1-50993-356-3
        ePub: 978-1-50993-357-0

Typeset by Compuscript Ltd, Shannon
Printed and bound in Great Britain by CPI Group (UK) Ltd, Croydon CR0 4YY

To find out more about our authors and books visit www.hartpublishing.co.uk. Here you will find
extracts, author information, details of forthcoming events and the option to sign up for our newsletters.

[P]rotecting the right to strike is not simply about States fulfilling their legal obligations. It is also about them creating democratic and equitable societies that are sustainable in the long run. The concentration of power in one sector – whether in the hands of government or business – inevitably leads to the erosion of democracy, and an increase in inequalities and marginalization with all their attendant consequences. The right to strike is a check on this concentration of power. I deplore the various attempts made to erode the right to strike at national and multilateral levels.

Maina Kiai, UN Special Rapporteur on Freedom of Association and Assembly (2011–17), 9 March 2017

PREFACE

Why the Right to Strike is Essential

Long before the emergence of any concept of human rights, working people collectively withheld their labour in order to overcome relations of oppression.[1] And so it continues. The modern histories of many countries record important strikes which, in the nineteenth and twentieth centuries, shifted the balance of power in the workplace and in society more broadly, at least for a time, towards greater equality (though often only for some). These strikes were led by militant women and men, working in mines and mills, in fields and factories, who risked their jobs and often their lives so that they might live with a modicum of dignity. In the Americas, the rebellions of enslaved workers, which were strikes at the most fundamental level, led to their collective emancipation and the abolition of the slave trade;[2] in the years following, black farm workers organised unions and went on strike throughout the southern States to improve wages and working conditions. Strikes have also led to the ouster of authoritarian regimes around the world.[3] It is no exaggeration, therefore, to claim that strikes have repeatedly changed the course of human history.

What is the Right to Strike?

Though lacking a precise legal definition, the common elements of the right certainly include: (1) the withdrawal of labour by workers (2) which is coordinated and (usually) simultaneous.[4] Beyond these two core elements, there is some

---

[1] The first recorded strike is commonly thought to be that of tomb-builders in Deir el Medina, Egypt in 1158 BCE. They apparently went on strike over repeated late payment of wages. See R David, *The Pyramid Builders of Ancient Egypt, A Modern Investigation of Pharaoh's Workforce* (London, Routledge, 1996) 73–75. With regard to strikes in ancient Rome see, eg, R MacMullen, 'A Note on Roman Strikes' (1963) 58 *The Classical Journal* 269. See also M Kittner, *Arbeitskampf – Geschichte, Recht, Gegenwart* (München, CH Beck, 2005).

[2] See, eg, E Loomis, *A History of America in Ten Strikes* (New York, New Press, 2018) 29–48.

[3] See ILO, *Report of the Commission of Inquiry* instituted under Article 26 of the Constitution of the ILO to examine the complaint on the observance by *Poland* of the Freedom of Association and Protection of the Right to Organise Convention, 1948 (No 87), and the Right to Organise and Collective Bargaining Convention, 1949 (No 98) *Official Bulletin*, Special Supplement Series B, Vol LXVII (1984) para 49; and *Report of the Fact-Finding Conciliation Commission on Freedom of Association concerning the Republic of South Africa* (Geneva, ILO, 1992).

[4] See, eg, T Novitz, *International and European Protection of the Right to Strike* (Oxford, Oxford University Press, 2003) 6. In this way, a strike is distinct from other forms of protest, like a public demonstration, which does not necessarily result in the cessation of work.

variation in the precise manner in which the right is formulated and regulated in legal systems around the world.

For example, while most legal systems treat strike action as a right, in others it is understood as a freedom, meaning that rather than a positive right, the law provides striking workers with immunities from the legal sanctions that an employer would otherwise have available in, for example, contract or tort law.[5] Examples of the latter include Austria, Japan, Australia and the United Kingdom. Some countries, such as Germany and Argentina, started by recognising a freedom and over time recognised a right. In some legal systems, the right to strike is an individual right, which is exercised at the initiative of the individual though almost always in concert with others.[6] The French system perhaps best represents this model, where the decision of a union is not required to authorise its exercise. Similarly, in Italy, Uruguay, South Africa and Hungary, the right requires no authorisation and may be exercised by any group of workers, unionised or not. In others, the right is a collective right which may only be exercised at the initiative of a trade union.[7] The German model exemplifies this approach. There, only a trade union is empowered to call a strike, and only if the union has the 'capacity to bargain'. In Greece and Turkey, the right to strike is also vested solely in a trade union.

In the end, the right to strike is probably best understood as a hybrid right, or what legal scholar Bernard Waas calls a 'double fundamental right', with individual and collective characteristics – both of which are protected.[8,9] In nearly 100 countries, the right to strike enjoys constitutional protection, while in nearly all countries it is protected in labour law.[10]

The Strike and its Philosophical Foundations

Just as there is some diversity in the regulation of the right to strike at the national level, there is also a diversity of opinion on its philosophical foundations.[11] In the classic liberal view, espoused by John Stuart Mill, 'from [the] liberty of each individual, follows the liberty, within the same limits, of combination among individuals; freedom to unite, for any purpose not involving harm to others'.[12] That is,

---

[5] See, eg, B Waas, *The Right to Strike, a Comparative View* (Alphen aan den Rijn, Woulters Kluwer 2014) 9–10.

[6] ibid, 14.

[7] ibid, 14–15.

[8] ibid, 8.

[9] This is the case under the European Convention on Human Rights, exemplified in *Hrvatski Liječnički Sindikat v Croatia* App No 36701/09 (27 November 2014) para 59; and *Ognevenko v Russia* App No 44873/09 (20 November 2018).

[10] See Annex III of this book.

[11] We do not attempt a comprehensive survey here but present some of the most cited arguments.

[12] JS Mill, *On Liberty* (Kitchener, Batoche Books, 2001) 16.

the full extent of individual liberty may be exercised by individuals acting together, but to the extent that it does not affect the liberty interests of others. Mill saw such freedom exercised to form voluntary combinations (unions) for the purpose of raising wages as a legitimate end, and that the right to strike was the instrument through which freedom of association was given effect. However, Mill saw strikes not as a fundamental challenge to the ordering of the capitalist free market but as a means of making it work more efficiently. He held that 'Strikes, therefore, and the trade societies which render strikes possible, are for these various reasons not a mischievous, but on the contrary, a valuable part of the existing machinery of society'.[13] Strikes, possible through combinations, were the means by which to discover the market rate of labour – they did not themselves challenge the market.

Legal theorist Sheldon Leader has argued that the right to strike is derived, both directly and indirectly, from the right to freedom of association, and, further, that the nature of the relationship between the two depends on the aspect of the right to strike in question.[14] For Leader, direct derivation would imply that the right to strike is a subset of the right to freedom of association, while indirect derivation could be understood as meaning the right to strike is a means of furthering the right to freedom of association.[15] He identified some aspects of the right to strike, which are constant, such as its collective quality and the fact that strikes are meant to exert pressure, which are directly related to the right to freedom of association and therefore deserve the highest protection in law.[16] These aspects of the right to strike are founded on the principle of symmetry between individual and collective action, a special status to be given to collective action, and that the right to freedom of association merits special interpretation.[17] Variable aspects, such as whether the strike is the exclusive domain of a union, or whether strikes must be

---

[13] JS Mill, *Principles of Political Economy with some of their Applications to Social Philosophy*, William James Ashley (ed), 7th edn (London, Longmans, Green and Co, 1909) 938. For further discussion on Mill and the derivation of the right to strike from the right to freedom of association, see S Leader, 'Can You Derive a Right to Strike from the Right to Freedom of Association?' (2009–10) 15 *Canadian Labour & Employment Law Journal* 271, 279.

[14] Leader, ibid; and S Leader, *Freedom of Association: A Study in Labour Law and Political Theory* (New Haven, CT, Yale University Press, 1992) ch 11.

[15] Leader, 'Can You Derive a Right to Strike from the Right to Freedom of Association?' (n 13 above) 273.

[16] ibid, 276–77.

[17] ibid, 279–86. The symmetry argument is based on the notion borrowed from Mill 'that from the liberty of each individual follows the liberty, within the same limits, of combination among individuals'. Thus, there should be no penalty in law for undertaking collectively what should be lawful if done individually. The argument on the special status for collective action recognises that right to act collectively may require being entitled to do more with others than when acting alone. Here, Leader cites the fact that the refusal to work through collective action results in the suspension of the employment relationship, while alone the employment relationship would be said to have been terminated. This rests on a claim of equality which 'calls for the equivalent treatment of a basic interest by different domains of law' namely torts and contracts. The argument with regard to the special status of freedom of association. Here, Leader identifies a qualified right, recognising that, among other justifications, in some cases it will be legitimate for one group to use its freedom to limit the freedom of another in order to overcome an imbalance in power.

related to a collective bargaining process, are matters which are indirectly related to the right to freedom of association, and as such legislatures have more latitude to regulate.[18] Regardless of the kind of derivation, Leader urges the recognition of a right to equal enjoyment of the right to strike.[19]

For James Gray Pope, the right to strike is founded on the freedom from forced or compulsory labour, and in particular finds it protected by the Thirteenth Amendment of the US Constitution, which abolished slavery and involuntary servitude (with the important exception as punishment for a crime, which was used to perpetuate the compulsory labour of black citizens long afterwards).[20] While the US Supreme Court has yet to rule on the right to strike under the Thirteenth Amendment, Pope argues that the principles of interpretation articulated in the Supreme Court decision *Pollock v Williams* are instructive, 'namely that a claimed right should be protected if it is necessary to provide workers with the "power below" and employers the "incentive above" to prevent a harsh overlordship or unwholesome conditions of work'.[21] Pope explains that the freedom from involuntary servitude depends on workers possessing the 'power below' to ensure that employers provide decent work. If this cannot be accomplished by the labour market, ie, by going elsewhere, then 'nonmarket rights' such as the right to freedom of association, is necessary, including to engage in concerted activity – namely to strike.[22]

For Alan Bogg and Cynthia Estlund, the right to strike 'rests on a dynamic normative interaction between three basic liberties ... to leave one's employment, to associate with others and to express what one thinks'.[23] These liberties, which they call 'voice, association and exit' are inextricably linked to form a 'republican right to strike'. As they explain:

> The expressive dimension of striking may warrant heightened legal protection because of its proximity to republican concerns about involuntary servitude. Collective withdrawals of labour might attract special protection under freedom of association precisely because of their expressive quality. The expressive dimension of a strike might require strong protections against private reprisals.[24]

Bogg and Estlund ground their theory on Philip Pettit's theory of freedom as nondomination, not only from the state, as in classical liberal thinking, but from private actors as well. As freedom requires equal civic status, such freedom is limited when

---

[18] ibid, 277–79, 286–94.

[19] ibid, 275.

[20] JG Pope, 'Contract, Race, and Freedom of Labor in the Constitutional Law of "Involuntary Servitude"' (2010) 119 *Yale Law Journal* 1474.

[21] ibid, 1566, citing 322 US 4, 18 (1944).

[22] ibid, 1566–67.

[23] See A Bogg and C Estlund, 'The Right to Strike and Contestatory Citizenship' in H Collins, G Lester and V Mantouvalou (eds), *Philosophical Foundations of Labour Law* (Oxford, Oxford University Press, 2019) 230.

[24] ibid.

one party has the ability to arbitrarily interfere in the choices of others. To attain a state of equal civic status requires the protection of 'basic liberties' between private individuals. They explain that the protection of the recourse to strike action is not simply a 'safeguard for insulating the employees "basic liberties" from private domination: it is itself derived from those "basic liberties"'. They note however that the question of domination is central to the understanding of the strike, even when mediated through the concept of basic liberties.[25]

Finally, Alex Gourevitch recently argued that the right to strike is fundamentally a right to resist the 'structural element of oppression in class societies'.[26] Framed this way, the right goes beyond one party gaining leverage over another at the bargaining table. Rather, the strike is a means to resist fundamentally the (intentionally) unequal ordering of the economy and society, which is expressed in three ways. First, a large majority of the population has no choice but to sell its labour to a small minority which has no such obligation (due to wealth accumulated or inherited), who may choose to work or not. Secondly, workers are forced to become subordinated to an employer (de jure or de facto). The third concerns the distributive impacts of structural and interpersonal oppression, which limit wealth accumulation and deepen dependency on the employer, constraining the freedom of one class by another.[27] The right to strike is thus framed as an effective means for reclaiming freedom against inherently illegitimate limitations.

While divergent in some respects, all these foundations share the common view that there is an asymmetry in power between labour and capital. For most, recognition of the right to strike is necessary to attain a status of equality by overcoming relations of domination – at least in the workplace, if not more broadly.

The Strike and Democracy

Of course, the protection of the right to strike is essential not only for the promotion of workplace democracy, but democracy writ large. Former UN Special Rapporteur for Freedom of Association and Assembly, Maina Kiai, importantly drew a direct link between the right to strike and enduring democracies.[28] Indeed, on numerous occasions, strikes have played an important role in the

---

[25] ibid, 231.

[26] A Gourevitch, 'The Right to Strike: A Radical View' (2018) 112 *American Political Science Review* 905.

[27] ibid, 909.

[28] UN Press Release, 'UN rights expert: Fundamental right to strike must be preserved', 9 March 2017. ('[P]rotecting the right to strike is not simply about States fulfilling their legal obligations. It is also about them creating democratic and equitable societies that are sustainable in the long run. The concentration of power in one sector – whether in the hands of government or business – inevitably leads to the erosion of democracy, and an increase in inequalities and marginalization with all their attendant consequences'.) Available at: www.ohchr.org/EN/NewsEvents/Pages/DisplayNews.aspx?NewsID=21328&LangID=E.

destabilisation of repressive or authoritarian governments, and ushered in new, democratic possibilities. Trade unions have accomplished this because of their organisation, structure and capacity for mobilisation, based on common workers' interests and solidarity. The union's ability to strike also disrupts the capitalist accumulation on which the maintenance of the status quo depends.[29]

For example, political scientist Ruth Collier has underscored the important role of trade unions in the third democratisation wave (mid- 1960s to 1980s) in Latin America and Southern Europe. Rather than seeing democratisation as resulting from the strategic choices of elites, as many had posited, she explained that labour's role was central and not indirect and ancillary to workplace demands:

> [I]n all third wave cases the working class was an important actor in the political opposition, explicitly demanding a democratic regime. Beyond that, labor often played an autonomous role in affecting the rhythm and pace of the transitions, and in some cases working-class protest for democracy contributed to a climate of ungovernability and delegitimisation that led directly to a general destabilization of authoritarian regimes.[30]

In ushering out the old order, the role of strikes was key. She notes:

> In one pattern of third wave democratization, characterizing Peru, Argentina, and Spain, massive labor protests destabilized authoritarianism and opened the way for the establishment of democracy. In these cases, the working class was the initial and most important anti-authoritarian actor, leading an offensive in the form of strikes and protests against the regime. Regime incumbents were unable to ignore such working-class opposition or formulate a response to these challenges from below.[31]

The Arab Spring represents perhaps the most recent democratisation wave, and one in which trade unions were important actors.[32] Indeed, the participation of the *Union Générale Tunisienne du Travail* (UGTT) rank and file in strikes in the years preceding the Arab Spring and in its early days following the self-immolation of Mohammed Bouazizi was critical to the success of the revolution and the ouster of President Ben Ali.[33] Afterwards, the UGTT pushed the transitional

---

[29] JS Valenzuela. 'Labor Movement in Transitions to Democracy: A Framework for Analysis' (1989) 21 *Comparative Politics* 445. See also, E Huber, D Rueschemeyer and JD Stephens, 'The Impact of Economic Development on Democracy' (1993) 7 *Journal of Economic Perspectives* 71 (finding that class formation during periods of economic development (and formation of unions) was an important factor in restraining the preferences of landed elites, which was necessary to sustain political democracy).

[30] See RB Collier and J Mahoney, 'Labor and Democratization: Comparing the First and Third Waves in Europe and Latin America' (1995) Institute for Research on Labor and Employment, UC Berkeley, Working Paper No 62, 2. Collier developed this paper into her seminal work, *Paths Toward Democracy: Working Class and Elites in Western Europe and South America* (Cambridge, Cambridge University Press, 1999).

[31] ibid, 36.

[32] See A Alexander and M Bassiouny, *Bread, Freedom, Social Justice: Workers & the Egyptian Revolution* (London, Zed Books, 2014); see also J Beinin, *Workers and Thieves* (Stanford, CA, Stanford University Press, 2016).

[33] See G Del Panta, 'Labour Movements and the Arab Uprisings: Comparing Egypt, Morocco, and Tunisia', available at: www.sisp.it/docs/convegno2016/203_sisp2016_partecipazione-movimenti-sociali.pdf.

government to make fundamental changes which helped prevent a return to the old order.[34] In Egypt, despite few trade unions outside the official, pro-regime Egyptian Trade Union Federation (ETUF), the number and length of strikes by independent unions had steadily climbed in the period leading up to 2011. In the days before, during and after the 'Days of Rage', trade union strikes throughout the country, in the public and private sectors, contributed to the destabilisation of the Mubarak regime and led to his eventual ouster. The revolution was short-lived, however. With a small and fractured independent labour movement unable to push back, the military toppled the failing Morsi government and resumed control in 2013.[35]

The Demise of the Right to Strike?

Until recently, the exercise of the right to strike had been on the decline in many industrialised countries, in some to the point of near obsolescence. In the United States, for example, there had been a long-term decline in the frequency of major strikes, from a peak of 470 strikes in 1952 involving 2.75 million workers and resulting in nearly 49 million lost work days to seven strikes in 2017, involving 25,000 workers and 440,00 lost work days.[36] A similar pattern is observed in the United Kingdom, where the 1979 'Winter of Discontent' (29.5 million lost work days) and the 1984–85 miners' strike (27 million lost work days) were significant exceptions to an otherwise long-term decline in strike action since the 1926 General Strike.[37] A similar story is repeated through much of the 'Anglo-Saxon' world, including Canada, Australia and New Zealand, where both the frequency and duration of strikes peaked in the late 1970s and early 1980s.[38] Of course, there are outliers like France, where the frequency of strikes has been and continues to be relatively high. The decline can be explained in some countries by regressive labour reforms (eg, the United Kingdom) which made the resort to the strike far more difficult, while in others (eg, the United States), policy changes, such as the exploitation of the absence of legal restriction on the use of replacement workers was used by the

---

[34] See, eg, T Schmidinger, *Unionism and Revolution in the Arab World, in Trade Unions in the Democratic Process: 10 International Contributions* (Dusseldorf, Hans-Böckler-Stiftung, 2013).

[35] Del Panta (n 33 above) 12–17; see also, Alexander and Bassiouny (n 32 above); and Beinin (n 32 above).

[36] US Department of Labor, Bureau of Labor Statistics, 'Work stoppages involving 1,000 or more workers, 1947–2017', available at: www.bls.gov/news.release/wkstp.t01.htm.

[37] UK, Office for National Statistics, 'Labour Disputes in the UK: 2017, Historical Context', available at: www.ons.gov.uk/employmentandlabourmarket/peopleinwork/workplacedisputesand workingconditions/articles/labourdisputes/2017#historical-context.

[38] E Tucker, 'Can Worker Voice Strike Back? Law and the Decline and Uncertain Future of Strikes' (2013) Comparative Research in Law & Political Economy Research Paper No 58, available at: www. digitalcommons.osgoode.yorku.ca/cgi/viewcontent.cgi?referer=&httpsredir=1&article=1300&context =cipe.

US government in the PATCO (air traffic controllers') strike in 1981, which gave employers in the private sector a green light to do the same.[39]

With the decline in the power of unions to bargain collectively and to strike, constraints on income inequality have obviously loosened. The result has been historically high wealth and income inequality, and diminished democracy in much of the industrialised world. Indeed, while corporate executives saw extraordinary rises in wages, for most workers, the real wage is largely the same as it was 40 years ago in terms of purchasing power.[40] It is well understood that the rise in income inequality is in part the result of a sharp decline in labour's power.[41] In the United States, research demonstrates that unions at their peak had the ability to constrain income inequality not only for their members, but to the company, the industry and the broader workforce.[42]

As Oxfam International reported in 2019, 'The wealth of the world's billionaires increased by $900bn in the last year alone, or $2.5bn a day. Meanwhile the wealth of the poorest half of humanity, 3.8 billion people fell by 11%'.[43] According to the Swiss bank, UBS, 'The past 30 years have seen far greater wealth creation than the Gilded Age'.[44] In 2017 alone, UBS noted that billionaires' wealth *increased* by $1.4 trillion, now standing at combined total wealth of $8.9 trillion.[45] Within countries, the distribution of wealth follows a similar pattern. In the United States, for example, three people hold the combined wealth of the bottom half of the population.[46]

As to income inequality, pay data collected by the US Securities and Exchange Commission, required under the 2010 'Dodd–Frank' law, show that the average CEO-to-median-worker pay ratio among Fortune 500 companies in 2017 was 339:1, up from a 20:1 ratio in 1965.[47] At the extremes, the pay ratio at fast food giant

---

[39] ibid.

[40] Drew Desilver, 'For most US workers, real wages have barely budged in decades', Pew Research Center, 7 August 2018, available at: www.pewresearch.org/fact-tank/2018/08/07/for-most-us-workers-real-wages-have-barely-budged-for-decades/.

[41] See, eg, Florence Jaumotte and Carolina Osorio, 'Inequality and Labor Market Institutions' (2015) IMF Staff Discussion Notes 15/14, International Monetary Fund.

[42] Henry S Farber, Daniel Herbst, Ilyana Kuziemko, Suresh Naidu, 'Unions and Inequality Over the Twentieth Century: New Evidence from Survey Data', Princeton University Industrial Relations Section, May 2018 (concluding, 'Our results show that over the last nine decades, when unions expand, whether at the national level or the state level, they tend to draw in unskilled workers and raise their relative wages, with significant impacts on inequality').

[43] See: oxfamilibrary.openrepository.com/bitstream/handle/10546/620599/bp-public-good-or-private-wealth-210119-en.pdf?utm_source=indepth, 28.

[44] UBS, 'Billionaires Report 2018', available at: www.ubs.com/global/en/wealth-management/uhnw/billionaires-report.html, 24.

[45] ibid, 6.

[46] Noah Kirsch, 'The 3 Richest Americans Hold More Wealth Than Bottom 50% Of The Country, Study Finds, Forbes, 9 November 2017, available at: www.forbes.com/sites/noahkirsch/2017/11/09/the-3-richest-americans-hold-more-wealth-than-bottom-50-of-country-study-finds/#64ac57eb3cf8.

[47] See: Rep Keith Ellison, 'Rewarding or Hoarding? An Examination of Pay Ratios Revealed by Dodd-Frank' (2018), available at: inequality.org/wp-content/uploads/2019/01/Ellison-Rewarding-Or-Hoarding-Full-Report.pdf.

McDonald's – a company known for low wages, irregular scheduling practices, and for its aggressive anti-union posture – is a shocking 3,101:1. While the pay ratio is narrower in European countries, the gap is still significant and growing.[48]

The concentration of power and wealth is also impacting the quality of democracy. As Colin Crouch has argued, many advanced industrial nations have become 'post-democratic', meaning that while the basic features of democracy are in place, such as open elections and universal suffrage, 'politics and government are increasingly slipping back into the control of privileged elites in the manner of pre-democratic times'.[49] Economic globalisation has strengthened the bargaining power of business and de-industrialisation has weakened that of trade unions. One result has been that political parties which used to respond to the needs of labour have sought support from business and have become increasing more responsive to their views.

It is in this political and economic context that the very existence of the right to strike is being contested by employers gathered at the International Labour Organization (ILO), with implications not only for the workplace, but inequality and indeed the maintenance of meaningful democracy. With the fall of the Soviet Union and the 'triumph' of Western capitalism, employers began to express opposition to the scope of the right to strike as defined by the ILO under its Constitution and conventions, and by 2012 opposed the very recognition of that right. As we explain in this book, the employers' legal reasoning contesting the existence of the right to strike is erroneous and were this issue to be adjudicated by the International Court of Justice, the right would be upheld. Apart from the legal question, and as we discuss in the conclusion, the last few years have seen a dramatic rise in the exercise of the right to strike, in some countries at levels not seen in decades. Thus, regardless of the existence of the right, as seen throughout history, workers will strike when pushed too far.

---

[48] Anders Melin and Wei Lu, 'CEOs in US, India Earn the Most Compared with Average Workers' (*Bloomberg*, 28 December 2017). According to *Bloomberg*, the ratio is 201:1 in the UK; 171:1 in the Netherlands; and 136:1 in Germany: www.bloomberg.com/news/articles/2017-12-28/ceos-in-u-s-india-earn-the-most-compared-with-average-workers.

[49] C Crouch, *Post-Democracy* (Cambridge, Polity Press, 2004) 6.

ACKNOWLEDGEMENTS

Jeffrey Vogt would like to extend his profound appreciation to his co-authors for seeing this book to completion. He also thanks the International Trade Union Confederation, where he worked as its legal director from 2011 to 2016, for supporting the initial research on the right to strike and for advocating for the referral of the dispute to the International Court of Justice. He also thanks the Chair and members of the Workers' Group at the ILO. Most importantly, he thanks his partner Tova Wang for her continued support and encouragement in the writing of this book.

CONTENTS

PART III
A REBUTTAL: THE INDISPUTABLE CASE
FOR THE RIGHT TO STRIKE

PART IV
WHERE TO FROM HERE?

TABLE OF CASES

Regional

Americas

Council of Europe

European Free Trade Association

EFTA Court

European Union

National

TABLE OF LEGISLATION

PART I

An Introduction

The aim of this book is to establish that the right to strike is protected in international law – first and foremost by the Constitution of the International Labour Organization (ILO) and ILO conventions. Other international and regional human rights instruments, ratified by ILO Member States, reinforce the existence of the right to strike in ILO instruments, as well as demonstrate a complementary body of law in support of this right. In fact, the right to strike has in our view become customary international law.

Before we proceed, however, a basic understanding of the ILO supervisory system is necessary to fully appreciate our arguments. Thus, we start with an introduction to the ILO that should help to guide the reader throughout the book.

1

Understanding the International Labour Organization (ILO)

I. An ILO Primer

The ILO was founded in 1919 in the aftermath of the First World War. Its purpose was clearly stated in the Preamble to its Constitution:

> [W]hereas conditions of labour exist involving such injustice, hardship and privation to large numbers of people as to produce unrest so great that the peace and harmony of the world are imperilled; and an improvement of those conditions is urgently required; as, for example, by the regulation of the hours of work, including the establishment of a maximum working day and week, the regulation of the labour supply, the prevention of unemployment, the provision of an adequate living wage, the protection of the worker against sickness, disease and injury arising out of his employment, the protection of children, young persons and women, provision for old age and injury, protection of the interests of workers when employed in countries other than their own, recognition of the principle of equal remuneration for work of equal value, recognition of the principle of freedom of association, the organization of vocational and technical education and other measures.[1]

In pursuit of these objectives, the ILO has adopted and supervised international labour standards through a tripartite process, meaning that ILO instruments are developed and monitored with the input not only of the Member States but also of representatives of trade unions and employer associations.[2] The ILO's shared governance structure is unique in the UN system and adds legitimacy and weight to its conventions and recommendations as well as the observations and conclusions of its supervisory bodies.

---

[1] See Preamble, ILO Constitution of 1919, available at: www.ilo.org/public/libdoc/ilo/1920/20B09_18_engl.pdf.

[2] A unique feature of ILO supervision arises from the tripartite nature of the Organization. Unlike all other international supervisory procedures, the ILO's non-governmental constituents – organisations of employers and of workers – have standing under Article 23 of the ILO Constitution to submit their own reports on governments' performance under a ratified convention, and these comments form an important part of the supervisory process. It is important to recognise that this is a full right of participation and is not limited to providing additional information or informing supervisory bodies, as is the case in purely intergovernmental organisations.

A. ILO Instruments

There are two kinds of ILO instrument: Conventions and Recommendations. The former have the status of a treaty and thus create binding international obligations for those Member States that ratify them. The latter are non-binding guidance, often providing further detail as to the proper implementation of a companion convention.[3] Conventions and recommendations are negotiated and adopted by delegates to the annual International Labour Conference, as provided for in the ILO Constitution.[4] At the time of writing, the ILO has adopted 190 conventions covering a wide range of topics concerning the world of work (though there are now fewer in force as some conventions have since been consolidated or abrogated as outdated).[5]

The ILO Governing Body has deemed eight conventions as 'fundamental',[6] including those related to freedom of association, collective bargaining, the elimination of discrimination in employment, and the abolition of child labour and forced labour. ILO conventions, and in particular the eight fundamental conventions, have been ratified widely, and inform national laws and the jurisprudence of national, regional and international tribunals. Currently, there are 1,381 ratifications of the fundamental conventions among the 187 Member States, representing nearly 93 per cent of the possible number of ratifications. In order to reach universal ratification, a further 115 ratifications are required.[7]

Our concern here is with the right to freedom of association, which is regulated by several conventions. These include ILO Convention 87 on Freedom of Association and Protection of the Right to Organise,[8] adopted in 1948, which has been interpreted consistently by the ILO supervisory system to protect the right to strike; and ILO Convention 98 on the Right to Organize and Collective Bargaining,[9] adopted in 1949, which has been invoked to further define the scope of the right to strike. Convention 87 has been ratified by 155 Member States,[10] while ILO Convention 98 has been ratified by 167 Member States,[11] making them

---

[3] See ILO, *Rules of the Game: An introduction to the standards-related work of the International Labour Organization* Centenary edition (Geneva, ILO, 2019) 18, available at: www.ilo.org/wcmsp5/groups/public/---ed_norm/---normes/documents/publication/wcms_672549.pdf.

[4] ibid, 20–24.

[5] ILO, 'Conventions', available at: www.ilo.org/dyn/normlex/en/f?p=1000:12000:9583788065169::::P12000_INSTRUMENT_ SORT:4.

[6] See *Rules of the Game* (n 3 above) 18–19.

[7] ILO, 'Ratification of Fundamental Conventions by Country', available at: www.ilo.org/dyn/normlex/en/f?p=NORMLEXPUB:10011:::NO:10011:P10011_DISPLAY_BY,P10011_CONVENTION_TYPE_CODE:1,F.

[8] ILO, 'Convention 87', available at: www.ilo.org/dyn/normlex/en/f?p=NORMLEXPUB:12100:0::NO::P12100 _ILO_CODE:C087 and excerpted in Annex 1 of this book.

[9] ILO, 'Convention 98', available at: www.ilo.org/dyn/normlex/en/f?p=NORMLEXPUB:12100:0::NO::P12100_INSTRUMENT_ ID:312243.

[10] ILO, 'Ratifications of Convention 87', available at: www.ilo.org/dyn/normlex/en/f?p=1000:11300:0::NO:11300: P11300_INSTRUMENT_ID:312232.

[11] ILO, 'Ratifications of Convention 98', available at: www.ilo.org/dyn/normlex/en/f?p=1000:11300:0::NO:11300: P11300_INSTRUMENT_ID:312243.

among the most widely accepted of all ILO instruments. Together with the ILO Constitution, in which the urgent recognition of the right to freedom of association was deemed necessary for peace and social justice, the right to strike has been part of the ILO's DNA from its foundation in 1919.

B. ILO Supervision

In addition to the negotiation and adoption of conventions and recommendations, the ILO is also responsible for their supervision in order to assist Member States to comply with the obligations they have voluntarily undertaken. To this end, the *regular* supervisory system publishes observations and conclusions on the extent of a Member State's level of compliance. The foundation for these observations is Article 22 of the Constitution, which provides that each Member State must report annually to the International Labour Office 'on the measures which it has taken to give effect to the provisions of conventions to which it is a party'.[12] These reports should be sent to representative organisations of workers and employers in the States in question, to enable comments to be made which may challenge the government's account of the level of compliance. The *special* supervisory system comes into play when a complaint has been filed by a constituent organisation, often a trade union, which concerns specific violations of a ratified convention in law and/or in practice. These two systems are complementary, as the observations and conclusions of the special supervisory system are followed up through the regular supervisory system, and the observations and conclusions by the regular supervisory system inform the special supervisory system.

i. Regular Supervisory System

The Committee of Experts on the Application of Conventions and Recommendations (Committee of Experts) was formed in 1926 by a resolution of the International Labour Conference.[13] The Committee of Experts is normally composed of 20 members who are eminent jurists and are appointed by the tripartite Governing Body for a term of three years.[14] The Committee of Experts meets annually to examine the Article 22 reports submitted by governments, as well as employers and workers, on, among other matters, the measures taken to give effect to ratified conventions. Its work is to indicate the extent to which the law and practice of each Member State are in conformity with these conventions.[15] In so doing,

---

[12] ILO Constitution, Article 22, available at: www.ilo.org/dyn/normlex/en/f?p=1000:62:0::NO:62:P62_LIST_ENTRIE_ID: 2453907:NO#A22.

[13] See *Rules of the Game* (n 3 above) 106.

[14] ibid.

[15] ibid.

it is guided by principles of independence, objectivity and impartiality. Due to the large volume of ratified conventions, it cannot examine annually all instruments by which a country is bound. As a result, the supervision of each of the fundamental conventions occurs every three years, with the supervision of all others every six years (though more frequently under special circumstances).[16] Each year, the Committee of Experts publishes its *Annual Report*, which contains its observations on Member States' compliance with ratified conventions, and its *General Survey*, which reports on Member States' national law and practice on a chosen subject.[17]

Each June, the ILO convenes the International Labour Conference (the Conference or ILC), during which, among other activities, new standards may be negotiated and adopted and where existing standards are supervised.[18] The ILO's Conference Committee on the Application of Standards (CAS), also established in 1926, is a standing tripartite body of the Conference and is constituted each year by the Conference.[19] Based on the technical examination of conventions contained in the *Annual Report*, the tripartite constituents in the CAS have an opportunity to examine further the manner in which Member States have complied with their obligations. The Employers' Group and Workers' Group, the 'social partners' in the ILO system, negotiate a 'short list' of roughly 25 cases[20] drawn from the *Annual Report* to which governments are then called upon to provide additional information to the CAS. Based on the report and additional information, the Employers' and Workers' Groups negotiate and adopt conclusions on those cases, which direct the government concerned and ILO to take specific follow-up measures.[21] The CAS report is published in the Proceedings of the Conference each year and is discussed by Conference delegates. The CAS discussion is in turn taken into account by the Committee of Experts when it next examines the application of the convention concerned.

A full discussion of the history and mandates of these two committees, and the relationship between them, is undertaken in chapter three.

ii. *Special Supervisory System*

Under Article 24 of the ILO Constitution, a *representation* may be filed if a country 'has failed to secure in any respect the effective observance within its jurisdiction of any Convention to which it is a party'.[22] A representation may only be filed

---

[16] ibid.

[17] ibid. See also 117.

[18] ILO, 'About the ILC', available at: www.ilo.org/ilc/AbouttheILC/lang--en/index.htm.

[19] See *Rules of the Game* (n 3 above) 110; See also, ILO, 'The Committee on the Application of Standards of the International Labour Conference, A Dynamic and Impact Built on Decades of Dialogue and Persuasion' (ILO, Geneva, 2011) 11–12, available at: www.ilo.org/wcmsp5/groups/public/---ed_norm/---normes/documents/publication/wcms_154192.pdf.

[20] By cases, we refer here to selected observations of the Committee of Experts with regard to a convention which the social partners have chosen for further examination.

[21] See *Rules of the Game* (n 3 above) 103; and *A Dynamic and Impact* (n 19 above) 12.

[22] See *Rules of the Game* (n 3 above) 106.

against a State that has ratified the convention concerned. After a representation has been declared receivable, an ad hoc tripartite committee appointed by the Governing Body from among its members examines the substance of the representation.[23] When all information from both parties has been received, or if no reply is received within the time limits set, the Committee makes its findings on compliance and makes recommendations to the Governing Body.[24] If the Governing Body decides that the government's explanations are not satisfactory, it publishes the representation and the government's reply, along with its own discussion of the case. Representations concerning the application of Conventions 87 and 98 are usually referred for examination to the Committee on Freedom of Association (CFA), in accordance with the procedure for the examination of representations.[25] The issues raised in a representation may be followed up by the ILO's regular supervisory machinery, for example, by the Committee of Experts, if the government has failed to take the requested measures.

For the most serious situations where a Member State is not 'securing the effective observance of any Convention' it has ratified, a *complaint* may be filed under Article 26 of the ILO Constitution to establish a Commission of Inquiry. The complaint procedure may be instituted by governments that have ratified the same convention, by delegates to the Conference, or by the Governing Body on its own motion.[26] Once a complaint has been deemed receivable, a vote may be been taken by the Governing Body to establish the Commission of Inquiry. A Commission of Inquiry is composed of three prominent and independent persons.[27] It is tasked with preparing a report in which it makes findings, conclusions and recommendations which is then presented to the parties (Article 28 of the Constitution). Its conclusions are expected to be followed by the Member State under supervision, though the Member State may refer the matter to the International Court of Justice (ICJ) under Article 29 if it does not accept the Commission's recommendations. Once referred, the decision of the ICJ is final, per Article 31 of the Constitution. The ICJ may, per Article 32, 'affirm, vary, or reverse the findings or recommendations of the Commission of Inquiry'.

Article 33 of the Constitution contains the only provision allowing the ILO to take action to compel compliance with a convention:

> In the event of any Member failing to carry out within the time specified the recommendations, if any, contained in the report of the Commission of Inquiry, or in the decision of the International Court of Justice, as the case may be, the Governing Body may recommend to the Conference such action as it may deem wise and expedient to secure compliance therewith.[28]

---

[23] ibid.
[24] ibid.
[25] ibid.
[26] ibid, 112.
[27] There have been 13 Commissions of Inquiry established in the ILO's 100-year history.
[28] ILO Constitution, Article 33, available at: www.ilo.org/dyn/normlex/en/f?p=1000:62:0::NO:62:P62_LIST_ENTRIE_ID:2453907:NO#A33.

Article 33 has been used only once in the history of the ILO, in 2000, concerning the failure of the military government of Myanmar to end the exaction of forced labour.[29]

Finally, the CFA is charged with addressing questions concerning the right to freedom of association, to organise and to collective bargaining. The CFA was established by agreement with the UN Economic and Social Council in 1951, following the adoption of Conventions 87 and 98.[30] It is composed of nine titular and nine deputy members of the Governing Body, three titular and three deputies from each of the government, worker and employer groups, with an independent chair.[31] It examines complaints filed by workers' or employers' organisations, *regardless of whether the country concerned has ratified any relevant convention*. Although it bases its work on the ILO Constitution, the CFA frequently refers to Conventions 87 and 98. As explained in detail through this book, the CFA has interpreted the ILO Constitution and Convention 87 to protect a right to strike and has specified the boundaries of that right with reference also to Convention 98.

---

[29] ILO Press Release, 'ILO Governing Body opens the way for unprecedented action against forced labour in Myanmar', 17 November 2000, available at: www.ilo.org/global/about-the-ilo/newsroom/news/ WCMS_007918/lang--en/index.htm.

[30] *Rules of the Game* (n 3 above) 110.

[31] ibid.

2

The Ill-Founded Challenge
to the Right to Strike in 2012

I. The Showdown at the 2012
International Labour Conference

At the commencement of the Conference on 30 May 2012, the spokespersons for the Employers' and Workers' Groups in the Committee on the Application of Standards (CAS) met to finalise the shortlist. Although the spokespersons had been in contact since March, the Employers' Group spokesperson announced at the Conference, without warning, that they would refuse to agree to a shortlist that included any case on freedom of association where the Committee of Experts had made observations regarding the right to strike. This was unprecedented. While there have been disagreements between the Employers' Group and Workers' Group over the years on the inclusion of specific cases on the shortlist, this marked the first time that any group flatly refused to discuss the application of an entire area of law, based on its own, unique beliefs on the interpretation of a convention.

In addition, the Employers' Group sought a 'disclaimer' on the Committee of Experts' *General Survey*. In 2012, the *General Survey* had focused on the eight fundamental ILO conventions and, among other things, confirmed the long-standing view of the Committee of Experts that ILO Convention 87 protects the right to strike. The competing arguments of the Employers' Group and Workers' Group on this issue were also both reported and evaluated in the *General Survey*.[1] The proposed disclaimer stated, 'The General Survey is part of the regular supervisory process and is the result of the Committee of Experts' analysis. It is not an agreed or determinative text of the ILO tripartite constituents'.[2]

---

[1] ILO, Report of the Committee of Experts on the Application of Conventions and Recommendations, *General Survey on the Fundamental Conventions concerning rights at work in light of the ILO Declaration on Social Justice for a Fair Globalisation 2008*, Report III (Part 1B); International Labour Conference, 101st Session, 2012 (*General Survey* 2012), available at: www.ilo.org/wcmsp5/groups/public/---ed_norm/---relconf/documents/ meetingdocument/wcms_174846.pdf.

[2] See International Organisation of Employers (IOE), *Do ILO Conventions 87 and 98 Recognize a Right to Strike?*, October 2014, 9, available at: www.ioe-emp.org/index.php?eID=dumpFile&t=f&f=111 630&token= d3f4de458d8a4b740afa01b449c44cb11761654b.

The purpose of this disclaimer was twofold: to diminish the persuasive authority of the Committee of Experts' observations and to establish a (novel) hierarchy of the political, tripartite body, the CAS, over the independent, quasi-judicial Committee of Experts. The Employers' Group threatened to block any agreement over a list of cases unless the Workers' Group accepted the proposed disclaimer (in addition to foregoing any discussion on cases dealing with the right to strike). These conditions made it impossible to proceed with the work of the CAS. As a result, the CAS failed to examine any cases during the Conference – the first time since it was established over 90 years ago.

The Employers' Group distributed a short statement at the Conference on 4 June explaining its actions.[3] The Employers' Group's text draws heavily upon the work of Alfred Wisskirchen, who served as the Employers' Group spokesperson and Vice-Chairperson of the CAS from 1983 to 2004.[4] The Employers' Group's statement made the following three claims:

1.   The mandate of the Experts is to comment on the 'application' of conventions, not to 'interpret' them. Only the International Court of Justice can provide a definitive interpretation.[5]
2.   The General Survey and the Annual Report of the Committee of Experts are not agreed or authoritative texts of the ILO tripartite constituents. Specifically, it is not the Committee of Experts which supervises labour standards but rather the ILO tripartite constituents. Thus, it is the tripartite constituents who ultimately decide upon the meaning of the ILO conventions.[6]
3.   Convention 87 is silent on the right to strike and therefore it is not an issue upon which the Committee of Experts should express an opinion. Given the absence of any reference to a right to strike in the actual text of ILO Convention 87, the internationally accepted rules of interpretation require Convention 87 to be interpreted without a right to strike.[7]

In addition to the entire Workers' Group, several members of the Government Group[8] and even the ILO Director-General,[9] through his representative, expressed sharp disagreement with the Employers' Group's views at the Conference. After

---

[3] See Employers' Statement in the Committee on the Application of Standards of the International Labour Conference on 4 June 2012, available at: www.uscib.org/docs/2012_06_04_ioe_clarifications_statement.pdf.

[4] Wisskirchen's views have been expressed in several papers in German and English. See, eg, A Wisskirchen, 'The Standard-setting and Monitoring activity of the ILO: Legal Questions and Practical Experience' (2005) 144 *International Labour Review* 253.

[5] See ILO, Report of the Committee on the Application of Standards, 19Rev (Part 1), International Labour Conference, 101st Session, 2012, 22 and 35, available at: www.ilo.org/wcmsp5/groups/public/---ed_norm/---relconf/documents/meetingdocument/wcms_183031.pdf.

[6] ibid, 34.

[7] ibid, 34–36.

[8] ibid, 24 (right to strike was a fundamental right); 42–43 (IMEC supporting mandate of experts and supervisory system).

[9] ibid, 44–45.

shutting down the CAS, the Employers' Group claimed that the entire supervisory system was now 'in crisis'[10] and called for an overhaul to its functioning.[11] Since 2012, the CAS has plodded forward. In 2014, the issue of the right to strike again caused the CAS to fail to reach negotiated conclusions, this time in 19 out of 25 cases. As explained later, the Workers' Group put on the agenda of the Governing Body, during its November 2014 session, the referral of the dispute over the interpretation of the ILO Constitution and Convention 87 as to the right to strike to the International Court of Justice (ICJ). The lock-step opposition by the Employers' Group and insufficient support from the Government Group ultimately doomed this effort. A special February 2015 tripartite meeting on the right to strike resulted in governments reaffirming the existence of the right to strike, and its linkage to freedom of association. Since 2015, the CAS has operated under a tenuous bipartite 'peace' agreement. There has been no resolution, however, on the central question of the existence of the right to strike.

II. Why Then?

ILO Convention 87 entered into force on 4 July 1950 and, for nearly 40 years after 1952, when the Committee on Freedom of Association (CFA) began to function, there was no challenge by the Employers' Group on the right to strike as developed by the Committee of Experts and the CFA.[12] Indeed, the CFA had routinely published conclusions, by tripartite consensus, affirming the right to strike and regulated its exercise. The Committee of Experts' observations on the right to strike were also routinely approved by the tripartite constituents at the Conference. Until the end of the Cold War, the Employers' Group did not question the existence of the right to strike as protected by ILO instruments.

However, with the collapse of the Soviet Union, the Cold War alliance between the Employers' and Workers' Groups formed in opposition to the Eastern Bloc repression of trade union rights, served no further purpose. The Employers' Group's acceptance of a right to strike recognised and protected by the ILO began to evaporate once striking Polish shipbuilders organised under Solidarność succeeded in bringing about free elections in 1990.[13] Employers' Group complaints about the

---

[10] See ILO, 'Matters arising out of the work of the International Labour Conference' (2013), Governing Body, 317th Session, GB.317/INS/4/1, 7, available at: www.ilo.org/wcmsp5/groups/public/---ed_norm/---relconf/documents/meetingdocument/wcms_206599.pdf.

[11] See IOE Press Release: 'Employers call for a change to the Functioning of the ILO Regular Supervisory System', 2 February 2013.

[12] See T Novitz, 'Connecting Freedom of Association and the Right to Strike: European Dialogue with the ILO and its Potential Impact' (2009–10) 15 *Canadian Labour & Employment Law* Journal 476; C La Hovary, 'Showdown at the ILO? A Historical Perspective on the Employers' Group's 2012 Challenge to the Right to Strike' (2013) 42 *Industrial Law Journal* 338.

[13] For a description of how the end of the Cold War and the dominance of neo-liberalism have adversely impacted on trade union rights, see S Kang, *Human Rights and Labor Solidarity: Trade Unions in the Global Economy* (Philadelphia, PA, University of Pennsylvania Press, 2012) 33–40.

right to strike began to surface in 1989 and 1992. In 1994, with the publication of a General Survey on Freedom of Association and Collective Bargaining, the Employers' Group elaborated a lengthy critique on the right to strike as it had been developed by the supervisory system and in particular by the Committee of Experts.[14]

Importantly, the Employers' Group had clarified that 'they were not so much criticizing the fact that the Committee of Experts wanted to recognize the right to strike in principle, but rather that it took as a point of departure a comprehensive and unlimited right to strike'.[15] Of course, neither the Committee of Experts nor the CFA had ever posited an unlimited right to strike and have in fact recognised numerous limitations on the right over the years.[16] Three years later, in 1997, the Employers' Group again 'acknowledged that the principle of industrial action, including the right to strike and lockouts, formed part of the principles of freedom of association as set out in Convention No 87'.[17] Not until 2012 did the Employers' Group argue that an international right to strike did not exist *at all*.

The Employers' Group's stance appears motivated in part by the fact that ILO jurisprudence, once largely self-contained within meeting rooms in Geneva, was now taking on a robust life outside the ILO.[18] Worker advocates were busily advancing novel arguments about the right to strike in litigation before national courts, citing to ILO jurisprudence.[19] Consequently, national and regional courts turned more frequently to the views of the ILO supervisory system to ascertain the scope of freedom of association under their own laws and instruments. Indeed, the European Court of Human Rights (ECtHR) used ILO conventions as a basis for the construction of the European Convention on Human Rights (ECHR) and to create a common standard across a number of international obligations.

---

[14] ILO, Record of Proceedings No 25, ILC, 81st Session, Geneva, 1994, 31–37.

[15] ibid, 33, para 121.

[16] The ILO Committee on Freedom of Association's *Compilation of Decisions* (and previously the *Digest*) is replete with cases where the CFA interpreted the ILO Constitution and/or Convention 87 to include limitations on the right to strike, including recourse to mediation and conciliation prior to a strike (paras 793–98); reasonable notice prior to a strike (paras 799–804); the limitation or prohibition of strikes in public services and essential services (paras 826–52); the maintenance of minimum services during a strike (paras 866–85). Convention 98 has been interpreted to shape the scope of the right to strike. For example, the CFA found that strikes wholly unrelated to industrial relations are not protected under Conventions 87 and 98. See para 761 ('Strikes of a purely political nature do not fall within the protection of Conventions Nos 87 and 98'); Convention 98 has also been found to constrain employers from retaliating against workers who have conducted a lawful strike. See para 957 ('The dismissal of workers because of a strike constitutes serious discrimination in employment on grounds of legitimate trade union activities and is contrary to Convention No 98'.)

[17] Record of Proceedings No 19, ILC, 85th Session, Geneva, 1997, 35.

[18] Report of the Committee on the Application of Standards 2012 (n 5 above) 13 and 34.

[19] See, eg *Metrobus Ltd v UNITE the Union* [2009] IRLR 851, [2010] ICR 173 (CA). Also, in Canada, see on the relevance of ILO standards to interpretation of Article 2(d) of the Canadian Charter of Rights and Freedoms, *Health Services and Support-Facilities Subsector Collective Bargaining Association v British Columbia* [2007] 2 SCR 391.

By the time of the Employer Group's challenge in 2012, the ECtHR had recognised the existence of a right to strike under the ECHR in *Enerji Yapi-Yol Sen v Turkey* and developed the right in subsequent cases.[20] The ECtHR noted that the right to strike had been recognised by the supervisory bodies of the ILO as an 'essential corollary' to the right of freedom of association protected by ILO Convention 87.[21] *Enerji Yapi-Yol Sen* built upon a prior case of the ECtHR, *Demir and Baykara v Turkey*, which referred to ILO Conventions 87 and 98, as well as the observations of the Committee of Experts and the CFA, to find that Turkey violated Article 11 of the ECHR when it interfered with the right of municipal civil servants to form a trade union and to enter into a collective bargaining agreement.[22]

In the Americas, the Inter-American Court of Human Rights, in *Baena-Ricardo et al v Panama*,[23] had relied on the observations of the Committee of Experts and the CFA in ruling that the government of Panama violated the right to freedom of association guaranteed by Article 16 of the American Convention on Human Rights when it issued a decree dismissing 270 workers for having gone on strike.[24] At the national level, Canadian employers were deeply concerned about innovative litigation used to challenge jurisprudence from the 1980s holding that the right to freedom of association as set forth in the Canadian Charter of Rights and Freedoms did not embrace the right to strike.[25] As described later, that litigation proved successful in 2015, when the Supreme Court of Canada found the right to strike was protected under the Charter, making direct reference to ILO conventions.

It was not just that national and regional courts had relied on the jurisprudence of the Committee of Experts, but that the Committee of Experts had also called into question important rulings where employers had succeeded in limiting the right to strike in their respective countries. It is no coincidence that the Employers' Group made their stand only two years after the Committee of Experts questioned the reasoning in the decisions of the European Court of Justice in the *Viking* and *Laval* cases. As these cases had firmly subordinated the right to strike to commercial interests under European Union (EU) instruments, they were of momentous significance for European workers.[26] The legitimacy of these rulings was directly called into question by the Committee of Experts, which made clear that EU law had been interpreted in a manner in breach of the obligations of EU Member States.[27]

---

[20] ECtHR (Third Section), *Enerji Yapi-Yol Sen v Turkey* App No 68959/01 (21 April 2009).

[21] ibid, para 24.

[22] ECtHR (Grand Chamber), *Demir and Baykara v Turkey* App No 34503/97 Judgment (12 November 2008) 28 EHRR 54.

[23] *Case of Baena-Ricardo et al v Panama*, Inter-American Court of Human Rights, Merits, Reparations and Costs, Judgment of 2 February 2001, Series C No 72.

[24] ibid, paras 162–63 and 214.

[25] See, eg, J Cameron, 'The Labour Trilogy's Last Rites: BC Health and a Constitutional Right to Strike' (2009–10) 15 *Canadian Labour & Employment Law Journal* 297.

[26] Case C-438/05 *ITF and FSU v Viking Line ABP* [2008] IRLR 143.

[27] ILO, Committee of Experts, Observation on *Freedom of Association and Protection of the Right to Organise Convention, 1948 (No 87) – Sweden*, published 102nd ILC session (2013), available at: www.ilo.org/dyn/normlex/en/f?p=1000: 13100:0::NO:13100:P13100_COMMENT_ID:3085286.

On the heels of the *Viking* and *Laval* cases, the Committee of Experts raised serious concerns about the United Kingdom in the *BALPA* case. There, British Airways had obtained an injunction against proposed industrial action by pilots on the basis of the *Viking* and *Laval* case law. The company threatened that were the work stoppage to take place, it would sue the union for damages estimated at £100 million per day. The Committee of Experts admonished the United Kingdom, explaining that the case had raised the need to ensure fuller protection of the right of workers to exercise legitimate industrial action, and that adequate safeguards and immunities from civil liability were necessary to ensure respect for this fundamental right.[28]

Apart from litigation, international labour standards had been included in other important documents. Trade unions and human rights and labour rights NGOs increasingly cited decisions of ILO supervisory bodies in attempting to hold multinational enterprises accountable for violations of the right to freedom of association.[29] Drafters of business and human rights guidelines and principles incorporated the rights and principles of the ILO fundamental conventions. The OECD Guidelines for Multinational Enterprises[30] and the UN Guiding Principles on Business and Human Rights (UNGPs)[31] both refer directly to the ILO's 1998 Declaration on Fundamental Principles and Rights at Work (which includes the principle of freedom of association).

The extent of an enterprise's duties under the OECD Guidelines or the UN Guiding Principles, and the assessment as to whether that duty was breached, would be ascertained through resort to the jurisprudence of the ILO. For example, the UNGPs Principle 12 states:

> The responsibility of business enterprises to respect human rights refers to internationally recognized human rights – understood, at a minimum, as those expressed in the International Bill of Human Rights and the principles concerning fundamental rights set out in the International Labour Organisation's Declaration on Fundamental Principles and Rights at Work.[32]

Corporations therefore have a responsibility not only to comply with human rights in general, but with the specific human rights set forth by the ILO. This means not only the broad principles, but also the detailed jurisprudence.

---

[28] ILO, Committee of Experts, Observation on *Freedom of Association and Protection of the Right to Organise Convention, 1948 (No 87) – United Kingdom,* published 100th ILC session (2011), available at: www.ilo.org/dyn/normlex/ en/f?p=1000:13100:0::NO:13100:P13100_COMMENT_ID:2322470.

[29] See, eg, Human Rights Watch, 'Discounting Rights: Wal-Mart's Violation of US Workers' Right to Freedom of Association' (2007), available at: www.hrw.org/reports/2007/us0507/.

[30] See eg, OECD Guidelines, Commentary on Employment and Industrial Relations, 43–46; UN Guiding Principles, Principle 12 and Commentary (stating that, 'The responsibility of business enterprises to respect human rights refers to internationally recognized human rights – understood, at a minimum, as those expressed in the International Bill of Human Rights and the principles concerning fundamental rights set out in the International Labour Organization's Declaration on Fundamental Principles and Rights at Work').

[31] *UN Guiding Principles on Business and Human Rights,* UN Doc A/HRC/17/31 (21 March 2011) annex (UNGPs).

[32] ibid.

Further, trade preference programmes and bilateral and regional trade agreements, especially those negotiated by or with the United States, Canada and the EU, have incorporated ILO conventions and/or the ILO Declaration of Fundamental Principles and Rights at Work. Some of these agreements can result in fines or suspension of trade benefits when national laws consistent with those international rights or principles are not adopted and effectively enforced.[33] By 2011, the United States had served notice on Guatemala to arbitrate a dispute under the Central American Free Trade Agreement for its failure to enforce its labour laws concerning, inter alia, the right to freedom of association.[34]

Together, these developments had the effect of slowly converting the 'soft' law of the ILO supervisory system to 'hard' law leading to real consequences for employers. The centrality of the ILO in the development of international labour instruments and jurisprudence in these various ways explains why, in 2012, employer representatives chose the ILO as the venue to challenge the existence of the right to strike as a matter of law. If legal certainty about the right could be called into question at the ILO, employers would have a basis to lobby Member States to limit or eliminate this most fundamental of labour rights everywhere.

III. And Now?

This book originates from a study undertaken for the International Trade Union Confederation (ITUC) from 2013 to 2014 on the foundations of the right to strike in international law, in which some of the authors were involved.[35] At the time, it appeared that the dispute over the interpretation of the ILO Constitution and Convention 87 would be referred to the ICJ for an Advisory Opinion. The ITUC study was meant to serve as the Workers' Group's brief to that court. As explained later, that effort failed. Nevertheless, this dispute remains very much alive, not only among legal academics, but in legal practice inside and outside the ILO with far-reaching, real-world consequences.

In the intervening years since 2012, employers have aggressively promoted the theory that there is no internationally protected right to strike.[36] While most scholars and courts have rebuffed the employers' arguments, it has been seized on by some governments to limit or deny this fundamental right. Further, the

---

[33] See, eg, ILO, *Social Dimensions of Free Trade Agreements* (Geneva, ILO, 2013) Chapter 2, available at: www.ilo.org/wcmsp5/groups/public/---dgreports/---inst/documents/publication/wcms_228965. pdf.

[34] USTR Press Release, 'US Trade Representative Ron Kirk Announces Next Step in Labor Rights Enforcement Case against Guatemala', August 2011, available at: www.ustr.gov/about-us/policy-offices/press-office/press-releases/2011/august/us-trade-representative-ron-kirk-announces-next-ste.

[35] ITUC, *The Right to Strike and the ILO: The Legal Foundations* (ITUC, 2014), available at: www. ituc-csi.org/new-legal-report-right-to-strike.

[36] See, eg, IOE, *Do ILO Conventions 87 and 98 Recognize a Right to Strike?* (n 2 above).

Employers' Group at the ILO continues its attack on the right to strike throughout the ILO supervisory system and governance structures, most notably in the CAS and the Committee on Freedom of Association. This has had the (intended) effect of destabilising the ILO itself and has led the organisation, which is based on tripartite consensus, to take a cautious approach on this right, as well as other issues which do not enjoy broad employer support.

In the following pages, we refute the Employers' Group's claim that the Committee of Experts has no mandate to provide authoritative determinations on the scope of Convention 87 (chapter three) and consider also how that mandate has been used to develop what is in practice a modest right, hedged by a number of qualifications and restrictions; if anything, the Committee has in our view been too cautious in its approach. We then identify the rules of interpretation governing this dispute (chapter four) and argue that the interpretation of Convention 87 to include the right to strike is consistent with the Vienna Convention on the Law of Treaties, having regard to both Article 31 (chapters five to nine), and Article 32 (chapter ten). In chapter eleven we argue that in any event the right to strike has been recognised as customary international law. Chapters twelve to thirteen conclude with some reflections on the settlement of the dispute, and its implications for the ILO and international labour standards more broadly.

Put simply, at the time of the Employers' Group's challenge in 2012, there was no question that the right to strike was protected by the Constitution and Convention 87 and international law more broadly. Developments since 2012 only lend additional support to this claim, including the direct or indirect repudiation of the employers' arguments by several high-level tribunals.

PART II

A Rebuttal: On the Question of Mandates

3

The ILO Committee of Experts has a Mandate to 'Interpret' ILO Conventions, not the Constituents

The Employers' Group has argued that the Committee of Experts has no constitutional mandate to provide 'binding' interpretations of ILO conventions, or indeed to interpret conventions in any meaningful sense. Secondly, they argue that it is the tripartite constituents, in the form of the Committee on the Application of Standards (CAS) and the delegates to the Conference, that have the final say as to what conventions mean, not the Committee of Experts.

While it is true that only the International Court of Justice (ICJ) may issue *binding* interpretations of ILO conventions,[1] the observations of the Committee of Experts must be viewed as authoritative if the system is to function unless and until the ICJ rules to the contrary. Of course, whether the Committee of Experts' interpretations are binding in any sense is a secondary question as to whether their task involves interpretation at all. The answer to this primary question is 'yes'. The Committee of Experts is the centrepiece of the ILO system, duly tasked by the Conference with assessing the application of Conventions and Recommendations by Member States. The Committee has done so, consistently applying the rules supplied by the Vienna Convention on the Laws of Treaties (VCLT). As to the employers' second argument, there is simply no constitutional support whatsoever for the notion that the CAS or the International Labour Conference (ILC) are the ultimate arbiters of the meaning of ILO conventions.

Before addressing the Employers' Group's arguments, we must underscore that for many years it had expressed support for the mandate of the Committee of Experts and that the latter's role involved some degree of interpretation. Thus, the Employers' Group's current position is undermined by their own words repeatedly expressed. In 2013, the Committee of Experts noted the following examples:

- In 1987, the Employers rejected claims by the USSR that the Committee of Experts had gone beyond its 1926 terms of reference, converting itself into 'a kind of supra-national tribunal, interpreting national laws and Conventions'.

---

[1] Article 37(1), ILO Constitution.

The Employers' spokesperson 'rejected the argument that the Committee of Experts had gone beyond its terms of reference' (paragraph 27) and both the Employers' and Workers' spokespersons 'supported the Committee's current methods of work' (paragraph 32).[2]

- In 1990, the Employers criticised the Committee's report that stated that the competence to interpret conventions absent an ICJ submission rests solely with the Committee (paragraph 22). The Employers explained that the Vienna Convention is 'the appropriate – in fact the only – yardstick to be used in interpreting ILO conventions. It was this yardstick that they invited the Committee to use in their interpretation of international labour standards' (paragraph 30).[3]

- In 1993, the Employers remarked that 'disagreements over the method and substance of interpretations arose in only a small proportion of the vast number of comments made over the years by the Committee of Experts' (paragraph 21).[4]

- In 2011, during the CAS, the Employers' group did not respond to the detailed discussion of the interpretive methods that the Committee of Experts had presented in paragraphs 10–12 of its *General Report*, which discussed in considerable detail: (a) the logical necessity of interpreting conventions in order to fulfil its mandate, (b) the necessity that its work remain committed to independence, objectivity, and impartiality, and (c) that the Committee constantly bore in mind all different methods of interpreting treaty law, especially the Vienna Convention.[5]

I. A Brief History

This is far from the first time the issue of the right to interpret conventions, and the relations between the Committee of Experts and the Conference Committee, have arisen. These issues arose with some frequency in the Governing Body early on. For instance, an extract from the Minutes of the Governing Body in 1930 provides:

5. Interpretation of Conventions

The Director said that he hoped there would not be, in connection with this question, a recrudescence of the discussions with which the Governing Body was familiar concerning the power of interpretation of the Governing Body and the Conference, and the functions of the Office in giving information concerning the interpretation of

---

[2] ILO, Report of the Committee of Experts on the Application of Conventions and Recommendations, *Application of International Labour Standards 2013*, Report III (Part 1A), International Labour Conference, 102nd Session, 2013 (*Annual Report* 2013) 13, para 34.
[3] ibid.
[4] ibid.
[5] ibid, 11, para 27.

Conventions. It had, however, been thought useful, in connection with the question now under consideration, to recall the fact that, according to Article 423 of the Treaty of Peace, the Permanent Court of International Justice alone was qualified to give authoritative interpretations of Conventions. All other interpretations, even those given by the Conference, might give rise to dispute. It might therefore be well to remind States of the possibility of appealing to the Permanent Court of International Justice.

It had been said that this was an expensive and cumbrous procedure, but even if the procedure were slow and costly, it was better to apply to the Court than to remain in a state of uncertainty.

The note of the Office also pointed out that the procedure for revision of Conventions offered an opportunity of interpreting them.[6]

The question flared up most prominently in 1990 when the Committee of Experts stated in its report:

The Committee has already had occasion to point out that its terms of reference do not require it to give definitive interpretations of Conventions, competence to do so being vested in the International Court of Justice by Article 37 of the Constitution of the ILO. Nevertheless, in order to carry out its function of determining whether the requirements of Conventions are being respected, the Committee has to consider and express its views on the content and meaning of the provisions of Conventions and to determine their legal scope, where appropriate. It therefore appears to the Committee that, in so far as its views are not contradicted by the International Court of Justice, they are to be considered as valid and generally recognised. The situation is identical as regards the conclusions or recommendations of commissions of inquiry which, by virtue of Article 37 of the Constitution, may be affirmed, varied or reversed by the International Court of Justice, and the parties can only duly contest the validity of such conclusions and recommendations by availing themselves of the provisions of Article 29, paragraph 2, of the Constitution. The Committee considers that the acceptance of the above considerations is indispensable to maintenance of the principle of legality and, consequently, for the certainty of law required for the proper functioning of the International Labour Organisation.[7]

The Employers' members of the Conference Committee reacted to this in 1990, in a discussion reported in the report of the Conference Committee that year:

22. The Employers' members ... feel that the opinion of the Committee of Experts that its evaluations are binding unless corrected by the International Court of Justice, could not be correct. One obvious reason was that, if this were the case, the present Committee would lose its fundamental purpose, and so would the Conference. A legal reason was that this was contradicted by the ILO Constitution and by the Standing Orders of the Conference concerning the submission of governments' reports and the terms of reference of the Conference Committee, which had an independent competence to examine reports.[8]

---

[6] ILO, Minutes of the Governing Body, 50th Session, October 1930, 656, 657.
[7] ILO, Report of the Committee of Experts on the Application of Conventions and Recommendations, *Application of International Labour Standards 1990*, Report III (Part 4A), International Labour Conference, 77th Session, 1990 (*Annual Report* 1990) para 7.
[8] ILC, Record of Proceedings No 27, 77th Session, Geneva, 1990, 6.

The ILO secretariat attempted to bring this discussion to a close on this point:

> The Conference Committee is not an appellate tribunal called upon to examine the opinion of the Committee of Experts, and its evaluations are not judgements. They arise instead from a spirit of dialogue with the ILO's constituents, based on the prior technical and legal advice given by the Committee of Experts, to achieve a better application of international labour standards.[9]

The Committee of Experts, in its 1994 report explained:

> 26. The Conference Committee has never operated as a review or appeals body vis-à-vis the Committee of Experts. The two bodies have different functions: the Committee of Experts is responsible for technical supervision, whereas the Conference Committee, which is tripartite, provides an opportunity for direct dialogue between governments, employers and workers, and can even mobilize international public opinion.[10]

The Employers' members then returned to this issue in 1996 in the Conference Committee:

> 10. The Employers' members noted that, although the present Committee had to take into account new information every year, its task remained the same. In accordance with Article 7 of the Standing Orders of the International Labour Conference, it was responsible for examining whether Member States were discharging their obligations under the ILO Constitution, as well as the obligations they had assumed through the ratification of Conventions. The Committee had been carrying out this task for around 70 years. The Committee's role concerned legal issues, and it was for this reason that the comments contained in the report of the Committee of Experts were important. However, the Conference Committee needed to make its own evaluation and arrive at its own conclusions. Its task was not confined to repeating the work of the Committee of Experts.[11]

This position, that the CAS had to act independently of the Committee of Experts, was not taken up by other members.

II. The Mandates of ILO Supervisory Bodies Establish No Hierarchy Among Them

The mandates of the Committee of Experts and the Committee on the Application of Standards were adopted, and have developed, in tandem. Until 1926, the plenary of the Conference reviewed governments' reports on ratified conventions, but this quickly became too heavy a burden for the Conference delegates. As a result, the

---

[9] ibid, 9.

[10] ILO, Report of the Committee of Experts on the Application of Conventions and Recommendations, *Application of International Labour Standards 1990*, Report III (Part 4A), International Labour Conference, 81st Session, 1994 (*Annual Report* 1994) para 26.

[11] ILC, Record of Proceedings No 14, 83rd Session, Geneva, 1996, 4.

Committee of Experts and the CAS were created, pursuant to a decision of the Conference in 1926, to relieve this burden. The 1926 resolution reads as follows:

> Proceedings of the International Labour Conference, 8th session, 1926, Appendix VII
>
> (1) Resolution concerning the methods by which the Conference can make use of the reports submitted under Article 408 of the Treaty of Versailles, submitted by the Committee on Article 408.[12]
>
> The Eighth Session of the International Labour Conference,
>
> Considering that the reports rendered by the State Members of the Organisation under Article 408 of the Treaty of Versailles are of the utmost importance,
>
> And that careful examination of the information contained therein is calculated to throw light upon the practical value of the Conventions themselves and to further their general ratification,
>
> Recommends that a Committee of the Conference should be set up each year to examine the summaries of the reports submitted to the Conference in accordance with Article 408,
>
> And requests the Governing Body of the International Labour Office to appoint, as an experiment and for a period of one, two or three years, a technical Committee of experts, consisting of six or eight members, for the purpose of making the best and fullest use of this information and of securing such additional data as may be provided for in the forms approved by the Governing Body and found desirable to supplement that already available, and of reporting thereon to the Governing Body, which report the Director, after consultation with the Governing Body, will annex to his summary of the annual reports presented to the Conference under Article 408.

A. Committee of Experts

The Committee of Experts was to (and still does) examine the actual reports received from governments. The CAS does not receive these reports but rather works on the basis of the *Annual Report* of the Committee of Experts and any supplementary information that governments may put before it which responds to observations by the Committee of Experts.[13] When a report submitted by a government directly to the CAS is detailed or contains technical questions, the CAS refers it to the Committee of Experts for examination.

---

[12] See *Proceedings*, 238–44, 247–60 and Appendix V. Article 408 of the Treaty of Versailles provided for the reporting requirement on ratified conventions and corresponds to Article 22 of the present ILO Constitution.

[13] Governments' reports are not now put before the Conference Committee, though they were until 1924. From then until the 1970s the Office forwarded summaries of governments' reports to the Conference, but this practice was discontinued for reasons of economy, as well as the fact that the Conference never examined them. This constitutional requirement is now met by forwarding a list of the reports requested and received, and by making the reports available to the Conference Committee should they wish to consult them. In practice, this occurs rarely if ever.

In 1946, the ILO Constitution was revised to add, inter alia, responsibility for reporting on unratified as well as ratified conventions (now Article 19 of the Constitution). In consequence, the Governing Body approved an expansion of the responsibilities of the Committee of Experts and the CAS.[14] When considered at the December Session of the Governing Body in 1947, the explanation given to the Governing Body by the Assistant Director-General was:

> With regard to the terms of reference of the Committee of Experts, it was suggested in the Office note that, in order to take account of the amendments to Article 7 of the Standing Orders of the Conference and of the consequent broadening of the functions both of the Conference Committee on the Application of Conventions and of the Committee of Experts, the latter should, in future, be known as the 'Committee of Experts on the Application of Conventions and Recommendations'. The functions of the Committee would include an examination of the annual reports made under Article 22 of the Constitution, the information concerning Conventions and Recommendations communicated in accordance with Article 19 of the Constitution, and the information and reports on the measures taken by States Members in accordance with Article 35 of the Constitution.[15] The Committee of Experts would make a report which, as at present, would be communicated to the Governing Body and the Conference.[16]

This decision was based on a note by the Office to the Governing Body, which was approved in the above-mentioned decision. That note read in relevant part:

> 36. It was in pursuance of a Resolution adopted by the Conference in 1926 that the Committee of Experts was set up by the Governing Body in the following year, as part of the mechanism of supervision of the application of Conventions, to carry out an examination of the annual reports submitted by Governments under Article 22 of the Constitution in preparation for the examination of these reports from a wider angle by the Conference, with the assistance of the three groups represented at the Conference. It has been recognised from the outset that the technical examination of the annual reports carried out by the Experts is an indispensable preliminary to the over-all survey of application conducted by the Conference through its Committee on the Application of Conventions. With the approval of the Governing Body, the report of the Committee of Experts is communicated to Governments and to the Conference.

> 37. It is accordingly suggested that, as from the coming into force of the amendments to the Constitution adopted by the Conference at its Montreal Session, 1946, the Committee of Experts on the Application of Conventions should be known as the 'Committee of Experts on the Application of Conventions and Recommendations', and that the Committee should be called upon to examine:

> (a)   the annual reports under Article 22 of the Constitution on the measures taken by Members to give effect to the provisions of Conventions to which they are parties, and the information furnished by Members concerning the results of inspections;

---

[14] ILO, Minutes of the Governing Body, 102nd Session, June–July 1947, 49.

[15] Article 35 refers to reports on the application of Conventions and Recommendations in non-metropolitan territories.

[16] ILO, Minutes of the Governing Body, 103rd Session, December 1947, 57.

(b)   the information and reports concerning Conventions and Recommendations communicated by Members in accordance with Article 19 of the Constitution;

(c)   information and reports on the measures taken by Members in accordance with Article 35 of the Constitution.

The Committee of Experts would make a report which the Director-General would submit in due course to the Governing Body and to the Conference.[17]

This remains today the mandate of the Committee of Experts. The Committee of Experts described its view of its responsibilities in its report to the 2013 Session of the Conference:

> The task of the Committee of Experts is to indicate the extent to which each Member State's legislation and practice are in conformity with ratified Conventions and the extent to which Member States have fulfilled their obligations under the ILO Constitution in relation to standards.[18]

The Experts' comments on the application of conventions therefore require it from time to time to find that a government is or is not in compliance with the Convention's requirements.

B.   Conference Committee on the Application of Standards

At the same time that it created the Committee of Experts in 1926, the ILO Governing Body created the Conference Committee on the Application of Conventions and Recommendations, a tripartite committee of the Conference. Its mandate today, following the 1946 revision of the Constitution, is described as follows in Article 7 of the Standing Orders of the Conference:

> Committee on the Application of Conventions and Recommendations
>
> 1.   The Conference shall as soon as possible appoint a Committee to consider:
>
> (a)   the measures taken by Members to give effect to the provisions of Conventions to which they are parties and the information furnished by Members concerning the results of inspections;
>
> (b)   the information and reports concerning Conventions and Recommendations communicated by Members in accordance with Article 19 of the Constitution;
>
> (c)   the measures taken by Members in accordance with Article 35 of the Constitution.
>
> 2.   The Committee shall submit a report to the Conference.

This mandate is similar to the mandate of the Committee of Experts, though as explained above the CAS does not directly examine governments' reports. It was described in the 1947 note as being responsible for the 'over-all survey of

---

[17] ibid, Appendix XII, 167 ff.

[18] Report of the Committee of Experts on the Application of Conventions and Recommendations, Report III (Part 4A), International Labour Conference, 102nd Session, 2013, 2.

application' and not with detailed supervision. The CAS bases its work on the Committee of Experts' report but, as evident from Article 7 above, the CAS does not occupy a superior, but rather a complementary, role in relation to the Committee of Experts.

Although neither committee is explicitly tasked with determining the extent of compliance with ratified conventions, both of them have elected over time to do so. The CAS adopts conclusions on each of the cases it discusses concerning compliance with the conventions concerned. It may classify some cases as 'continued failure over several years to eliminate serious deficiencies in the application of ratified Conventions'. For instance, in 2010 its report contained the following paragraph:

> 222. The Committee recalled that its working methods provide for the listing of cases of continued failure over several years to eliminate serious deficiencies, previously discussed, in the application of ratified Conventions. This year the Committee noted with great concern that there had been continued failure over several years to eliminate serious discrepancies in the application by Myanmar of the Freedom of Association and Protection of the Right to Organise Convention, 1948 (No 87).[19]

C. Relationship between Mandates

The Employers' Group maintains that the Committee of Experts' conclusions should be subordinated to those of the CAS (and the Conference). In the report of the 2012 Session of the Conference Committee, the Employers' group stated:

> 12. Moreover, while the Employer members recognized that the Committee of Experts was an independent body composed of legal experts, they recalled once again that the overall responsibility for the supervision of international labour standards lay with the International Labour Conference (ILC), through this Committee, which had to establish to this end an effective framework, including rules and methods. The Committee of Experts had a mandate to undertake preparatory tasks in this context – that were delegated to the Office – and to facilitate, not to replace, the tripartite supervision of this Committee. The supervision of international labour standards should be at the service of the ILO's tripartite constituents and reflect their needs, including the needs of workers and employers.

The following year, in a position paper presented at the 2013 Conference, the Employers' Group stated: 'The Committee of Experts has the task of preparing the supervisory work of the Committee on the Application of Standards (CAS) of the International Labour Conference (ILC)'.[20]

---

[19] ILC, Record of Proceedings No 16, Part I, 99th Session, Geneva, 2010, 1/62.

[20] ILC, 102nd Session of the International Labour Conference, 5–20 June 2013, Committee on the Application of Standards (CAS), 27 May 2013, Briefing Note for Governments.

As Lee Swepston, former Senior Adviser on Human Rights to the ILO, has explained, 'The mandate of neither Committee indicates a hierarchy between them, and, in particular, neither Committee is accorded the role of passing judgment on the findings of the other'.[21] The essential task of the Committee of Experts is to assess the conformity of national law and practice with the conventions each State has ratified.[22] The Committee of Experts works on the basis of the governments' reports and analyses their legislation and practice for conformity, taking into account any information furnished either by the government or by employers' and workers' organisations, or which is revealed by the research of the Committee's secretariat, the International Labour Office. This is the analytical function, and it is for this reason that the members of the Committee of Experts are eminent jurists.

The task of the CAS, which is composed of delegates of the governments, employers and workers, is to 'add a public and political element of direct discussions with selected governments in a tripartite setting to gather additional information and put additional pressure on them in a public setting to implement the Conventions they have ratified'.[23] Once the CAS has considered an individual case, it returns it to the Committee of Experts for further consideration, and cases may go back and forth between the two committees for many years. Each committee bases its work in large part on the work of the other, in a circular and complementary way. This relation between two independent but complementary supervisory bodies is one that is found nowhere else in the UN system.

It cannot be maintained convincingly that the Committee of Experts' work is merely preparatory for the Conference Committee's discussions. Again, as Swepston explained, the argument 'that the Experts' conclusions are not legally valid unless specifically endorsed by the Conference Committee [on the Application of Standards], do[es] not stand up to examination'.[24] Only a tiny portion of the Committee of Experts' observations are discussed in the Conference and none of its direct requests are supervised at all (which constitute by far the largest portion of its comments). It would be nonsensical that the ILO would have entrusted to the CAS, which again reviews the application of a handful of conventions each year, the fundamental role of determining the meaning of the entire corpus of international labour standards. Indeed, until the Employers' Group began criticising the views of the Committee of Experts on the right to strike, the CAS simply took all the Committee of Experts' observations as established and added an element of public discussion to a very few of them.

And to the present day, the CAS as a whole has never attempted to develop a distinct statement of the scope and effect of conventions.

---

[21] L Swepston, 'Crisis in the ILO Supervisory System: Dispute Over the Right to Strike' (2013) 29 *International Journal of Comparative Labour Law and Industrial Relations* 199, 202.

[22] Article 7(1)(a) of the Standing Orders of the International Labour Conference, available at: www. ilo.org/ public/english/standards/relm/ilc/ilc-so.htm#Article7.

[23] See Swepston (n 21 above).

[24] ibid, 215.

Finally, the extent to which the Conference has the last word on interpretation derives from its 'legislative' power. The question as to whether the Conference was best placed to both adopt and interpret conventions was discussed in a report submitted by the ILO to the Governing Body in 1993. The report noted that no conference can bind another and raised questions as to the composition of the conference which adopted an instrument and a subsequent conference which could be called upon to interpret it. The report also questioned whether interpretation by the Conference could result in a 'clandestine modification of meaning'. The report concluded that 'an interpretation by the Conference, if it is to be perfectly legitimate, should logically be recast – that is, through a revision'. This is to say, if the Conference does not like how an instrument has been interpreted, it is free to amend that instrument through its legislative function.[25] Thus, the Conference has the right to revise conventions to express exact meanings which the supervisory bodies would have to follow, subject to ratification of the revised instruments.

In sum, the complementarity of the roles of the two committees appears to be accepted by other ILO constituents without a need to decide whether one committee has ascendancy over the other. And indeed, the opinion expressed by the Committee of Experts in 1990 is in fact the way in which the committees have interacted.

III. The Committee of Experts and the Interpretation of Conventions

The Employers' Group has challenged the right of the Committee of Experts to 'interpret' conventions, specifically in relation to the question of the right to strike, a position adopted by no other part of the ILO structure. Their insistence on their own point of view without following the wider consensus threatens the operation of machinery that has functioned well since 1927.

All of the ILO's supervisory bodies perform an interpretive function, including whether the law and practice of a Member State falls within the ambit of an instrument. This includes both those bodies that supervise conventions, like the Committee of Experts, and those that supervise the implementation of the Constitution – which after all is also an international treaty, like the CFA. The most analytically authoritative interpretive function is confided to the two ILO supervisory bodies composed of independent jurists (the Committee of Experts and Commissions of Inquiry). As labour law scholar Claire La Hovary explained:

> While it is clear to everybody that the Committee of Experts does not have the legal mandate to interpret conventions, it is also clear that the Committee of Experts needs

---

[25] See ILO, Article 37, Paragraph 2, of the Constitution and the Interpretation of International Labour Conventions, Governing Body, 256th Session, May 1993, GB256/2/2, paras 22–24, available at: www.ilo.org/public/libdoc/ilo/GB/256/GB.256_SC_2_2_engl.pdf.

to interpret provisions of the conventions in the process of its work of evaluating the implementation of conventions. Indeed, a body that is created to verify the application of conventions must interpret these conventions, for the same reason that 'there is no application of law without interpretation'.[26]

Legal scholar Nicolas Valticos has also explained well the interpretive function of the Committee of Experts:

> This interpretative role is not based on any express authority but follows logically from its mandate and the nature of its task. It has increased over the years as the Organization has adopted texts in deliberately general terms in the interest of flexibility. The increasing generality of the terms used in international labour conventions has resulted in an increase in the interpretative role of the Committee of Experts, which is called upon to assess more accurately the meaning and scope of a convention in order to assess whether it is actually being respected. While the need and scope for interpretation are minimal in the case of technical agreements drafted in specific terms, such as those providing for a specific minimum age for admission to work or a certain duration of maternity leave or paid leave, they are considerable in the case of agreements establishing principles in general terms, which are also generally those that deal with fundamental issues.[27]

Following this is the question of the weight afforded to such interpretations. Again, while only interpretations rendered by the ICJ are binding in a technical sense, the observations of the Committee of Experts must be viewed as authoritative. This assertion is supported by the Committee's status in the ILO Constitution, its distinguished composition, the soundness of its reasoning, and the concordance of its observations with other bodies both within and without the ILO and the global respect given to its conclusions. If these observations were not treated in a practical sense as binding, Member States would have no certainty as to the requirements of ratified conventions in order to apply them (or the scope of the obligations States may consider ratifying). The accretion of these observations over the decades is properly viewed as a jurisprudence.[28]

---

[26] See C La Hovary, 'Showdown at the ILO? A Historical Perspective on the Employers' Group's 2012 Challenge to the Right to Strike' (2013) 42 *Industrial Law Journal* 338, 351, fn 44, citing G Scelle, *Précis de droit des Gens*, vol 2 (Paris, Sirey, 1932) 488. See also C Hofmann and N Schuster, 'It ain't over 'til it's over: the right to strike and the mandate of the ILO Committee of Experts revisited', Global Labour University, Working Paper No 40, ILO, Geneva 2016.

[27] N Valticos, *Droit international du travail* (Paris, Dalloz, 1983) 136, para 176 (authors' translation from the French text).

[28] With regard to the idea of international jurisprudence, again Valticos provides useful insight. See N Valticos, 'Le développement d'une jurisprudence internationale au sujet des normes établies par les organisations internationales (spécialement à propos des normes relatives au travail)' in *Memoriam Sir Otto Kahn Freund* (München, Beck, 1980) 715, 718: 'Between the formulation of the rule by the international standard-setting body (the Conference) and its application to particular cases, several stages of successive concretisation should intervene, at the international and national levels, their number and importance depending on the greater or lesser degree of generality of the international standard … This international concretisation can be construed as constituting an international jurisprudence in the widest sense, that is to say, insofar as it completes the international legal order by the information it provides about the scope of international standards'.

This is given further weight by the absence of any other mechanism which could provide interpretive guidance. In addition to a referral to the ICJ, Article 37(2) of the ILO Constitution provides for the creation of an in-house tribunal to settle questions or disputes relating to the interpretation of a convention. Though the creation of this in-house tribunal has been debated, it has not been established. The last time the issue was considered, the Employers' Group and several governments did not support its creation.[29] In the absence of recourse to the ICJ and given that the tribunal has not been established, the Committee of Experts necessarily has had to fill the gaps to 'settle day to day difficulties without having to go through the complex procedure of requesting an advisory opinion of the court'.[30]

It is of particular note that in 2014 the Employers' Group welcomed the Committee of Experts' restatement of its mandate, which in large part make our points above, and indeed requested that it be reproduced in all future volumes.

> The Committee of Experts undertakes an impartial and technical analysis of how the Conventions are applied in law and practice by member States, *while cognizant of different national realities and legal systems. In doing so, it must determine the legal scope, content and meaning of the provisions of the Conventions.* Its opinions and recommendations are non-binding, being intended to guide the actions of national authorities. *They derive their persuasive value from the legitimacy and rationality of the Committee's work based on its impartiality, experience and expertise. The Committee's technical role and moral authority is well recognized,* particularly as it has been engaged in its supervisory task for more than 90 years, by virtue of its composition, independence and its working methods built on continuing dialogue with governments taking into account information provided by employers' and workers' organizations. *This has been reflected in the incorporation of the Committee's opinions and recommendations in national legislation, international instruments and court decisions* (emphasis added).[31]

---

[29] ILO, Minutes of the Governing Body, 322nd Session, November 2014, GB322/PV, 17–28.

[30] Para 10; See, also F Maupain, L'interprétation des conventions internationales du travail dans Mélanges en l'honneur de Nicolas Valticos: Droit et justice (Paris Pedone, 1999) 571: 'elle note en particulier que, d'une part, la supervision comporte toujours une part d'interprétation et, d'autre part, que si les Etats ne sont pas d'accord avec ses interprétations, la Constitution comporte un mécanisme afin de mettre précisément un terme aux débats. Les Etats ou les parties concernes sont libres de ne pas se prévaloir de ce mécanisme, mais ils ne sauraient refuser alors d'assumer les conséquences de leur contestation sans mettre en péril la sécurité juridique. C'est pourquoi, aussi longtemps que les vues qu'elle exprime au sujet de la signification des dispositions d'une convention et de sa portée juridique ne sont pas contredites par la Cour internationale de Justice, elles sont réputées valables et communément admises'. ('One notes in particular that, on the one hand, supervision always involves interpretation and, on the other hand, that if States do not agree with its interpretations, the Constitution includes a mechanism precisely to end the debates. States or parties concerned are free not to avail themselves of this mechanism, but they cannot then refuse to assume the consequences of their challenge without jeopardising legal certainty. Therefore, as long as the views it expresses concerning the meaning of the provisions of a convention and its legal scope are not contradicted by the International Court of Justice, they are considered valid and generally accepted').

[31] See, ILO, Report of the Committee of Experts on the Application of Standards (Part I) (*General Report* 2014) para 46 stating that the Employers 'also welcomed the response of the Committee of Experts to the discussions in the Conference Committee and the clarification by the Committee of Experts in paragraph 31 of the *General Report* concerning the scope of their mandate. They further

This restatement makes clear the position of the Committee of Experts as a respected voice in the interpretation of ILO conventions, including of course Convention 87. It makes clear that the Committee must inevitably and logically interpret the scope, meaning and content of convention provisions while cognisant of different national realities and legal systems. It underscores its impartiality, experience and expertise, which give its observations and recommendations persuasive value. Finally, it underscores that national legislatures, national and transnational courts and other international instruments have adopted their reasoning, based on the authority of their views (and the correctness of their reasoning).

IV. Conclusion

The accumulation of the legally non-binding interpretations by all the ILO supervisory bodies has been so gradual, and so thorough, that it is difficult to imagine a challenge to the authority of the Committee of Experts to flesh out the words of conventions and to adapt their understanding of the meaning of these standards to new situations, sometimes nearly a century after the convention in question was adopted, unless a similar position was adopted by all the ILO supervisory bodies, and for all conventions.

Similar points can be made concerning the constitutional complaint procedures. There is the same circular relation among these bodies and the 'regular' supervisory machinery. Representations committees and Commissions of Inquiry carry out functions that are more similar to the Committee of Experts than to the CAS, by examining individual situations in relation to a given convention (or occasionally a set of conventions). One major difference is that neither the Committee of Experts nor the Commissions of Inquiry submits their conclusions for approval by a higher body, in spite of the employers' assertions concerning the relationship between the Committee of Experts and the CAS. Both the Committee of Experts and Commissions of Inquiry – the bodies with independent, expert legal membership – arrive at their own conclusions, which are then noted and acted upon by other bodies without being subject to challenge except by the ICJ. The other two committees, with tripartite, non-expert composition, adopt conclusions that must be approved, by the plenary of the Conference and by the Governing Body respectively.

---

encouraged the Committee of Experts to continue to set out this section of the text in bold, in all future reports, including the *General Survey*, as it was important to highlight its significance', available at: www.ilo.org/wcmsp5/groups/public/---ed_norm/---relconf/documents/meetingdocument/wcms_ 246781.pdf.

PART III

A Rebuttal: The Indisputable Case for the Right to Strike

4

The Rules of Interpretation: The Vienna Convention on the Law of Treaties (VCLT)

Elaborated within the UN system, the VCLT contains, inter alia, rules on the interpretation of international treaties, such as ILO Convention 87.[1] Articles 31–33 of the VCLT and other relevant provisions are set out in Annex III, but Articles 31 and 32, which principally guide our analysis, are set out below:

Article 31: General rule of interpretation

1. A treaty shall be interpreted in good faith in accordance with the ordinary meaning to be given to the terms of the treaty in their context and in the light of its object and purpose.
2. The context for the purpose of the interpretation of a treaty shall comprise, in addition to the text, including its preamble and annexes:
   (a) any agreement relating to the treaty which was made between all the parties in connection with the conclusion of the treaty;
   (b) any instrument which was made by one or more parties in connection with the conclusion of the treaty and accepted by the other parties as an instrument related to the treaty.
3. There shall be taken into account, together with the context:
   (a) any subsequent agreement between the parties regarding the interpretation of the treaty or the application of its provisions;
   (b) any subsequent practice in the application of the treaty which establishes the agreement of the parties regarding its interpretation;
   (c) any relevant rules of international law applicable in the relations between the parties.
4. A special meaning shall be given to a term if it is established that the parties so intended.

Article 32: Supplementary means of interpretation

Recourse may be had to supplementary means of interpretation, including the preparatory work of the treaty and the circumstances of its conclusion, in order to

---

[1] R Gardiner, *Treaty Interpretation* (Oxford, Oxford University Press, 2008) 5.

confirm the meaning resulting from the application of article 31, or to determine the meaning when the interpretation according to article 31:

(a)   leaves the meaning ambiguous or obscure; or

(b)   leads to a result which is manifestly absurd or unreasonable.

Importantly, the objective criteria (Article 31) are given priority over the history-oriented criteria such as *travaux préparatoires* (Article 32). The Employers' Group argue that the ILO supervisory system, and the Committee of Experts in particular, have failed to obey the relevant rules of the VCLT on treaty interpretation in observing a right to strike in Convention 87 and thereafter regulating its exercise.[2] This cannot be sustained. Both the Committee of Experts and the Committee on Freedom of Association (CFA) have recognised the existence of a right to strike in a manner which, on analysis, is entirely consistent with the rules of interpretation. Indeed, in giving deference as it does to the findings of the CFA, the Committee of Experts is already taking into account consensus-based tripartite opinion on interpretation of the ILO conventions in the light of the ILO Constitution.

I. Applicability of the VCLT

There is a preliminary question as to whether the VCLT, or at least its rules of interpretation, applies to the ILO. This question raises issues of retroactivity (*ratione temporis*),[3] material scope (*ratione materiae*)[4] and the personal scope (*ratione personae*).

A. Retroactivity

Article 4 provides for the general rule of non-retroactivity and, accordingly, the VCLT would not apply. Convention 87 was adopted in 1948. The VCLT was signed

---

[2] ILO, Report of the Committee of Experts on the Application of Conventions and Recommendations, *Application of International Labour Standards 2013*, Report III (Part 1A), International Labour Conference, 102nd Session, 2013 (*Annual Report* 2013) 13, para 34. 'While in 1990, the Employers criticized a statement in the Committee's report that they viewed as saying in substance that competence to interpret Conventions absent an ICJ submission rests solely with the Committee (paragraph 22), following extended discussion involving workers and governments as well, the Employers emphasized their view of the Vienna Convention as "the appropriate – in fact the only – yardstick to be used in interpreting ILO Conventions. It was this yardstick that they invited the Committee to use in their interpretation of international labour standards"'.

[3] Article 4, 'Non-retroactivity of the present Convention: Without prejudice to the application of any rules set forth in the present Convention to which treaties would be subject under international law independently of the Convention, the Convention applies only to treaties which are concluded by States after the entry into force of the present Convention with regard to such States'.

[4] Article 5, 'Treaties constituting international organizations and treaties adopted within an international organization: The present Convention applies to any treaty which is the constituent instrument

on 23 May 1969 and entered into force on 27 January 1980. However, Article 4 provides that the rules enshrined in the VCLT apply to a treaty 'under international law independently of the Convention'. Thus, if the interpretation rules contained in Articles 31–33 VCLT are considered 'international law' (as indeed they are), then the principle of non-retroactivity of the VCLT would not apply. Indeed, the requirement to give the ordinary meaning to the terms of an international treaty has been continuously observed for more than a century before the VCLT entered into force.

B. Material Scope

Article 5 of the VCLT, included at the insistence of the ILO, provides that the rules of the Convention shall apply to the constituent instruments of international organisations and any treaty adopted within an international organisation without prejudice to any relevant rules of the organisation.[5] The term 'rules' is to be understood in a broad sense.[6] The ILO is an international organisation[7] and Convention 87 is a treaty adopted[8] within the ILO. Therefore, the reservation applies. It follows that, as a principle, the rules of the ILO take precedence over the rules contained in the VCLT.

---

of any international organization and to any treaty within an international organization without prejudice to any relevant rules of the organization'.

[5] Indeed, then ILO Director General Mr Jenks, who attended the UN Conference on the Law of Treaties, stated that 'ILO practice on the interpretation had involved greater recourse to preparatory work than was envisaged' in the draft convention. The ILO supervisory bodies have indeed developed interpretive practices under which the preparatory work, as well as the comments of other supervisory bodies, has a role: see United Nations Conference on the Law of Treaties Vienna, First session 26 March–24 May 1968, UN DOC A/CONF.39/C.1/SR.7 (7th meeting of the Committee of the Whole), p 37 para 12, available at: https://undocs.org/en/A/CONF.39/11.

[6] 'At the first session of the Conference his delegation had proposed (A/CONF.39/C.1/.39) the addition of the words "and established practices" after the word "rules" in order to make it clear that the term "rules" was not to be understood in too restrictive a sense. His delegation had not pressed that amendment to the vote, because, as the Chairman of the Drafting Committee has pointed out at the 28th meeting of the Committee of the Whole, the Drafting Committee had taken the view that the term "rules" applied both to written and to unwritten customary rules' (Sir Francis Vallat, United Kingdom, United Nations, United Nations Conference on the Law of Treaties, Second Session Vienna, 9 April–22 May 1969, Official Records, New York 1970, 4).

[7] See the definition in Article 2 (i): '"international organisation" means an "intergovernmental organisation"' (see also the reference in Article 9(2) VCLT: 'The adoption of the text of a treaty at an international conference takes place by the vote of two-thirds of the States present and voting, unless by the same majority they shall decide to apply a different rule').

[8] 'Certain governments, in their comments on what was then part III of the draft articles (application, effects, modification and interpretation), expressed the view that care must be taken to avoid allowing the rules of international organizations to restrict the freedom of negotiating States unless the conclusion was part of the work of the organization, and not merely when the treaty was drawn up within it because of the convenience of using conference facilities. Noting these comments, the Commission revised the formulation of the reservation at its present session so as to make it cover only "constituent instruments" and treaties which are "*adopted*" within an international organisation"' Wetzel, Ralf Günter/Rauschning, Dietrich, The Vienna Convention on the Law of Treaties – Travaux Préparatoires – Die Wieder Vertragsrechtskonvention – Materialien zur Entstehung der einzelnen Vorschriften, Alfred Metzner Verlag, Frankfurt am Main, 1976.

C. Personal Scope

The VCLT is itself not legally binding on the ILO in general or on any of its supervisory bodies in particular. As international organisations/institutions, they are not (and cannot be) contracting parties to the VCLT. Indeed, Articles 81 ff of the VCLT provide for the ratification and accession by States only. Nevertheless, this limitation does not concern those parts of the VCLT which are considered customary international law, such as the rules on interpretation of treaties.

II.   VCLT Rules of Interpretation as Customary International Law[9]

The rules of interpretation have played an important role during the process of elaboration of the VCLT. The International Court of Justice (ICJ), in the *Kasikili/ Sedudu Island* case (1999), held that Article 31 of the VCLT on treaty interpretations reflected customary international law and therefore applied despite the fact that neither Botswana nor Namibia were parties to the VCLT and that the treaty in question entered into force in 1890:

> As regards the interpretation of that Treaty, the Court notes that neither Botswana nor Namibia are parties to the Vienna Convention on the Law of Treaties of 23 May 1969, but that both of them consider that Article 31 of the Vienna Convention is applicable inasmuch as it reflects customary international law. The Court itself has already had occasion in the past to hold that customary international law found expression in Article 31 of the Vienna Convention (see *Territorial Dispute (Libyan Arab Jamahiriya/ Chad), Judgment, ICJ Reports 1994*, p 21, para 41; *Oil Platforms (Islamic Republic of Iran v United States of America), Preliminary Objections, Judgment, ICJ Reports 1996 (II)*, p 8 12, para 23). Article 4 of the Convention, which provides that it 'applies only to treaties which are concluded by States after the entry into force of the … Convention with regard to such States', does not, therefore, prevent the Court from interpreting the 1890 Treaty in accordance with the rules reflected in Article 31 of the Convention.[10]

The ICJ clearly considers that the 'rules reflected in Article 31 of the Convention' constitute customary international law and applies them irrespective of any limitation against retroactivity under Article 4. This general proposition is confirmed by

---

[9] *Customary international law* refers to international legal obligations binding on all States which arise from (1) established State practice, and (2) *opinio juris* – meaning that States view the custom as obligatory, not as a mere courtesy or moral obligation. See Military and Paramilitary Activities in and Against Nicaragua (*Nicaragua v United States of America*) ICJ Rep 1986, 87–88, paras 183–87. See also 'Continental Shelf' (*Libyan Arab Jarnahiriyu v Malta*) ICJ Rep 1985, 29–30, para 27.

[10] See Judgment, 13 December 1999 *Kasikili/Sedudu Island (Botswana/Namibia)* ICJ Rep 1999, 1045, para 18. For more recent authority, see Preliminary Objections, Judgment, 2 February 2017 *Maritime Delimitation in the Indian Ocean (Somalia v Kenya)* ICJ Rep 2017, 3, para 63 and Judgment, 17 July 2019 *Jadhav Case (India/Pakistan)* para 71.

other international (regional) courts which have considered that the interpretation rules, in particular Article 31 have to be considered as 'international law'. Indeed, in an Advisory Opinion the Inter-American Court of Human Rights stated:

> 48. The manner in which the request for the advisory opinion has been framed reveals the need to ascertain the meaning and scope of Article 4 of the Convention, especially paragraphs 2 and 4, and to determine whether these provisions might be interrelated. To this end, the Court will apply the rules of interpretation set out in the *Vienna Convention*, which may be deemed to state the relevant *international law principles* applicable to this subject.[11]

At the European level, the European Court of Human Rights (ECtHR) refers extensively to the VCLT's rules of interpretation. In many judgments, it refers to the principles of these provisions,[12] albeit employing formulations which make it clear that these principles are not intended to be direct and totally binding, in particular as regards matters of interpretation. By formulating certain qualifications such as 'guided mainly by the rules'[13] or 'in the light of the rules'[14] of interpretation provided for in Articles 31–33 VCLT or qualifying them as a 'backbone for the interpretation',[15] the ECtHR obviously seeks to ensure that some degree of flexibility is retained. It appears that the ECtHR has in mind use of Article 5 VCLT without referring to it directly. This is, no doubt, to preserve the primacy of the ECHR as the 'relevant rules of the organisation'. The ECtHR is not the only European body to do so, however. The European Committee of Social Rights has

---

[11] 8.9.1983 – OC-3/83 – para 48 (emphasis added). In para 49 it quoted the relevant rules as follows: 'These rules specify that treaties must be interpreted "in good faith in accordance with the ordinary meaning to be given to the terms of the treaty in their context and in the light of its object and purpose"' [Vienna Convention, Article 31(1)]. Supplementary means of interpretation, especially the preparatory work of the treaty, may be used to confirm the meaning resulting from the application of the foregoing provisions, or when it 'leaves the meaning ambiguous or obscure or leads to a result which is manifestly absurd or unreasonable' (ibid, Article 32). It goes on in para 50: 'This method of interpretation respects the principle of the primacy of the text, that is, the application of objective criteria of interpretation. In the case of human rights treaties, moreover, objective criteria of interpretation that look to the texts themselves are more appropriate than subjective criteria that seek to ascertain only the intent of the Parties. This is so because human rights treaties, as the Court has already noted, are not multilateral treaties of the traditional type concluded to accomplish the reciprocal exchange of rights for the mutual benefit of the contracting States; "rather" their object and purpose is the protection of the basic rights of individual human beings, irrespective of their nationality, both against the State of their nationality and all other contracting States'.

[12] See ECtHR (Grand Chamber) Judgment, *Andrejeva v Latvia* App No 55707/00 (18 February 2009) para 18; see also paras 19–20; ECtHR (Third Section) Judgment, *Mirojubovs and others v Latvia* App No 798/05 (15 September 2009) para 62; ECtHR (First Section) Judgment, *Rantsev v Cyprus and Russia* App No 25965/04 (7 January 2010) paras 273–74.

[13] ECtHR (Grand Chamber), *Demir and Baykara v Turkey* App No 34503/97 (12 November 2008) 28 EHRR 54, para 65.

[14] ECtHR (Grand Chamber) *Cudak v Lithuania* App No 15869/02 (23 March, 2010) para 56. For more recent authority, see, eg, ECtHR (Grand Chamber), *Magyar Helsinki Bizottság v Hungary* App No 18030/11 (8 November 2016) para 118.

[15] ECtHR (Grand Chamber) *Andrejeva v Latvia* (n 12 above) para 19.

regularly used the VCLT in interpreting the European Social Charter, including on matters relating to labour law.[16]

III. ILO Practice

As for the ILO's 'internal rules', the Committee of Experts has tended to refer expressly to Article 31 VCLT:

'[T]he Committee constantly bore in mind all different methods of interpreting treaty law, *especially the Vienna Convention*'.[17]

With regard to the views put forward that the preparatory work would not support the inclusion of the right to strike, the Committee would first observe that the absence of a concrete provision is not dispositive, as the terms of the Convention must be interpreted in the light of its object and purpose. While the Committee considers that the preparatory work is an important supplementary interpretative source when reviewing the application of a particular Convention in a given country, it may yield to the other interpretative factors, in particular, in this specific case, to the subsequent practice over a period of 52 years (see Articles 31 and 32 of the Vienna Convention on the Law of Treaties).[18]

and

'In responding to the request to clarify the methods followed when expressing its views on the meaning of the provisions of Conventions, the Committee reiterates that it constantly and consistently bears in mind all the different methods of interpreting treaties recognized under international public law, and in particular under the Vienna Convention on the Law of Treaties, 1969. In particular, the Committee has always paid due regard to the textual meaning of the words in light of the Convention's purpose and object as provided for by Article 31 of the Vienna Convention, giving equal consideration to the two authentic languages of ILO Conventions, namely the English and French versions (Article 33 of the Vienna Convention). In addition, and in accordance with Articles 5 and 32 of the Vienna Convention, the Committee takes into account the Organization's practice of examining the preparatory work leading to the adoption of the Convention. This is especially important for ILO Conventions in view of the tripartite nature of the Organization and the role that the tripartite constituents play in standard setting.'[19]

Further, in its General observation – Indigenous and Tribal Peoples Convention, 1989 (No 169) the Committee of Experts used nearly the same wording.[20]

---

[16] See, K Lörcher, 'Interpretation' in N Bruun, K Lörcher, I Schömann and S Clauwaert (eds), *The European Social Charter and the Employment Relation* (Oxford, Hart Publishing, 2017).

[17] Committee of Experts Report 2013, Part I, para 27 (emphasis added).

[18] ILO, Report of the Committee of Experts on the Application of Conventions and Recommendations, *General Survey on the Fundamental Conventions concerning rights at work in light of the ILO Declaration on Social Justice for a Fair Globalisation 2008*, Report III (Part 1B) para 118.

[19] Committee of Experts Report 2011, Part I, para 12.

[20] See also General observation – Indigenous and Tribal Peoples Convention, 1989 (No 169) ibid, 783 ('The Committee of Experts has, on a number of occasions, stated that, although its mandate does

The analysis of the applicability of the VCLT's interpretation rules has shown that they are 'international law independently of the Convention' in the sense of Article 4 of the VCLT and are to be applied, in general, without any restriction *ratione temporis*. Equally, it is therefore irrelevant that the ILO is not (and cannot) be a party to the VCLT (*ratione personae*). However, there remains a question as to the extent to which the interpretation rules enshrined in Articles 31–33 VCLT have to be altered or nuanced by the ILO 'internal rules' (Article 5 VCLT – *ratione materiae*).

In 2007, the Committee of Experts made note of the different methods of interpreting conventions. In interpreting Convention 29 as to questions of modern-day slavery, it stated:

> In interpreting conventions, the terms and purposes had to be taken into consideration, as they were living instruments which had not to be solely interpreted in the context of prevailing conditions which existed at the time of their adoption. Indeed, a review of the Committee of Experts' methodology confirms a more flexible approach to interpretation, including the actual terms in their own context and in light of the purpose of the convention, as well as preparatory work, the views of the Office and the other supervisory mechanisms.[21]

The Committee of Experts referred to these issues again in 2011, responding to a request to clarify the methods followed when expressing its views on the meaning of the provisions of Conventions. It reiterated that:

> It constantly and consistently bears in mind all the different methods of interpreting treaties recognized under international public law, and in particular under the Vienna Convention on the Law of Treaties, 1969. In particular, the Committee of Experts has always paid due regard to the textual meaning of the words in light of the Convention's purpose and object as provided for by Article 31 of the Vienna Convention. In addition, and in accordance with Articles 5 and 32 of the Vienna Convention, the Committee takes into account the Organization's practice of examining the preparatory

not require it to give definitive interpretation of ILO Conventions, in order to carry out its function of determining whether the requirements of Conventions are being respected, it has to consider and express its views on the legal scope and meaning of the provisions of Conventions, where appropriate. In doing so, the Committee has always paid due regard to the textual meaning of the words in light of the Convention's purpose and object as provided for by Article 31 of the Vienna Convention on the Law of Treaties, giving equal consideration to the two authoritative texts of ILO Conventions, namely the English and French versions (Article 33 of the Vienna Convention). In addition, and in accordance with Articles 5 and 32 of the Vienna Convention, the Committee takes into account the Organization's practice of examining the preparatory work leading to the adoption of the Convention. This is especially important for ILO Conventions in view of the tripartite nature of the Organization and the role the tripartite constituents play in standard setting'). Endnote 1: '1 – See ILC, 63rd Session, 1977, Report III (Part 4A), Report of the Committee of Experts on the Application of Conventions and Recommendations, para 32; ILC, 73rd Session, 1987, Report III (Part 4A), Report of the Committee of Experts on the Application of Conventions and Recommendations, para 21; ILC, 77th Session, 1990, Report III (Part 4A), Report of the Committee of Experts on the Application of Conventions and Recommendations, para 7; ILC, 78th Session, 1991, Report III (Part 4A), Report of the Committee of Experts on the Application of Conventions and Recommendations, paras 11 and 12'.

[21] Provisional Record No 22, ILC, 96th Session, Geneva, 2007, Part I, 40, para 133.

work leading to the adoption of the Convention. This is especially important for ILO Conventions in view of the tripartite nature of the Organization and the role that the tripartite constituents play in standard setting.[22]

The Committee of Experts has for many years confirmed that its interpretation of Convention 87 as including the right to strike was in conformity with (and indeed required by) the VCLT's rules of interpretation. The Committee of Experts appears to be the only supervisory body in the ILO which has considered the VCLT in any detail.

---

[22] CEACR Report, 100th Session, ILC 2011 (Part IA, Report III) para 12.

5

The Ordinary Meaning
of Convention 87 Supports
the Existence of a Right to Strike

The Employers' Group asserts that there is no right to strike to be found in Convention 87 because such a right is not expressed explicitly in those terms. Further, they claim that the rules of interpretation enshrined in Article 31 of the Vienna Convention on the Law of Treaties (VCLT) do not support the conclusion that Convention 87 includes the right to strike.[1] This is not a legally tenable position.[2]

The primary element in the rules of interpretation of Article 31 VCLT is that 'the ordinary meaning [is] to be given to the terms of the treaty in their context and in the light of its object and purpose'. Recognition of the requirement to interpret international treaties in accordance with the 'plain and obvious meaning' of words is long-standing and dates from well before the VCLT and was recorded as long ago as 1855.[3] 'The plain meaning of the words' was observed to be the primary guide for the interpretation of treaties in 1895.[4] Judicial practice giving primacy to the ordinary meaning of words in international treaties was noted in 1936.[5]

The principle was illustrated in the *Acquisition of Polish Nationality* case, where the Permanent Court of International Justice (PCIJ) stated that it was

> bound to apply this clause as it stands, without considering whether other provisions might with advantage have been added to or substituted for it … To impose an

---

[1] See International Organisation of Employers (IOE), *Do ILO Conventions 87 and 98 Recognize a Right to Strike?* October 2014, available at: www.ioe-emp.org/index.php?eID=dumpFile&t=f&f=11 1630&token=d3f4de458d8a4b740afa01b449c44cb11761654b, fn 15, stating: '[T]he Employers have consistently argued that a right to strike is not provided for in the text of ILO Conventions 87 and 98 and, according to all applicable methods of interpretation stated in the Vienna Convention on the Law of Treaties, it would be difficult to consider it to be implicit or customary law'.

[2] Article 31(2) VCLT is not relevant to our analysis as there was no agreement relating to Convention 87 between all the parties nor any instrument made by one or more parties in connection with the conclusion of Convention 87 and accepted by the other parties as an instrument related to the Treaty.

[3] See Sir Robert Phillimore, *Commentaries on International Law*, Vol II (Philadelphia, PA, T and JW Johnson, 1855) 73.

[4] WE Hall, *A Treatise on International Law* (Oxford, Clarendon Press, 1895) 350.

[5] M Jokl, *De l'Interpretation des traits normatifs d'aprés de la doctrine et la jurisprudence internationals* (1936) 24.

additional condition not provided for in the Treaty [under consideration] would be equivalent not to interpreting the Treaty but to reconstructing it.[6]

However, the literal rule is subject to exceptions. In the *Polish Postal Service in Danzig* case, the PCIJ stated (at paragraph 113) that:

It is a cardinal principle of interpretation that words must be interpreted in the sense which they would normally have in their context, unless such interpretation would lead to something unreasonable or absurd.[7]

This was the basis for the dissent of judges Anzilotti and Huber in the *Wimbledon* case.[8] There, the minority were only prepared to reject the literal meaning preferred by the majority on the basis that words cannot be presumed 'to express an idea which leads to contradictory or impossible consequences'. Even those sceptical of the literal rule concede that so long as no other common intention can be found, then the words must be given their literal meaning.[9]

Applying these rulings, we now turn to the relevant text of Convention 87.

Article 2 of ILO Convention 87 provides that:

Workers and employers, without distinction whatsoever, shall have the right to establish and, subject only to the rules of the organisation concerned, to join organisations of their own choosing without previous authorisation.

Article 3 provides that:

1. Workers' and employers' organisations shall have the right to draw up their constitutions and rules, to elect their representatives in full freedom, to organise their administration and activities and to formulate their programmes.

2. The public authorities shall refrain from any interference which would restrict this right or impede the lawful exercise thereof.

The *only limitations* on the rights described in Article 3 are found in Articles 8 and 9. Article 8 provides that in exercising those rights, those concerned 'shall respect the law of the land' though the latter 'shall not be such as to impair, nor shall it be so applied as to impair' those rights. Importantly, Article 9, which concerns the possible exclusion of the armed forces and the police, is *the only* provision in Convention 87 that specifies that the extent to which the guarantees of the Convention apply 'shall be determined by national laws and regulations'.[10]

---

[6] *Acquisition of Polish Nationality* Advisory Opinion of 15 September 1923, PCIJ Series B, No 6, 20.

[7] *Polish Postal Service in Danzig* Advisory Opinion of 16 May 1925 PCIJ Series B, No 11, 39.

[8] *SS Wimbledon* Dissenting Opinion of 17 August 1923 PCIJ Series A, No 1, 36.

[9] J Stone, 'Fictional Elements in Treaty Interpretation – A Study in the International Judicial Process' (1954) 1 *Sydney Law Review* 344, 355–56.

[10] There are provisions in a number of other ILO conventions which make it similarly explicit that particular rights, or protections, or obligations, are to be set exclusively through national laws or regulations, or that national governments have the option of limiting the scope of their obligations under a convention in certain respects. See Convention 182, Article 4(2) which provides that the types of hazardous work which children shall not perform are to be determined by national law. See also

No other provision of Convention 87 provides for the exclusive role of national laws and regulations to determine the scope of the right. It must therefore be the case, following the principle of *expressio unis*, that no other occupations are to be so regulated by national law. Rather, like almost all convention provisions, it is expected that their application in law and practice be influenced by the observations and recommendations of the Committee of Experts, which are, per its mandate, intended to guide the actions taken by national authorities.

Article 10 is an interpretation clause and significantly provides that:

> In this Convention the term organisation means any organisation of workers or of employers for furthering and defending the interests of workers or of employers.

The words of Article 3 provide the right to draw up constitutions and rules, organise activities and formulate programmes. Thus, the words of Article 3 confer on trade unions (and employers' associations) the right to draw up their *rules and constitutions* on any subject matter whatever. The first five meanings of the noun 'rule' given by the *Oxford English Dictionary* (*OED*) are:[11]

(i) a principle, regulation, or maxim governing individual conduct;
(ii) the code of discipline or body of regulations observed by a religious order or congregation;
(iii) a principle regulating practice or procedure;
(iv) an order made by a judge or court (hence irrelevant here);
(v) a regulation framed or adopted by a corporate body, public or private, for governing its conduct and that of its members.

Convention 138, Article 2, which provides that the minimum age for employment shall be specified by each country, so long as such age is tied to the age for compulsory schooling. Convention 158, Article 2(2), provides that States may exclude certain categories of workers from the protection against termination. Convention 102, Article 2, provides that States may choose to accept certain articles while rejecting others, leaving such matters to national law.

[11] The authors of this brief have considered the meanings of the relevant words in some of the non-English translations of Article 3(1) of Convention 87, but to the best of their understanding there are no relevant distinctions between the languages so far as the relevant meaning of the relevant words is concerned. The phraseology of Article 3(1) in some of the principal European languages is: Les organisations de travailleurs et d'employeurs ont le droit d'élaborer leurs statuts et règlements administratifs, d'élire librement leurs représentants, d'organiser leur gestion et leur activité, et de formuler leur programme d'action; Las organizaciones de trabajadores y de empleadores tienen el derecho de redactar sus estatutos y reglamentos administrativos, el de elegir libremente sus representantes, el de organizar su administración y sus actividades y el de formular su programa de acción; Die Organisationen der Arbeitnehmer und der Arbeitgeber haben das Recht, sich Satzungen und Geschäftsordnungen zu geben, ihre Vertreter frei zu wählen, ihre Geschäftsführung und Tätigkeit zu regeln und ihr Programm aufzustellen; As organizações de trabalhadores e de entidades patronais têm o direito de elaborar os seus estatutos e regulamentos administrativos, de eleger livremente os seus representantes, organizar a sua gestão e a sua actividade e formular o seu programa de acção; 'Организации работников и работодателей имеют право вырабатывать свои уставы и административные регламенты, свободно выбирать своих представителей, организовывать свой аппарат и свою деятельность и формулировать свою программу действий.

In relation to the word 'constitution', only the third, sixth and seventh meanings in the *OED* have any relevance:

(iii) a decree, ordinance, law, regulation: usually, one made by a superior authority, civil or ecclesiastical;
(vi) the mode in which a state is constituted or organised;
(vii) the system or body of fundamental principles according to which a nation, state, or body politic is constituted or governed.

Legal dictionaries shed no further light. In relation to 'rules'. *Duhaime's Legal Dictionary*, *Black's Law Dictionary* and *Stroud's Judicial Dictionary* identify only a variety of sets of rules of law or procedure. As to 'constitution' *Duhaime's* 100 references are almost without exception references to the constitutions of nations, and states and provinces within them save for a reference to *United States v White*[12] in which Justice Murphy in the US Supreme Court held of the typical labour union:

> It normally operates under its own constitution, rules and bylaws, which, in controversies between member and union, are often enforced by the courts. The union engages in a multitude of business and other official concerted activities, none of which can be said to be the private undertakings of the members.

There is nothing inherent therefore in the ordinary meaning of 'constitution' or 'rules' which would preclude making whatever provision in such instruments as those drafting it and the members thereof desire.

Of course, Article 3 is not dealing with constitutions or rules at large but those of voluntary organisations of civil society. The rules and constitutions of trade unions and employers' associations (indeed, practically every kind of organisation) invariably set out the structure of those organisations, their objects and their powers. Some of these may, of course, be implicit. It cannot therefore be seriously argued that Article 3, in referring to constitutions and rules, does other than give trade unions and employers' associations the right to prescribe in their governing documents at least the structure by which they will operate and make and implement decisions, their purposes and, if not all, then some of the ways in which they have agreed to seek to achieve their purposes.

Article 3 imposes no limitations on the above by requiring the inclusion of certain rules or constitutional provisions, or by specifying that certain rules or constitutional provisions are impermissible. On a literal reading, trade unions (and employers' associations) may draw up their constitutions and rules so as to make any provision they wish – without limitation.[13] The words are therefore not merely capable but do mean that both organisations may provide, for example,

---

[12] *US v White* 322 US 694 (1944).

[13] Of course, it is not suggested that trade unions could adopt any rules whatsoever, particularly rules that would limit workers' rights, such as racially discriminatory membership rules.

that one of their objects is to bargain collectively. By the same token, the words also mean that unions have the right to draw up constitutions which provide that their purposes or some of them may be achieved by organising and supporting industrial action, and the right to have rules which prescribe the conditions under which industrial action will be organised or supported. Indeed, the words mean that a trade union may have, not merely as a means to an end, but as an objective in itself, the organisation and support of industrial action.

The contrary argument would be that since the right under Article 3 to draw up rules and a constitution does not specify that they may include provision for the organisation or support of industrial action, there is no right to have such rules. However, if that construction was correct then neither trade unions nor employers' associations could have a rule or constitutional provision about anything at all, since no particular rules are specified by Article 3. Thus, an employers' association, for example, could not have any particular object or, specifically, the purpose of collective bargaining. It could not even have rules for the admission of members. No rules would be permitted for raising funds by subscriptions from members, and none for lobbying governments. Such a construction by which a general right is interpreted as having no effect in the absence of specification of particular rights is not merely untenable but absurd. A literal construction of the words simply cannot sustain an interpretation which negates any content being given to an express right.

The right to organise their administration and *activities* is the second feature of Article 3 to require consideration. Leaving aside administration, 'activities' is a word of wide compass. The first meaning of 'activity', according to the *OED*, is 'the state of being active; the exertion of energy, action'. The fourth (and only other relevant) meaning given is 'anything active; an active force or operation'. The nature of the actions encompassed in 'activity' is notably not specified in the dictionary meaning. The case of *White* above gives a natural and wide scope to the notion of trade union activities. It is significant, though, that in UK law, for example, protection is given against discrimination by an employer against an employee for participating in the 'activities of an independent trade union'.[14] Such activities have been held (without controversy) to include both planning and participation in industrial action.[15]

---

[14] ss 146 and 152, Trade Union and Labour Relations (Consolidation) Act 1992.

[15] *Winnett v Seamarks Bros Ltd* [1978] IRLR 387, [1978] ICR 1240, EAT; *Britool Ltd v Roberts* [1993] IRLR 481, EAT (though the legislative constraint that the activity must take place 'at an appropriate time' means that no successful claim has thus far been recorded in relation to participation in a strike). This analysis is fortified by s 170(1) of the 1992 Act which entitles a union member, in certain circumstances, to be permitted time off work to engage in 'trade union activity' but in that context it is specifically enacted that there is no right to claim time off for 'activities which themselves consist of industrial action' (s 170(2)). The inescapable inference is that, but for that proviso, union 'activity' in that context would naturally include industrial action. It must follow that the expression, 'the activities of an independent trade union', in the absence of a similar exclusionary proviso must include participation in a strike.

The literal meaning of activities thus leaves open to trade unions and employers' associations a free and unlimited election as to which activities they choose to organise. However, it is implicit from the juxtaposition of the right to draw up constitutions and rules, that the right to organise administration and activities is confined to those permitted by the rules and constitution. This would be normal and accord with law in most, if not every, jurisdiction. It follows that trade unions have the right to organise, among other of their activities authorised by their constitutions, the activities of industrial action and collective bargaining.

The contrary proposition advanced by the Employers' Group is that since the right to organise industrial action is not specified as one of the activities a trade union has the right to organise, there is no right to organise industrial action. But again, as pointed out above, if such a rule of construction was tenable and applied, since Article 3 does not specify *any* particular activities, it must follow that the right conferred on trade unions and employers' associations to organise their activities contained no right to organise any specific activity. This conclusion, of course, would empty Article 3 of any meaning or effect.

The right of trade unions and employers' associations to formulate their *programmes* needs consideration next. The *OED* offers the following relevant meanings of 'programme':

(i) a public notice;
(ii) a descriptive notice, issued beforehand, of any formal series of proceedings ... a prospectus, syllabus, ... a definite plan or scheme of any intended proceedings; an outline or abstract of something to be done (whether in writing or not).

The literal meaning of the words thus confers an unqualified right on the part of unions and employers' associations to include whatever they wish in their plans for the future. This must include the right, for example, to plan for collective bargaining and, for trade unions, the right to plan for industrial action. There is no basis within the words used for excluding from the right of a trade union to formulate within its programme, a plan which includes the organisation of or support for industrial action.

Once again, the contrary proposition is that because Article 3 does not specify the right to plan industrial action, no such right is to be found in the right to formulate a union's programme. Once again, however, the words are incapable of bearing such a meaning which would, if correct, have the consequence that the right to formulate a plan about any particular matter, or to plan to do any particular thing, was necessarily excluded from the protection of Article 3, since the Article does not authorise a plan to do any particular thing. This would mean that the right of employers' associations and unions to formulate their programmes was devoid of substance since every particular plan would fall foul of the proposed canon of construction.

6

The Object and Purpose of Convention 87 Supports the Existence of a Right to Strike

Article 31(1) of the Vienna Convention on the Law of Treaties (VCLT) provides that the words of a term of a treaty must be construed in its 'context and in the light of its object and purpose'. The context of a treaty term had been used for interpretation purposes well before the VCLT. Indeed, the Permanent Court of International Justice (PCIJ) had used context for interpretation purposes in an early Advisory Opinion and stressed that the context is not merely the article or section of the treaty in which the term occurs, but the treaty as a whole:

> In considering the question before the Court upon the language of the Treaty, it is obvious that the Treaty must be read as a whole, and that its meaning is not to be determined merely upon particular phrases which, if detached from the context, may be interpreted in more than one sense.[1]

The PCIJ also stated, inter alia, that Part XIII of the Treaty of Versailles – the Constitution of the ILO – expressly declared that the design of the Contracting Parties was to establish a permanent labour organisation, and that fact strongly militated against the argument that agriculture, then employing more than half of the world's wage earners, was to be considered outside the scope of the ILO merely because it was not expressly mentioned by name.[2] The PCIJ concluded that it was unable to find in Part XIII of the Treaty, read as a whole, any ambiguity, and it had no doubt that agricultural labour was included therein.[3]

The context in which the relevant words are found (and the object and purpose of the provisions in question) can be considered at a number of levels. It is self-evident that freedom of association is essential to the tripartite constitutional structure of the ILO, which entails representation of both employers' and workers' organisations. It is therefore no surprise that Article 427 (in Part XIII) of the Treaty

---

[1] *Competence of the ILO to Regulate Agricultural Labour*, PCIJ (1922) Series B, Nos 2 and 3, 23, available at: www.icj-cij.org/pcij/serie_B/B_02/ Competence_OIT_Agriculture_Avis_consultatif.pdf.

[2] See PCIJ Advisory Opinion, 23, 25.

[3] See E Odieke, 'Ultra Vires Acts in International Organizations – The Experience of the International Labour Organization' (1976) 48 *British Yearbook of International Law* 259, 265.

of Versailles 1919 stated explicitly that, among the 'methods and principles' that all industrial communities should endeavour to apply was, 'The right of association for all lawful purposes by the employed as well as by the employers'. However, more than this, the adoption of the first Constitution of the ILO was a response to the realities of industrial relations at the time (explored later in chapter ten), namely that

> conditions of labour exist involving such injustice, hardship, and privation to large numbers of people as to produce unrest so great that the peace and harmony of the world are imperilled; and an improvement of those conditions is urgently required.

One key way in which to improve them was explicitly said (in the Preamble to Part XIII) to be 'recognition of the principle of freedom of association'. This was, of course, not only so that workers' organisations could participate in ILO standard-setting and other deliberative structures on an equal standing to that of employers but because, in the industrial setting, organisation in trade unions provided safety in numbers for those who sought to collectively negotiate terms and conditions of employment. Further, the proclamation of freedom of association alongside freedom of expression as a 'fundamental principle' in the Declaration of Philadelphia can be seen as an assertion that trade unions are intrinsically linked to democratic processes. Many countries in the developed world had encouraged collective bargaining as an important means of overcoming the economic and social ills of the Great Depression of the 1930s.[4] It also has to be read in tandem with the idea of social justice as well as the reference in Article 3 to 'the effective recognition of the right of collective bargaining, the cooperation of management and labour in the continuous improvement of productive efficiency, and the collaboration of workers and employers in the preparation and application of social and economic measures', which blends the social, economic and political functions of trade unions.[5]

It is inconceivable that the endorsement of freedom of association did not recognise that trade union membership (as an aspect of freedom of association) involved trade union action towards attaining those concrete objectives, including the use of strike action.[6] This was clearly also part of the context of Convention 87.

---

[4] The re-emergence of Joint Industrial Councils in Britain was a reflection of this. The Ministry of Labour's *Annual Report* for 1934 (at 74) affirmed that, 'It has been the policy of the Department to take every opportunity of stimulating the establishment of joint voluntary machinery or of strengthening that already in existence'. During the Second World War, the collective bargaining system was heavily relied upon to enhance Britain's war effort with the introduction of Order 1305, a compulsory measure which provided the legal machinery to extend collective agreements to non-parties. In the United States, the National Industrial Recovery Act of 1933 also promoted collective bargaining. In France, the 1936 Matignon Accords provided for both the rights to strike and to bargain collectively.

[5] For the development and explanation of these arguments, see J Bellace, 'The ILO and the Right to Strike' (2014) 153 *International Labour Review* 29. See also, C La Hovary, 'Showdown at the ILO? A Historical Perspective on the Employers' Group's 2012 Challenge to the Right to Strike' (2013) 42 *Industrial Law Journal* 338.

[6] The primary purpose of trade union membership (as the membership of many other associations) is to influence the 'outside world', and in the case of trade unions, most particularly the employers.

Freedom of association is part of the title of Convention 87 of 1948, the '*Freedom of Association and Protection of the Right to Organise Convention*'. Freedom of association is reiterated in its Preamble. Indeed, the Preamble reinterprets the ILO Constitution by stating that: 'The Preamble to the Constitution of the International Labour Organisation declares "recognition of the principle of freedom of association" to be a means of improving conditions of labour'. It is self-evident that freedom of association was intended to comprehend actions by which such conditions could be improved; equally obviously this was by way of collective bargaining and, where necessary, strike action. This too is part of the context of Convention 87.[7]

Article 10 of Convention 87 also forms part of the context for Article 3. It specifies the objective of workers' organisations: to further and defend the interests of workers. Trade union constitutions, rules, activities and programmes must therefore be capable of furthering and defending workers' interests. The context also requires reference to Article 3(2) of Convention 87 which prohibits 'any interference which would restrict this right or impede the lawful exercise thereof'. In a more general way (concerning all the rights contained in the Convention) Article 8(2) confirms this approach by stating that the 'law of the land shall not be such as to impair, nor shall it be so applied as to impair, the guarantees provided for in this Convention'. The breadth of the right conferred is thus emphasised by the drafters' insistence on prohibiting restriction or impairment of it.

With these aspects in mind, the question to be asked is whether the literal meaning of Article 3 which contains within it the right to strike, as identified above, when set in context, must be expanded, contracted or otherwise adapted. The answer is a resounding 'no'. There is nothing which suggests that the literal meaning of those rights must be expanded, contracted or otherwise adapted by the reiteration of the concept of freedom of association as it would have been understood in 1919, 1944, 1948 or, indeed, any time subsequently, nor in the notion that the trade unions to which are given the rights in Article 3 have as their purpose that of furthering and defending workers' interests. Indeed, the context only fortifies the literal meaning adduced above.

The other side of the coin is that there is certainly nothing in the context which could support the proposition for which the Employers' Group contend, namely that Article 3 is to be read as meaning that:

(i) Though trade unions have the right to draw up their constitutions and rules, that right specifically excludes the right to draw up constitutional provisions permitting the organising or supporting of strikes.

---

[7] The first signatory to Convention 87 was the British Foreign Secretary, Ernest Bevin, on behalf of the United Kingdom. The idea that he, former General Secretary of the giant Transport and General Workers Union, signed Convention 87 under the impression that it did not confer the right to strike on his former members is hard to accept. Equally significantly, the Australian government by reason of its legislative system of collective awards which thereby limited access to industrial action considered that, for that reason, it could not initially ratify ILO Convention 87 or 98, only doing so in 1973.

(ii) Though trade unions have the right to organise their activities, that right specifically excludes the right to organise or support strike action.
(iii) Though trade unions have the right to formulate their programmes, that right specifically excludes the right to formulate a programme of strike action.

Those exclusions could have been written into Convention 87, but they were not. It must be presumed that such exclusions were not intended.

More generally, ILO Convention 87 must certainly be interpreted in the context of industrial relations, which it was adopted to regulate. The Employers' Group's argument relies on a deeply flawed understanding of the right to freedom of association. The Employers' Group takes a very narrow view, where freedom of association is a self-contained, individual right, divorced from the context of industrial relations. For it, freedom of association confers no more than the right to gather together into organisations, be they book clubs or trade unions. However, the right to freedom of association has long been understood as a collective right, particularly in the context of industrial relations, and indeed is a bundle of rights exercised jointly and protected individually which enable those in the association to further the purposes for which it was formed. The right to associate in a trade union is understood to include the right to strike (and to bargain collectively). Indeed, without the attendant derivative rights, the right to association in the industrial relations context would be wholly meaningless. This view, shared by the ILO and indeed the great majority of tribunals and scholars, is why the Committee of Experts is on solid footing in articulating a right to strike in the text of Convention 87.

Freedom of association has been espoused as a fundamental liberty which is the right of every human being,[8] but also as one which has particular significance and relevance to trade unions in the context of industrial relations. It is therefore not surprising that the ILO supervisory bodies, as part of an institution devoted to concern with the 'conditions of labour'[9] alongside 'sustained progress' and 'social justice',[10] have taken a more substantive view of the rights and freedoms which follow from a bare guarantee of freedom of association. The theory of freedom of association applied in the industrial relations context by the Committee on Freedom of Association and the Committee of Experts is specific to the context of the workplace and what has been described as 'the special role trade unions play in our society'.[11]

Combination in a trade union may be a function of individual liberty, but this liberty has little meaning if workers are unable to pursue their own interests through such organisations. Worker solidarity allows workers to overcome the

---

[8] See JS Mill, 'On Liberty' in JS Mill, *Utilitarianism* (Glasgow, Fontana Place, 1962) 138; Universal Declaration of Human Rights, GA res 217A (III), UN Doc A/810 at 71 (1948) Article 20.

[9] See ILO Constitution, Preamble.

[10] See Declaration of Philadelphia 1944, Article I(b) and II (appended to the ILO Constitution).

[11] C Summers, 'Book Review: Sheldon Leader, Freedom of Association: A Study in Labor Law and Political Theory' (1995) 16 *Comparative Labor Law and Policy Journal* 262, 268.

limitations inherent in entering individual contracts of employment, to achieve fair conditions of employment and to participate in making decisions which affect their own lives and society at large. In the absence of a right to strike, it remains difficult (if not impossible) for workers to achieve these goals given the unequal power in the employment relationship. From this premise stems the view that freedom of association implies not only the right of workers and employers to form freely organisations of their own choosing, but also the right to pursue collective activities for the defence of workers' occupational, social and economic interests.

This point was made eloquently by the Canadian Supreme Court in relation to section 2(d) of the Canadian Charter which provides constitutional protection for freedom of association:[12]

> [53] In *Mounted Police*,[13] this Court recognized that the Charter values of '[h]uman dignity, equality, liberty, respect for the autonomy of the person and the enhancement of democracy' supported protecting the right to a meaningful process of collective bargaining within the scope of s 2(d). And, most recently, drawing on these same values, in *Mounted Police*[14] it confirmed that protection for a meaningful process of collective bargaining requires that employees have the ability to pursue their goals and that, at its core, s 2(d) aims
>
>> to protect the individual from 'state-enforced isolation in the pursuit of his or her ends' … The guarantee functions to protect individuals against more powerful entities. By banding together in the pursuit of common goals, individuals are able to prevent more powerful entities from thwarting their legitimate goals and desires. In this way, the guarantee of freedom of association empowers vulnerable groups and helps them work to right imbalances in society. It protects marginalized groups and makes possible a more equal society.
>
> [54] The right to strike is essential to realizing these values and objectives through a collective bargaining process because it permits workers to withdraw their labour in concert when collective bargaining reaches an impasse. Through a strike, workers come together to participate directly in the process of determining their wages, working conditions and the rules that will govern their working lives.[15] The ability to strike thereby allows workers, through collective action, to refuse to work under imposed terms and conditions. This collective action at the moment of impasse is an affirmation of the dignity and autonomy of employees in their working lives.
>
> [55] Striking – the 'powerhouse' of collective bargaining – also promotes equality in the bargaining process.[16] This Court has long recognized the deep inequalities that

---

[12] *Saskatchewan Federation of Labour v Saskatchewan* 2015 SCC 4, 53–55.

[13] *Health Services and Support – Facilities Subsector Bargaining Assn v British Columbia* 2007 SCC 27 (CanLII), [2007] 2 SCR 391, para 81.

[14] *Mounted Police Association of Ontario v Canada (Attorney General)* 2015 SCC 1 (CanLII), [2015] 1 SCR 3, para 58.

[15] Citing here: J Fudge and E Tucker, 'The Freedom to Strike in Canada: A Brief Legal History' (2009–10) 15 *Canadian Labour & Employment Law Journal* 333, 334.

[16] Citing here: G England, 'Some Thoughts on Constitutionalizing the Right to Strike' (1988) 13 *Queen's Law Journal* 168, 188.

structure the relationship between employers and employees, and the vulnerability of employees in this context. In the *Alberta Reference*,[17] Dickson CJ observed that

> [t]he role of association has always been vital as a means of protecting the essential needs and interests of working people. Throughout history, workers have associated to overcome their vulnerability as individuals to the strength of their employers.

And this Court affirmed in *Mounted Police*[18] that

> s 2(d) functions to prevent individuals, who alone may be powerless, from being over-whelmed by more powerful entities, while also enhancing their strength through the exercise of collective power. Nowhere are these dual functions of s 2(d) more pertinent than in labour relations. Individual employees typically lack the power to bargain and pursue workplace goals with their more powerful employers. Only by banding together in collective bargaining associations, thus strengthening their bargaining power with their employer, can they meaningfully pursue their workplace goals.

> The right to a meaningful process of collective bargaining is therefore a necessary element of the right to collectively pursue workplace goals in a meaningful way … [The] process of collective bargaining will not be meaningful if it denies employees the power to pursue their goals.

> … [I]t is 'the possibility of the strike which enables workers to negotiate with their employers on terms of approximate equality'.[19] Without it, 'bargaining risks being inconsequential – a dead letter'.[20]

While some have sought to argue that freedom of association should be regarded as a mere individual liberty without reference to its context, here the industrial context,[21] this is not a view which has held sway in academic[22] or judicial opinion.[23]

The unquestioned (and unquestionable) international right to collective bargaining gives further support to the existence of the right to strike as a derivative right of freedom of association. While the right to strike is not to be confined to the advancement or defence of collective bargaining,[24] the right to collective

---

[17] *Reference re Public Service Employee Relations Act (Alta)* 1987 CanLII 88 (SCC), [1987] 1 SCR 313, 368.

[18] 2015 SCC 1 (CanLII), [2015] 1 SCR 3, paras 70–71.

[19] Fudge and Tucker (n 15 above) 333.

[20] Prof Michael Lynk, 'Expert Opinion on Essential Services', para 20; AR, vol III,145.

[21] B Langille, 'Is there a Constitutional Right to Strike in Canada?' in B Langille (ed), *Special Symposium Issue* (2010) 15 *Canadian Labour & Employment Law Journal* 129. See also FA Hayek, *Law, Legislation and Liberty* (London, Routledge, 1980); and FA Hayek, *1980s, Unemployment and the Unions*, 2nd edn (London, Institute of Economic Affairs, 1984).

[22] See, eg, A Bogg and K Ewing, 'A (Muted) Voice at Work? Collective Bargaining in the Supreme Court of Canada' (2011–12) 33 *Comparative Labor Law & Policy Journal* 379, 392–97; see also T Novitz, 'Workers' Freedom of Association' in J Gross and L Compa (eds), *Human Rights in Labor and Employment Relations: International and Domestic Perspectives* (Champaign, IL, LERA, 2009) 125–28.

[23] See, eg, *Wilson, Palmer, and others v UK* App No 30668/96 (30 January 2002) 35 EHRR 20, where the European Court of Human Rights held that, contrary to the ruling of the House of Lords in *Associated Newspapers Ltd v Wilson, Palmer and others* [1995] 2 AC 454, the right to trade union membership meant more than the right merely to hold a membership card and involved the right for the union to strive to be heard on behalf of its members, including the right to strike in order to do so (paras 44–46).

[24] As the jurisprudence of the European Convention on Human rights makes clear, see KD Ewing and J Hendy, *Days of Action, The Legality of Protest Strikes against Government Cuts* (Liverpool, Institute of Employment Rights, 2011) 19.

bargaining is, on the workers' side, without practical effect in the absence of a right to strike. Without the latter right, a right to collective bargaining amounts to no more than a right to 'collective begging'.[25] As legal scholar Eric Tucker has noted, that notion has a very long history, which he traces back as far as 1921, being popularised in the 1940s.[26] Given the palpable threats of dismissal and relocation which could be presented by an employer, the corresponding threat of temporary withdrawal of labour was all that most workers could offer in return. Certainly, as early as 1924, the ILO 'Nicod' Report considered freedom of association in tandem with industrial action, self-evidently seeing the two as linked.[27] And, the stated view of the International Labour Office by 1927 was that there was an 'intimate relationship between the right to combine for trade union purposes and the right to strike' with a strong case being made for international legislation relating to both.[28]

This interdependence has been universally recognised. In the United Kingdom, for example, as long ago as 1942, the House of Lords in *Crofter Hand Woven Harris Tweed v Veitch* held that 'the right of workmen to strike is an essential element in the principle of collective bargaining'.[29] In *South Africa*, with its constitutional right to strike, the Constitutional Court has held that:

> Collective bargaining is based on the recognition of the fact that employers enjoy greater social and economic power than individual workers. Workers therefore need to act in concert to provide them collectively with sufficient power to bargaining effectively with employers. Workers exercise collective power primarily through the mechanism of strike action.[30]

And in another case, it held that

> it is through industrial action that workers are able to assert bargaining power in industrial relations. The right to strike is an important component of a successful collective bargaining system.[31]

---

[25] German Federal Labour Court (Bundesarbeitsgericht) Judgment 10 June 1980 (Case 1 AZR 822/79): 'Against the background of this conflict of interests collective bargaining without the right to strike in general would be nothing more than collective begging (Blanpain)'. (Original German: ‚Bei diesem Interessengegensatz wären Tarifverhandlungen ohne das Recht zum Streik im allgemeinen nicht mehr als kollektives Betteln (Blanpain)'.

[26] E Tucker, 'Can Worker Voice Strike Back?' in A Bogg and T Novitz, *Voices at Work: Continuity and Change in the Common Law World* (Oxford, Oxford University Press, 2014) 456.

[27] J Nicod, 'Freedom of Association and Trade Unionism: An Introductory Survey' (1924) 9 *International Labour Review* 467.

[28] *Freedom of Association: Report and Draft Questionnaire* (Geneva, ILO, 1927) ILC, 10th Session, 75, 138 and 143.

[29] *Crofter Hand Woven Harris Tweed v Veitch* [1942] AC 43, Lord Wright, 463.

[30] In re *Certification of the Constitution of South Africa* [1996] (4) SA 744, para 66.

[31] *NUMWSA v Bader POP (pty) Ltd and Minister of Labour* [2003] (2) BCLR 182 (CC).

7

The Subsequent Agreement
and Practice between the Parties
Concerning Convention 87 Supports
the Existence of a Right to Strike:
ILO Jurisprudence

I. Some History

This element of Article 31 of the Vienna Convention on the Law of Treaties (VCLT) makes it necessary to consider any subsequent practice which establishes the agreement of the parties regarding the interpretation of Convention 87. It is important to note that the predecessor of the International Court of Justice (ICJ), the Permanent Court of International Justice (PCIJ), looked to the ILO as a guide to construction long before the advent of the VCLT. In its Opinion on the Competence of the ILO to Regulate Agricultural Labour it stated: 'If there were any ambiguity, the Court might for the purpose of arriving as the true meaning, consider the action which has been taken under the Treaty'.[1] As for the substance of the subsequent practice, the PCIJ referred to the practice of the ILO Member States (in confirmation of the meaning which it had deduced from the text and which it considered to be unambiguous):

> The Treaty was signed in June 1919, and it was not until October 1921, that any of the Contracting Parties raised the question whether agricultural labour fell within the competence of the International Labour Organization. During the intervening period the subject of agriculture had repeatedly been discussed and had been dealt with in one form and another. All this might suffice to turn the scale in favour of the inclusion of agriculture, if there were any ambiguity.[2]

By 1947, the American Federation of Labor wrote to the Economic and Social Council (ECOSOC) of the United Nations and explicitly raised the question: 'to what extent is the right of workers and their organizations to resort to strikes

---

[1] PCIJ (1922) Series B, No 2, 39.
[2] ibid, 40–41.

recognized and protected?'[3] However, the answer was assumed rather than explicitly stated in the two interlinking instruments subsequently adopted by the ILO, namely ILO Convention 87 and ILO Convention 98. Rather, there was a consensus that the right to strike was encompassed in these provisions, a consensus borne out by subsequent interpretation of these guarantees by the tripartite Committee on Freedom of Association (CFA) and subsequently the Committee of Experts. Indeed, for 60 years the CFA applied this mutual agreement in determining the cases before it. The significance of this to the application of the VCLT cannot be underestimated.

As explained in chapter 2, there was no challenge made by the Employers' Group to ILO jurisprudence on the right to strike as developed by the Committee of Experts and CFA in relation to Convention 87 for nearly 40 years. Nor was there any apparent basis for such a challenge, given that CFA cases are decided by tripartite consensus, that is, CFA conclusions and recommendations have always required the consent of the employer representatives. As there has been no disparity between CFA case law and the findings of the Committee of Experts, the principles espoused by the latter were also understood to meet with the approval of employers represented at the ILO.

II. The Right to Strike is Enshrined in Convention 87

From Article 3 of Convention 87, which makes provision (among other entitlements) for workers' organisations to 'organise their administration and activities and formulate their programmes', both the CFA and the Committee of Experts have, since the 1950s, regarded Article 3 as encompassing protection of a right to strike, albeit a circumscribed and carefully defined entitlement, which seeks to balance the needs of employer, worker and citizen.

A. Committee of Experts

The Employers' Group maintains that the Committee of Experts has incorrectly concluded that the right to strike is derived from Convention 87. According to the Employers' Group's position paper submitted to the International Labour Conference in 2013:

> Employers have always asserted that article 3 of the 'Freedom of Association and Protection of the Right to Organise Convention', No 87, does not contain, nor implicitly recognise, a right to strike. Strong support for this view can be found in the historical background of the Convention, in which it is evident from the Conference reports that

---

[3] Reported and discussed by R Ben-Israel, *International Labour Standards: The Case of Freedom to Strike* (Deventer, Kluwer, 1988) 38–39.

'the proposed Convention relates only to the freedom of association and not to the right to strike'. An extensive interpretation of Convention 87, which includes the right to strike, has however been developed over time by the ILO 'Committee of Experts on the Application of Conventions and Recommendations' (Committee of Experts).

The Committee of Experts has explained its position on a number of occasions. By 1959, less than a decade after Convention 87 came into force, the Committee of Experts, in the first General Survey to review in detail freedom of association, provided analysis on the right to strike in the section corresponding to Article 3 of the Convention. It found in particular that the 'prohibition of strikes by workers other than public officials acting in the name of public powers ... may sometimes constitute a considerable restriction of the potential activities of trade unions'.[4] The Committee of Experts also found that prohibitions on the right to strike run counter to Articles 8 and 10 of Convention 87.[5]

In the 1983 *General Survey*, the Committee of Experts reiterated a conclusion that the CFA had already reached, namely that 'the right to strike is one of the essential means available to workers and their organisations for the promotion of their social and economic interests'.[6] This met with no opposition from employers at that time. Indeed, the tripartite CFA shortly afterwards stressed again the connection to be made between Convention 87 and the right to strike.[7]

In its 1994 *General Survey on the Freedom of Association*, the Committee of Experts stated:

> 147. As early as 1959, the Committee expressed in its General Survey the view that the prohibition of strikes by workers other than public officials acting in the name of the public powers 'may sometimes constitute a considerable restriction of the potential activities of trade unions ... There is a possibility that this prohibition may run counter to Article 8, paragraph 2, of the Freedom of Association and Protection of the Right to Organize Convention, 1948 (No 87)'. This position was subsequently reiterated and reinforced: 'a general prohibition of strikes constitutes a considerable restriction of the opportunities opened to trade unions for furthering and defending the interests of their members (Article 10 of Convention No 87) and of the right of trade unions to organize their activities'; 'the right to strike is one of the essential means available to workers and their organizations for the promotion and protection of their economic and social interests. These interests not only have to do with better working conditions and pursuing collective demands of an occupational nature, but also with seeking solutions to economic and social policy questions and to labour problems of any kind which are of direct concern to the workers'. The Committee's reasoning is therefore based on the recognized right of workers' and employers' organizations to organize their activities

---

[4] Report of the Committee of Experts on the Application of Conventions and Recommendations, ILC, 43rd Session, 1959, Part I, Report III, 114.

[5] ibid, 115.

[6] *General Survey on the Freedom of Association and Collective Bargaining*, Report III (Part 4B), ILC, 69th Session, 1983, 62.

[7] See CFA, *Digest of Decisions* 3rd edn (1985) paras 361 and 363.

and to formulate their programmes for the purposes of furthering and defending the interests of their members (Articles 3, 8 and 10 of Convention No 87).

148. The promotion and defence of workers' interests presupposes means of action by which the latter can bring pressure to bear in order to have their demands met. In a traditional economic relationship, one of the means of pressure available to workers is to suspend their services by temporarily withholding their labour, according to various methods, thus inflicting a cost on the employer in order to gain concessions ... [early on the Committee was led] to the view that the right to strike is one of the essential means available to workers and their organizations to promote their economic and social interests.[8]

The Committee of Experts has repeated and expanded on the same position several times, most recently in the 2012 *General Survey on the Fundamental Conventions Concerning Rights at Work in Light of the ILO Declaration on Social Justice for Fair Globalizations,* 2008,[9] which was the proximate cause for the Employers' Group to withhold its cooperation in the selection and discussion of cases and to launch its present campaign. Though the Committee of Experts has repeated and developed the position stated in the 1994 *General Survey* above, they have not changed it.

The Committee of Experts' position is thus that the terms of Convention 87 are broadly stated and encompass the right to strike, as well as other means of promoting and protecting the economic and social interests of workers. The right to strike is also derived from the very concept of freedom of association. The Committee also recognises that the right to bargain collectively is dependent on the right to strike.

The Employers' Group argues that the preparatory materials for Convention 87 show that 'the right to strike is not provided for in either Convention 87 or Convention 98 and was not intended to be' and that because the CAS has not reached consensus on the existence and extent of this right, it cannot be held to exist. As concerns the adoption of Convention 87, there was only occasional reference to the right to strike during the preparatory stages, and it appears clear that the Conference refrained from including a mention of this right in the instrument. The Office analysis of replies to the questionnaire for the adoption of Convention 87 included the following:

> It may be observed, in this latter connection, that the Governments were also consulted on the question whether it would be desirable to provide in the international regulations that the recognition of the right of association of public officials should in no way prejudice the question of the right of such officials to strike. Several Governments, while

---

[8] Report of the Committee of Experts on the Application of Conventions and Recommendations, *General Survey on Freedom of Association and Collective Bargaining,* Report III (Part 4B), International Labour Conference, 81st Session, 1994 (*General Survey* 1994) 66, para 148.

[9] International Labour Conference, 101st Session, 2012 (*General Survey* 2012), available at: www.ilo.org/wcmsp5/groups/public/---ed_norm/---relconf/documents/ meetingdocument/wcms_174846.pdf, 46 ff.

giving their approval to the formula, have nevertheless emphasised, justifiably it would appear, that the proposed Convention relates only to the freedom of association and not to the right to strike, a question which will be considered in connection with Item VIII (conciliation and arbitration) on the agenda of the Conference.

In these circumstances, it has appeared to the Office to be preferable not to include a provision on this point in the proposed Convention concerning freedom of association.[10]

This is, however, a much more limited decision than is implied by the Employers' Group and may be argued to show the opposite. The question put to the constituents in the questionnaire related only to whether the right of association of public officials would prejudge the question of the right of such officials to strike. There was a presumption of the existence of the right to strike inherent in this question, which was intended to address only the right of public officials to strike and not to address the right of all workers to strike.

As to the second presumption – that the lack of consensus in the CAS means that there is no right to strike implied by Convention 87 as the Committee of Experts has contended – this is instead evidence of exactly the contrary conclusion. If the Committee of Experts has been stating since 1959 that Convention 87 can be fully applied only if the right to strike is an inherent part of the right to freedom of association, and if the CAS as a whole has been discussing general surveys and individual cases on the basis of the Experts' comments every year since then, then the conclusion must be that the CAS as a whole does not dispute the Committee of Experts' findings. If some members disagree, but their opinions are not followed, then it is only by stopping the work of the CAS (ironically, by staging what is analogous to a strike) that the Employers' Group is able to stop the CAS from continuing its acceptance of the Committee of Experts' position.

Clearly, there is no provision in the text stating that the right to strike is not covered by Convention 87. Moreover, Bernard Gernigon, Former Chief of the Freedom of Association Branch of the ILO, has noted that at no point in the proceedings prior to the adoption of Convention 87 was the right to strike ever expressly denied.[11] Were there any uncertainty, the 'subsequent agreement between the parties' and the 'subsequent practice' in the application of the treaty (Article 31(3) of the Vienna Convention) are dispositive. Again, the ILO Committee of Experts has addressed this point. In particular, it found:

With regard to the views put forward that the preparatory work would not support the inclusion of the right to strike, the Committee would first observe that the absence of a concrete provision is not dispositive, as the terms of the Convention must be interpreted in the light of its object and purpose. While the Committee considers that the preparatory work is an important supplementary interpretative source when reviewing

---

[10] ILC, 31st Session, Freedom of Association and the Protection of the Right to Organize, Seventh Item on the Agenda, Report VII, Geneva, 1948, 87.

[11] B Gernigon, et al, 'ILO Principles Concerning the Right to Strike' (1998) 137 *International Labour Review* 441, 442, fn 4.

the application of a particular Convention in a given country, it may yield to the other interpretative factors, in particular, in this specific case, to the subsequent practice over a period of 52 years (see Articles 31 and 32 of the Vienna Convention on the Law of Treaties).[12]

B. Committee on Freedom of Association

Following an agreement between ECOSOC and the ILO, the ILO created the Fact-Finding Conciliation Commission on Freedom of Association (FFCC) in 1950, with near unanimous support from the International Labour Conference, to receive complaints regarding violations of freedom of association. The CFA was created the following year to undertake the preliminary examination of allegations concerning violations of freedom of association, which would then be referred to the FFCC.[13] It was not long before these bodies found that the right to strike was clearly within their jurisdiction. In a number of cases the CFA has made a direct reference to Article 3 of Convention 87 as forming part of its own reasoning.

Indeed, according to a 1988 study by Ruth Ben-Israel:

> In approximately 500 cases dealt with by the CFA since 1951, the CFA relied upon [a] three-dimensional concept to infer from Article 3 of the convention that workers organizations shall have the right to organize their administration and activities and to formulate their programs without the interference of public authorities which might restrict this right or impede the lawful exercise thereof. The CFA recognized the right to strike as being included within these activities and determined its limits.[14]

It is unsurprising, of course, that the CFA relied on Conventions 87 and 98 in considering the concept of freedom of association. Prior to 1953, the Office had been giving advice on what freedom of association meant. In 1953, the Director-General informed the Governing Body that the Office would no longer perform this function, as this was now entrusted to the CFA.[15] The view of the CFA (arrived at by tripartite consensus from 1952 onwards and as set out in its *Compilation of Decisions* in its sixth revised edition of 2018)[16] is as follows:

> 210. Protests are protected by the principles of freedom of association only when such activities are organized by trade union organizations or can be considered as legitimate trade union activities as covered by Article 3 of Convention No 87.

---

[12] *General Survey 2012* (n 16 above) 48.
[13] The FFCC was a body of independent experts empowered to perform a quasi-judicial function, namely the examination of specific allegations concerning violations of trade union rights. However, as the FFCC could only act with the infrequently given consent of the party complained against (absent ratification of the relevant conventions, which could then lead to referral to a commission of inquiry under Article 26), the CFA began to evolve as the pre-eminent body.
[14] Ben-Israel (n 3 above) 66.
[15] See ILO, Minutes of the Governing Body, 122nd Session, May–June 1953, 110.
[16] ILO Committee on Freedom of Association, *Compilation of Decisions* (Geneva, ILO, 2018), available at: www.ilo.org/wcmsp5/groups/public/---ed_norm/---normes/documents/publication/wcms_632659.pdf.

754. The right to strike is an intrinsic corollary to the right to organize protected by Convention No 87.

805. With regard to the majority vote required by one law for the calling of a legal strike (two-thirds of the total number of members of the union or branch concerned), non-compliance with which might entail a penalty by the administrative authorities, including the dissolution of the union, the Committee recalled the conclusions of the Committee of Experts on the Application of Conventions and Recommendations that such legal provisions constitute an intervention by the public authorities in the activities of trade unions which is of such a nature as to restrict the rights of these organizations, contrary to Article 3 of the Convention.

967. The Committee considered that some of the temporary measures taken by the authorities as a result of a strike in an essential service (prohibition of the trade union's activities, cessation of the check-off of trade union dues, etc) were contrary to the guarantees provided for in Article 3 of Convention No 87.

Importantly, all of the conclusions referenced above from the 2018 *Compilation of Decisions* were brought forward from the CFA's *Digest of Decisions* of 2006, though the numbering has changed.[17] This reflects the continuity of the Committee's jurisprudence before and after the Employers' Group's challenge in 2012 to the right to strike. The Employers' Group had attempted to block the inclusion of Section 10 concerning the right to strike in the *Compilation* but was ultimately unsuccessful – further reaffirming the existence of the right protected by the Constitution and Convention 87.

C. Commissions of Inquiry

Commissions of Inquiry are expressly provided for at Article 26 of the ILO Constitution. Within the supervisory system, they are the highest level of supervision of ratified conventions as the ILO itself lacks any more authoritative interpretative organ. As noted elsewhere, no tribunal pursuant to Article 37(2) of the ILO Constitution currently exists and the ILO has yet to refer a question on the right to strike to the ICJ under Article 37(1). As such, the Commissions' recognition of the right to strike on the basis of the interpretation of ILO supervisory bodies must be considered a constitutional acknowledgement of the right to strike.

It is therefore of great relevance that in the complaint against Poland, the Commission of Inquiry explicitly shared the views of the Committee of Experts in respect of the right to strike:

Convention No 87 provides no specific guarantee concerning strikes. The supervisory bodies of the ILO, however, have always taken the view – which is shared by the

---

[17] The numbering to the above referenced cases in the *Digest of Decisions*, 5th edn are paras 135, 523, 555 and 669 respectively. The 2006 *Digest* is available at: www.ilo.org/wcmsp5/groups/public/---ed_norm/---normes/documents/publication/wcms_090632.pdf.

Commission – *that the right to strike constitutes one of the essential means that should be available to trade union organisations* for, in accordance with Article 10 of the Convention, furthering and defending the interests of their members. An absolute prohibition of strikes thus constitutes, in the view of the Commission, a serious restriction on the right of trade unions to organise their activities (Article 3 of the Convention) and, moreover, is in conflict with Article 8, paragraph 2, under which 'the law of the land shall not be such as to impair, nor shall it be so applied as to impair, the guarantees provided for (by the Convention)' (emphasis added).[18]

In the Commission of Inquiry against Zimbabwe, the Commission stated that:

[It] is obliged to observe that the right to strike is not fully guaranteed in law or practice. In particular, the Commission is concerned that the legislation includes disproportionate sanctions for the exercise of the right to strike and an excessively large definition of essential services; and that in practice the procedure for the declaration of strikes is problematic and that it appears that the security forces often intervene in strikes in Zimbabwe. *The Commission wishes to confirm that the right to strike is an intrinsic corollary of the right to organize protected by Convention No 87* (emphasis added).[19]

Several other Commissions of Inquiry concerning Convention 87 have had an opportunity to confirm that the right to strike is protected by the Convention. In the case of Greece, the Commission found:

The Commission observes that Convention No 87 contains no specific guarantee of the right to strike. On the other hand, the Commission accepts that an absolute prohibition of strikes would constitute a serious limitation of the right of organisations to further and defend the interest of their members (Article 10 of the Convention) and could be contrary to Article 8, paragraph 2, of the Convention, under which 'the law of the land shall not be such as to impair, nor shall it be so applied as to impair, the guarantees provided for in this Convention, including the right of unions to organise their activities in full freedom (Article 3)'.[20]

---

[18] ILO, *Report of the Commission of Inquiry* instituted under Article 26 of the Constitution of the ILO to examine the complaint on the observance by *Poland* of the Freedom of Association and Protection of the Right to Organise Convention, 1948 (No 87), and the Right to Organise and Collective Bargaining Convention, 1949 (No 98) *Official Bulletin*, Special Supplement Series B, Vol LXVII (1984) para 517.

[19] *Report of the Commission of Inquiry* appointed under article 26 of the Constitution of the International Labour Organization to examine the observance by the Government of *Zimbabwe* of the Freedom of Association and Protection of the Right to Organise Convention, 1948 (No 87), and the Right to Organise and Collective Bargaining Convention, 1949 (No 98) (Vol XCIII, 2010, Series B, Special Supplement) para 575.

[20] *Report of the Commission of Inquiry* appointed under article 26 of the Constitution of the International Labour Organization to examine the complaints concerning the observance by *Greece* of the Freedom of Association and Protection of the Right to Organise Convention, 1948 (No 87), and the Right to Organise and Collective Bargaining Convention, 1949 (No 98) (Vol LIV, 1971, No 2, Special Supplement) para 261.

The Commission of Inquiry concerning Nicaragua[21] cited favourably the jurisprudence of the Committee of Experts and the CFA in drawing conclusions on the right to strike. It found:

> The Committee of Experts had noted the provision requiring a majority of 60 per cent of the workers for the calling of a strike (section 225 of the Labour Code); the prohibition of strikes in rural occupations when produce may be damaged if it is not immediately disposed of (section 228(1)); the provision enabling the authorities to impose compulsory arbitration to end a strike that has lasted 30 days (section 314). These are restrictions on the right to strike which go beyond what is accepted by the ILO supervisory bodies and which infringe the right of trade unions to organise their activities (Article 3 of the Convention) for the purposes of promoting and defending the interests of their members (Article 10).[22]

III. The ILO Constitution

An examination of the ILO Constitution explains how the CFA came to draw this link between freedom of association and the right to strike. The primary aim of the ILO under the Constitution is 'social justice', which is to take precedence over other economic goals.[23] It is apparent from the ILO Constitution that social justice involves the improvement of conditions of work and the ability of workers to participate in making the decisions which affect their working lives, either by means of collective bargaining or tripartite consultation. While the Constitution makes no explicit reference to the right to strike, it recognises the principle of freedom of association in the Preamble. Further, the Organization is obligated under Part III of the Declaration of Philadelphia to further

> (e) the effective recognition of the right of collective bargaining, the cooperation of management and labour in the continuous improvement of productive efficiency, and the collaboration of workers and employers in the preparation and application of social and economic measures.

As we explain in detail in Chapter 10, the drafters of the ILO Constitution understood that the right to freedom of association was inclusive of a right to strike. As such, it would be truly remarkable if the International Labour Conference had adopted a convention which they knew to be narrower than the corresponding rights afforded under the Constitution and would weaken those rights. There is

---

[21] *Report of the Commission of Inquiry* appointed under article 26 of the Constitution to examine the observance by *Nicaragua* of the Freedom of Association and Protection of the Right to Organise Convention, 1948 (No 87), the Right to Organise and Collective Bargaining Convention, 1949 (No 98) and the Tripartite Consultation (International Labour Standards) Convention, 1976 (No 144) (Vol LXXIV, 1991, Series B, Special Supplement) paras 500–09.

[22] ibid, para 506.

[23] See Preamble to Part XIII of the Treaty of Versailles 1919 and Declaration of Philadelphia 1944, Article II(c).

no evidence that drafters intended Convention 87 to be narrower than the corresponding provisions of the ILO Constitution. It is relevant to bear in mind that Article 19(8) of the ILO Constitution provides:

> In no case shall the adoption of any Convention or Recommendation by the Conference, or the ratification of any Convention by any Member, be deemed to affect any law, award, custom or agreement which ensures more favourable conditions to the workers concerned than those provided for in the Convention or Recommendation.

The idea that ratifying Convention 87 materially reduces the rights available under the Constitution is patently unsustainable.

A. CFA Jurisprudence under the Constitution

The right to strike can be derived not only from Convention 87 but more directly from the provisions in the Constitution setting out the priority to be given to freedom of association (as the Employers' Group previously recognised). The Constitution has long been established as the source of the CFA mandate to address issues relating to 'freedom of association', certainly following the constitutional challenge to the competence of the CFA made by the then South African government in *Case No 102 (South Africa)*.[24] The South African government had not ratified Conventions 87 and 98 and therefore objected to a complaint being heard before the CFA. The Committee responded that, by virtue of the Constitution, all ILO Members were bound to abide by the principle of freedom of association. The CFA also relied on Article 19(5) of the ILO Constitution which states that ILO Members can be required to report to the Director-General on the position of their law and practice in relation to unratified conventions.[25] This was obviously a decision adopted by tripartite consensus between the government, employer and worker representatives and has since been reiterated repeatedly.[26] The CFA has made direct reference to the ILO's constitutional objectives when interpreting the constitutional provision for freedom of association.[27]

The CFA has over the years opined on the right to strike, and without specific reference to Convention 87 and instead explicitly or implicitly relying on the

---

[24] *Case No 102 (South Africa)*, 15th Report of the CFA (1955) para 128.

[25] ibid paras 130–32.

[26] See, eg, *Case No 2524 (US)*, 349th Report (2008) para 846. ('[T]he Committee recalls as it had done when examining Cases Nos 2227 and 2460 [332nd Report, para 600 and 344th Report, para 985], that since its creation in 1951, it has been given the task to examine complaints alleging violations of freedom of association whether or not the country concerned has ratified the relevant ILO Conventions. Its mandate is not linked to the 1998 ILO Declaration – which has its own built-in follow-up mechanisms – but rather stems directly from the fundamental aims and purposes set out in the ILO Constitution. The Committee also recalls in this respect that when a State decides to become a Member of the Organization, it accepts the fundamental principles embodied in the Constitution and the Declaration of Philadelphia, including the principles of freedom of association.')

[27] See *Digest of Decisions*, 5th edn (Geneva, ILO, 2006) paras 1, 2, 8, 11, and 12.

ILO Constitution. As early as their second meeting in 1952, the CFA held that the right to strike was an *'essential [element] of trade union rights'*.[28] In Case 28 (UK–Jamaica), for example, the CFA held that:

> The right to strike and that of organising union meetings are essential elements of trade union rights, and measures taken by the authorities to ensure the observance of the law should not, therefore, result in preventing unions from organising meetings during labour disputes.[29]

That the CFA observed that the right to strike was an essential element of the right to freedom of association, thus giving it competency to review the case, generated no controversy at the time. The same report also examined several other cases where legislation related to the right to strike was noted.

In subsequent cases, the CFA was explicit in asserting its competence to address complaints regarding the right to strike. In 1958, in Case No 163 (Burma), the CFA declared 'allegations relating to prohibitions to the right to strike are not outside its competence when the question of freedom of association is involved'.[30] It further stated, 'the right of workers and workers' organisations to strike as a legitimate means of defence of their occupational interests is generally recognised'.[31]

In case after case in the subsequent decades, the CFA has found that the right to strike by workers and their organisations is not only a legitimate but an essential means for defending occupational interests. This jurisprudence is thoroughly discussed in ILO publications including *ILO Principles Concerning the Right to Strike*[32] and *The Committee of Freedom of Association: Its Impact over 50 years*.[33]

As set forth in the CFA's *Compilation of Decisions* (2018):

> 752. The Committee has always recognized the right to strike by workers and their organizations as a legitimate means of defending their economic and social interests.

> 753. The right to strike is one of the essential means through which workers and their organizations may promote and defend their economic and social interests.[34]

Thus, the basis on which the CFA has found that the right to strike exists is the general recognition of the rights to organise in order to promote and protect workers' economic and social interests – the same recognition, in less detail, as is contained in Convention 87. The Employers' Group's participation in the work of the CFA, and its explicit endorsement over many years of the right to strike as a

---

[28] *Second Report*, 1952, Case No 28 (Jamaica) para 68; endorsed in *23rd Report*, 1956, Case No 111 (USSR) paras 4, 227, and many other cases; more recently *327th Report*, 2002, Case No 1581 (Thailand) para 111.

[29] CFA Report No 2 (1952), Case No 28 (UK–Jamaica) para 68.

[30] CFA Report No 27 (1958), Case No 163 (Burma) para 51.

[31] ibid.

[32] Gernigon (n 18 above).

[33] See E Gravel et al, *The Committee of Freedom of Association: Its Impact Over 50 Years* (Geneva, ILO, 2001).

[34] These principles were included in the *Digest of Decisions* (2006) paras 521–22.

necessary corollary of the rights to organise and bargain, cannot easily be reconciled with their reasoning in relation to the Committee of Experts.

B. Fact-Finding and Conciliation Commission

In extraordinary circumstances involving violations of freedom of association, the ILO Governing Body may appoint a Fact-Finding and Conciliation Commission (FFCC). Only six such commissions have been named since such a commission was first established in 1950.[35] The FFCC, in a case filed against Chile following the 1973 coup d'état, affirmed the right to strike and discussed how various measures taken and laws proposed by the regime of Augusto Pinochet violated that right.[36] These measures included the imprisonment and murder of trade union leaders, dissolution of trade unions, police and military surveillance of union meetings, and prohibitions on collective bargaining and the right to strike.

The Commission stressed the importance of freedom of association as 'a customary rule above the conventions' in a passage often cited to affirm the primacy of freedom of association among ILO norms:

> Chile has not ratified the Freedom of Association and Protection of the Right to Organise Convention, 1948 (No 87), which, accordingly, has no binding effect for this country. However, by its membership of the International Labour Organisation, Chile is bound to respect a certain number of general rules which have been established for the common good of the peoples of the twentieth century. Among these principles, freedom of association has become a customary rule above the Conventions.[37]

It concluded that, 'the Government should recognise in law and in practice ... the right to bargain collectively and to strike, so that trade unions may effectively further and defend the rights of the workers'[38] – echoing Article 10 of Convention 87.

> 524. On the basis of all the information and viewpoints compiled, including those expressed by those officials most favourably disposed towards the present Government, the Commission has come to the conclusion that there is a general feeling that there should be a return to normal as soon as possible in the trade union and industrial relations field. To achieve this it is considered necessary that the Government should recognise in law and in practice the right to elect trade union executive committees in full freedom, so that the workers may choose for themselves the leaders they wish

---

[35] See ILO, 'Fact-Finding and Conciliation Commission on Freedom of Association', available at: www.ilo.org/global/standards/information-resources-and-publications/WCMS_160778/lang--en/index.htm.

[36] Chile did not ratify Convention 87 until 1999.

[37] ILO, *Report of The Fact-Finding and Conciliation Commission on Freedom of Association Concerning the Trade Union Situation in Chile*, GB 196/4/9, 196th session (May 1975).

[38] ibid, 118, para 524.

to represent them, and these leaders may have the feeling that they are performing their functions with a legitimate mandate from their members; the right to hold meetings without hindrance in order to discuss freely problems and economic and social demands; and the right to bargain collectively and to strike, so that trade unions may effectively further and defend the rights of the workers.

Concerning the right to strike specifically, it held:

> 535. As regards the right to strike, the Commission considers that the Provisions of the draft Labour Code are construed in very general terms and could lead in practice, to considerable restrictions of this right. The Commission recommends the Government to re-examine the provisions on this question concerning which the Office has already transmitted its comments to the Government.

The FFCC also concluded that 'the function of the International Labour Organization in regard to trade union rights is to contribute to the effectiveness of the general principle of freedom of association as one of the primary safeguards of peace and social justice'.[39]

Chile is not the only such example. The FFCC's 1992 report on South Africa[40] expressed concern over numerous violations of the right to strike and drew on the jurisprudence of both the Committee of Experts and Committee on Freedom of Association, including their observations on Convention 87 and Convention 98.[41] For example, the FFCC held that the dismissal of trade unionists for exercising the right to strike which was stated to be 'contrary to the principle of freedom of association',[42] as was the failure to make legislative provision for reinstatement.[43] The FFCC concluded that the then unfair labour practice provisions of the Labour Relations Act should be amended to provide 'appropriate protection against dismissal' not only for 'strikers engaged in a legal strike' but also 'strikers where the strike, although technically illegal, was in all other respects legitimately called for the promotion of the workers' economic and social interests' including the end to apartheid'.[44]

IV. The Right to Strike in Subsequent ILO Instruments

Subsequent ILO instruments, adopted by the tripartite constituents, contain supplementary provisions affirming the existence of a right to strike protected

---

[39] ibid, 108, para 466.

[40] ILO, *Report of the Fact-Finding Conciliation Commission on Freedom of Association concerning the Republic of South Africa* (Geneva, ILO, 1992).

[41] ibid paras 639–70.

[42] ibid, para 668.

[43] ibid, para 669.

[44] ibid, para 670. See also T Novitz, 'The International and Regional Framework' in B Hepple, R Le Roux and S Sciarra, *Laws Against Strikes: The South African Experience in an International and Comparative Perspective* (Milan, Franco Angeli, 2015).

by the ILO. This is inconsistent with the Employers' Group's contention to the contrary. For example, Article 7 of Voluntary Conciliation and Arbitration Recommendation 92 of 1951 states that none of its provisions should be interpreted as limiting the right to strike.[45] Article 1 of the Abolition of Forced Labour Convention 105 of 1957 specifies that forced or compulsory labour is prohibited 'as a punishment for having participated in strikes'.[46] In addition, various resolutions of the International Labour Conference have referred (with the support, of course, of the Employers' Group) to the right to strike.[47] These subsequent instruments and resolutions are directly relevant to how the Vienna Convention, explored below, applies to this situation.

In addition, the large majority of States that have ratified Convention 87 have done so since the CFA (in 1952) and the Committee of Experts (in 1959) recognised the right to strike contained within that Convention. Indeed, of the 152 Member States that have ratified Convention 87, 138 did so after 1952 when the CFA first established its jurisprudence on the right to strike. Furthermore, 116 out of those 152 ratifications were made after the publication by the Committee of Experts of the first *General Survey on Freedom of Association* in 1959 mentioned above. Those States may thus be presumed to have accepted that the right to strike is inherent in Convention 87.

V. 2015 Tripartite Meeting on the Right to Strike

Following the 2012 International Labour Conference, the ILO established a schedule of informal tripartite discussions in addition to formal discussions at the regular sessions of the ILO Governing Body in an effort to find a way out of the impasse. While the Employers' Group did agree to discuss a list of cases in 2013, they did not back down on any of their demands. The Swiss government facilitated a series of bilateral meetings between the Employers' Group and Workers' Group to try and see if some consensus on the way forward could be reached between the social partners prior to resuming tripartite consultations. These meetings, held in May, June and September of 2013, failed to resolve the issues.

At the 2013 Conference, the Employers' Group reiterated its position that the right to strike was not regulated by Convention 87.[48] The Workers' Group again

[45] ILO, Voluntary Conciliation and Arbitration Recommendation 92 of 1951, available at: www.ilo.org/dyn/normlex/en/f?p=NORMLEXPUB:12100:0::NO::P12100_ILO_CODE:R092.

[46] ILO, Abolition of Forced Labour Convention 105 of 1957, available at: www.ilo.org/dyn/normlex/en/f?p=NORMLEXPUB:12100:::NO:12100:P12100_ILO_CODE:C105:NO.

[47] Resolutions of the International Labour Conference referring to the right to strike include the Resolution concerning the Abolition of Anti-Trade Union Legislation 1957, and the Resolution Concerning Trade Union Rights and their Relation to Civil Liberties 1970. These are discussed in ILO, *General Survey* (1994) 63.

[48] See, ILO, Report of the Committee on the Application of Standards, Part I, *General Report* (2013) para 50, available at: www.ilo.org/wcmsp5/groups/public/---ed_norm/--relconf/documents/meeting-document/ wcms_216379.pdf.

maintained the opposite position.[49] However, both the Workers' and Employers' Group were under intense pressure from governments and the ILO secretariat to avoid another breakdown in the CAS, as some worried that another failure to agree to a list would permanently derail the CAS's work. The CAS did in fact function in 2013, but only with the Workers' Group agreeing to a 'disclaimer' in the Committee report with regard to those cases where the Committee of Experts had made observations on the right to strike.[50] Thus, in the summary of the CAS debate on Belarus, Canada, Egypt, Fiji, Swaziland and Zimbabwe, the following text appeared: 'The Committee did not address the right to strike in this case, as the employers do not agree that there is a right to strike recognized in Convention No 87'.[51]

The Workers' Group made clear that this was a one-time exception and that any dispute on the interpretation of the Convention be addressed via the ILO Constitution – namely the ICJ.[52] Indeed, in October 2013, the General Council of the International Trade Union Confederation resolved to seek to refer to the ICJ the question as to whether the right to strike was protected by Convention 87. The Workers' Group chair had similarly challenged the Employers' Group over the course of 2012–13 to exercise the judicial options available to it including the ICJ.[53]

In March 2014, the ILO Governing Body again discussed potential ways forward from the dispute arising out of the 2012 International Labour Conference. Among other measures, the Governing Body authorised the ILO Director-General to

> prepare a document for its 322nd Session (November 2014) setting out the possible modalities, scope and costs of action under articles 37(1) and 37(2)(referral to the ICJ)

---

[49] ibid, para 51.

[50] ibid, para 232 ('In 2013, the Worker members had therefore had to accept a procedure that was similar to the issue already raised in 2012 by the Employer members concerning the inclusion of a disclaimer in the report of the Committee of Experts. The conclusions of some cases relating to the application of Convention No 87 therefore included the wording that "the Committee did not address the right to strike in this case as the employers do not agree that there is a right to strike recognized in Convention No 87". It should be noted in this regard that the Committee had never commented in its conclusions on the basis of the right to strike and the Employer members were the only ones to disagree on this point. If the Employer members wanted to go further in challenging the mandate of the Committee of Experts and the right to strike, they should seek a solution in other tools available in the ILO Constitution, such as the recourse to article 37(2)').

[51] ILO, Provisional Record No 16, Part 2Rev, Report of the Committee on Application of Standards, 102nd Session, Geneva, June 2013, available at: www.ilo.org/wcmsp5/groups/public/---ed_norm/---relconf/documents/meetingdocument/wcms_216456.pdf.

[52] ILO, Report of the Committee on the Application of Standards, Provisional Record, 16 Rev, Part One (2013 Geneva) paras 232–33, available at: www.ilo.org/wcmsp5/groups/public/---ed_norm/---relconf/documents/ meetingdocument/wcms_216379.pdf; ILO, Report of the Committee on the Application of Standards, Provisional Record, 13, Part One (2014 Geneva) paras 7–8, available at: www.ilo.org/wcmsp5/groups/public/---ed_norm/---relconf/documents/meetingdocument/wcms_246781.pdf.

[53] See, eg, Provisional Record 16 Rev, Part One (n 60 above) para 86.

of the ILO Constitution to address a dispute or question that may arise in relation to the interpretation of an ILO Convention.[54]

The urgency to resolve the dispute increased when in 2014, the CAS again broke down over the right to strike, with the Workers' and Employers' Groups unable to agree to conclusions in 19 of the 25 cases.[55]

On the basis of the ILO's modalities paper,[56] the ILO Governing Body debated in November 2014 whether to refer the dispute on the interpretation of Convention 87 on the right to strike to the ICJ. After some debate, the ILO presented a draft decision which included the proposed question to be referred to the ICJ as well as a number of initiatives which the employers had requested, including a tripartite meeting on the right to strike as well as to initiate a Standards Review Mechanism process through which the constituents would classify the status of ILO conventions.[57] While the draft decision had the full support of the Workers' Group,[58] the Employers' Group adamantly refused the referral to the ICJ.[59]

The employers made a number of dubious claims to support their view.[60] They claimed for example that referral to the ICJ would damage the credibility of the ILO supervisory system, even though the ILO Constitution itself provides for referral to the ICJ for just these circumstances; as such, the ICJ is an integral part of the supervisory process. Moreover, the Employers' Group had attacked the supervisory system as 'in crisis' for the past two years, making their concern for its reputation incredible.

They also argued that if the ICJ found the right to strike protected by Convention 87, then countries would be obligated to revise their laws, which they argue constituted a breach of national sovereignty in industrial relations. This too is a curious argument. First, States which have ratified the convention are already expected to comply with the legal obligations flowing from it, as determined by

---

[54] Decision on the fourth item on the agenda: The standards initiative: Follow-up to the 2012 ILC Committee on the Application of Standards, GB.320/LILS/4, paras 40–43, available at: www.ilo.org/gb/decisions/GB320-decision/ WCMS_239960/lang--en/index.htm.

[55] See, ILO, Report of the Committee on the Application of Standards, Part I, *General Report* (2014) paras 201–19, available at: www.ilo.org/wcmsp5/groups/public/---ed_norm/---relconf/documents/meetingdocument/ wcms_246781.pdf.

[56] ILO, 'The standards initiative: Follow-up to the 2012 ILC Committee on the Application of Standards', GB.322/INS/5, 16 October 2014, available at: www.ilo.org/wcmsp5/groups/public/---ed_norm/---relconf/documents/meetingdocument/wcms_315494.pdf.

[57] ILO, 'The standards initiative: Follow-up to the 2012 ILC Committee on the Application of Standards', GB.322/INS/5(Add), 8 November 2014, available at: www.ilo.org/wcmsp5/groups/public/---ed_norm/---relconf/documents/meetingdocument/wcms_318810.pdf.

[58] ILO, Institutional Section, Draft Minutes of the Governing Body, 322nd Session, October–November 2014, para 50. (The Worker Spokesperson explained that 'his group had reached the inescapable conclusion that referral of the interpretation dispute to the International Court of Justice (ICJ) for an advisory opinion, as a matter of urgency, was the necessary way forward'). See: www.ilo.org/wcmsp5/groups/public/---ed_norm/---relconf/ documents/meetingdocument/wcms_331068.pdf.

[59] ibid, paras 58–59.

[60] ibid.

the regular supervisory system such as the Committee of Experts. An affirmative decision by the ICJ would impose no new obligation but only reaffirm the decades-old ILO jurisprudence. If a country failed to comply, it would be subject only to further scolding by the ILO supervisory system. Secondly, it is an exercise of national sovereignty to ratify conventions, undertaken voluntarily, with the attendant obligations that flow from that instrument. It is difficult to discern how sovereignty would be undermined. Instead, the Employers' Group proposed a 'tripartite declaratory statement' which would recognise the right to strike as a right existing at the national level. Of course, such a statement is contrary to law, would be non-binding, and further the Employers' Group erroneous theory that it is the tripartite constituents that determine the meaning of conventions.

Among governments, most European[61] and Latin American[62] governments spoke in favour of the referral; however, the lack of support from Asia,[63] Africa and, behind the scenes the United States, which did not want to be associated with a decision to refer any matter to the ICJ (whose jurisdiction it does not recognise) in the end doomed the effort. Given the lack of a majority for a referral, the ILO presented to the parties at the closing minutes of the Governing Body session a new, third draft resolution which did not include the referral to the ICJ but included the remaining items which the Workers' Group agreed to only in exchange for the referral.[64] Presented with no other options, the Governing Body supported the revised resolution though the Workers' Group expressed deep disappointment that the referral was stripped from the final decision document.[65]

In response to the Employers' opposition, workers around the world mobilised on 18 February 2015 to make clear to governments and employers' associations the critical importance of an international right to strike and workers' determination to defend it.[66] As a result of that action, and mounting employer losses in courts on the right to strike, and a desire by governments and workers to see the supervisory system get back on track, particularly following the failure of the CAS in 2014 to agree to conclusions in a majority of the cases, the Workers' and Employers' Groups agreed to a so-called 'ceasefire' in late February 2015, on the eve of a tripartite meeting on the modalities on the right to strike.[67] The joint statement did not resolve the matter of whether the right to strike is protected by

---

[61] ibid, paras 81–84

[62] ibid, para 64.

[63] ibid paras 70–72

[64] ILO, 'The standards initiative: Follow-up to the 2012 ILC Committee on the Application of Standards', GB.322/INS/5(Add2), 12 November 2014, available at: www.ilo.org/wcmsp5/groups/public/---ed_norm/---relconf/documents/meetingdocument/wcms_319583.pdf.

[65] Draft Minutes (n 65 above) paras 152–53.

[66] See International Trade Union Confederation, Hands Off Our Right to Strike Campaign, available at: www.ituc-csi.org/18feb?debut_news_577=5.

[67] See ILO Tripartite Meeting on the Freedom of Association and Protection of the Right to Organise Convention, Outcome of the Meeting, February 2015, Annex I, available at: www.ilo.org/ wcmsp5/groups/public/---ed_norm/---relconf/documents/meetingdocument/wcms_346764.pdf.

Convention 87. However, the employers did concede that workers do have a right to undertake 'industrial action'. Importantly, the joint statement also includes a commitment to respect the mandate of the Committee of Experts and to allow the ILO supervisory system to work unimpeded.

Given the agreement, the tripartite discussion on the right to strike was cut short, but it did provide an opportunity for governments collectively and individually to endorse the existence of the right to strike. The consensus government statement explained,

> the right to strike is linked to freedom of association which is a fundamental principle and right at work of the ILO. The Government Group specifically recognizes that without protecting a right to strike, Freedom of Association, in particular the right to organize activities for the purpose of promoting and protecting workers' interests, cannot be fully realized.[68]

The Government Group statement went on to recognise that the right to strike is not an 'absolute right'. Likely because the statement was the product of negotiation of disparate views of governments, the text provides that 'the scope and conditions of this right are regulated at the national level'. It is impossible to read the text in its entirety and argue, as the Employers' Group has, that this clause means that the right to strike is not protected by the ILO Constitution and conventions, or that the ILO has nothing to say on the content of that right. Rather, it must be read that limitations on the right to strike can be regulated at the national level, *consistent with the output of the ILO supervisory system.*

The Nordic governments went further, issuing a lengthy legal opinion on the protection of the right to strike by Convention 87.[69] The US government, which had opposed the referral to the ICJ, issued a strong defence of the right to strike:

> In the decades since the adoption of C 87, the Committee of Experts and the Committee on Freedom of Association have provided observations and recommendations with regard to the right to strike. Working within their mandates – through the examination of specific cases – they have observed that freedom of association, and in particular the right to organize their activities for the purpose of promoting and protecting workers' interests, cannot be fully realized without protecting the right to strike.

> This same logic has prevailed in the United States. Our National Labor Relations Act protects workers' right not only to form and join labor organisations and bargain collectively, but also 'to engage in other concerted activities for the purpose of collective bargaining or mutual aid or protection'. The United States Supreme Court has deemed strikes to be among the concerted activities protected ...

---

[68] ibid, Appendix II.

[69] ILO, Final Report of the Meeting, Tripartite Meeting on the Freedom of Association and Protection of the Right to Organise Convention, 1948 (No 87), in relation to the right to strike and the modalities and practices of strike action at national level, Geneva, 23–25 February 2015, para 15, available at: www.ilo.org/wcmsp5/groups/public/---ed_norm/---relconf/documents/meetingdocument/wcms_349069.pdf.

[The] Committee on Freedom of Association has confirmed and applied the relationship between the right to strike and the right to freedom of association in almost 3000 cases without any dissent from the social partners. It has been the express view of the committee that the right to strike is one of the essential means through which workers and their organizations may promote and defend their economic and social interests [and] the right to strike is an intrinsic corollary to the right to organize protected by Convention No 87.

We concur that the right to organize activities under Convention 87 protects the right to strike, even though that right is not explicitly mentioned in the Convention.[70]

The joint statement was adopted by the Governing Body in March 2015. While it does not pretend to resolve the central dispute, it has nevertheless allowed the constituents to resume the supervision of standards. The CAS was able to reach conclusions, without dissent from the Employers' Group, in all of its cases in 2015. And, while the Employers' Group has begun to challenge the jurisprudence of the Committee on Freedom of Association, it has nevertheless maintained its ability to function.

---

[70] Statement of the United States, Tripartite Meeting on the Freedom of Association and Protection of the Right to Organize Convention, 1948 (No 87), in relation to the right to strike and the modalities and practices of strike action at the national level, Geneva, 23–25 February 2015, available at: www.dol.gov/ilab/media/pdf/USGstatementatILOmeetingonFOAandrighttostrike-2-23-2015.pdf.

8

The Subsequent Agreement and Practice between the Parties Concerning Convention 87 Supports the Existence of a Right to Strike: Beyond the ILO

The right to freedom of association (and collective bargaining) is well established in international instruments other than those adopted by the ILO. They are indicia of the international context in which ILO conventions are situated and reflect the law and practice of States.

I. United Nations

The ILO and the UN have taken consistent, though not necessarily identical, approaches on human rights. The Universal Declaration of Human Rights, adopted a few months after the adoption of Convention 87 and a few months before the adoption of Convention 98, contains a brief but robust statement on trade union rights in Article 23(4), namely, 'Everyone has the right to form and to join trade unions for the protection of his interests'. This was given greater articulation in the two Human Rights Covenants adopted in 1966, with the notable inclusion in both Covenants of a clause providing for respect of ILO Convention 87 (see Article 8(3) of the International Covenant on Economic, Social and Cultural Rights (ICESCR) and Article 22(3) of the International Covenant on Civil and Political Rights (ICCPR)). And, before the adoption of the Covenants, the UN Economic and Social Council asked the ILO to adopt measures to deal with complaints of violations of trade union rights on behalf of both organisations.

A. International Covenant on Economic, Social and Cultural Rights

This Covenant provides as follows in Article 8:

> 1. The States Parties to the present Covenant undertake to ensure:
>
> (a)   The right of everyone to form trade unions and join the trade union of his choice, subject only to the rules of the organization concerned, for the promotion and protection of his economic and social interests. No restriction may be placed on the exercise of this right other than those prescribed by law and which are necessary in a democratic society in the interests of national security or public order or for the protection of the rights and freedoms of others;
>
> (b)   The right of trade unions to establish national federations or confederations and the right of the latter to form or join international trade-union organizations;
>
> (c)   The right of trade unions to function freely subject to no limitations other than those prescribed by law and which are necessary in a democratic society in the interests of national security or public order or for the protection of the rights and freedoms of others;
>
> (d)   The right to strike, provided that it is exercised in conformity with the laws of a particular country.
>
> 2. This article shall not prevent the imposition of lawful restrictions on the exercise of these rights by members of the armed forces or of the police or of the administration of the State.
>
> 3. Nothing in this article shall authorize States Parties to the International Labour Organization Convention of 1948 concerning Freedom of Association and Protection of the Right to Organize to take legislative measures which would prejudice, or apply the law in such a manner as would prejudice, the guarantees provided for in that Convention.

It is apparent that this provision was closely based on ILO Convention 87, and the basic drafting was completed very shortly after the adoption of the ILO Convention. Paragraph 3, found in both Covenants, further attests the close relationship between the ILO and UN standards.

While it is broadly compatible with the ILO standards, there are some differences.[1] In the first place, the Covenant does not cover employers as do the ILO standards.[2] Secondly, it explicitly protects the right to strike, though with the caveat that it should be 'exercised in conformity with the laws of a particular

---

[1] KD Ewing, 'Myth and Reality of the Right to Strike as a "Fundamental Labour Right"' (2013) 29 *International Journal of Comparative Labour Law and Industrial Relations* 145, 146.

[2] The reasons for this omission were essentially that the USSR and its allies did not want the forces of capital to be covered. See the detailed analysis of this history in H Dunning, 'The Origins of Convention No 87 on Freedom of Association and the Right to Organise' (1998) 137 *International Labour Review* 160.

country' (Article 8(1)(d)). This supplements the concern in Article 8(1)(c) that States Parties shall ensure

> [t]he right of trade unions to function freely subject to no limitations other than those prescribed by law and which are necessary in a democratic society in the interests of national security or public order or for the protection of the rights and freedoms of others.[3]

These calls for respect for the national legal order are not accompanied by the countervailing provision found in Article 8(2) of ILO Convention 87 that 'The law of the land shall not be such as to impair, nor shall it be so applied as to impair, the guarantees provided for in this Convention'.

The UN instruments set the conditions for the exercise of a certain class of human rights, but do not explore the uses to which these rights might be put, except that the ICESCR provides that the right of everyone to organise is 'for the promotion and protection of his economic and social interests'. In spite of minor differences, the ICESCR and ILO standards obviously cover the same ground and are intended to be compatible. Concerning the supervision of the ICESCR, this is carried out by the Committee on Economic, Social and Cultural Rights (CESCR) which reviews the compliance of ratifying States on a cyclical basis.[4] From time to time the CESCR publishes 'General Comments' which are authoritative interpretations of the text of the ICESCR. There is as yet no General Comment on Article 8; however, General Comment No 3 (1990) lists Article 8 among others which 'would seem to be capable of immediate application by judicial and other organs in many national systems',[5] and General Comment No 9 (1998) requires that the ICESCR provisions should be enforceable in the domestic legal system of ratifying States.[6] Thus, immediate implementation of Article 8 is required where this is legally possible. The most recent relevant General Comment, No 23 (2016), on the right to just and favourable conditions of work, emphasised the fundamental nature of the right to strike to the enjoyment of other labour rights including those protected under Article 7, finding, '[T]rade union rights, freedom

---

[3] There was debate within the drafting committee about the explicit inclusion of the right to strike. In the end, the majority believed that 'the right to strike was essential for the protection of the economic and social interests of workers' and that it was 'meaningless to try to guarantee trade union rights without a right to strike'. See M Craven, *The International Covenant on Economic, Social and Cultural Rights: A Perspective on its Development* (Oxford, Clarendon Press, 1995) 257 and fns 85 and 86. To accommodate those who had opposed the inclusion of the right to strike, the text included the limitation that the right be 'subject to the laws of the particular country' (ibid 259).

[4] Since the Committee's first meeting in 1987; before the Committee was established, supervision was carried out directly by a Working Group of ECOSOC.

[5] United Nations, General Comment No 3: The nature of States parties' obligations (Article 2, para 1, of the Covenant) 1990, available at: www.tbinternet.ohchr.org/layouts/treatybodyexternal/Download. aspx?symbolno=INT%2fCESCR%2fGEC%2f4758&Lang=en.

[6] United Nations, Draft General Comment No 9: The domestic application of the Covenant, E/C.12/1998/24, 3 December 1998, available at: www.tbinternet.ohchr.org/_layouts/treatybodyexternal/Download.aspx?symbolno=E%2fC.12%2f1998%2f24&Lang=en.

of association and the right to strike are crucial means of introducing, maintaining and defending just and favourable conditions of work.[7]

The Concluding Observations of the CESCR (the UN equivalent of the ILO Committee of Experts (CEACR)), show how the CESCR, on individual cases, understands the meaning of this Article. Notably, members of the ILO Committee of Experts have at times participated in the sittings of the CESCR when it reviewed a State's compliance with Articles 6–9 which related to work.[8] From the Concluding Observations it may be determined that the CESCR applies the same methods which the Employers' Group criticises when used by the ILO Committee of Experts. The CESCR has developed its jurisprudence on the meaning of Article 8 of the Covenant beyond the words alone on the page. The right to strike itself need not be inferred, since it is textually in the Covenant, but the CESCR has carried out the same process as the ILO supervisory bodies in using the bare words of the Covenant as a platform for laying down what is required to fully implement the right.

A sample of extracts from recent Concluding Observations of the CESCR show that the Committee's comments closely resemble the observations of the ILO Committee of Experts, though less detailed. Further, in doing so, it has taken care to retain compatibility with the jurisprudence of the ILO, in some cases explicitly. The UN Committee accepts that the right to strike is inherent in ILO Convention 87, as Observations with regard to Germany (below) make absolutely clear.

Germany (2011)

20. The Committee reiterates its concern … that the prohibition by the State party of strikes by public servants other than those who provide essential services constitutes a restriction of the activities of trade unions that is beyond the purview of the restrictions allowed under Article 8(2) of the Covenant (Art 8). The Committee once again urges the State party to take measures to ensure that public officials who do not provide essential services are entitled to their right to strike in accordance with Article 8 of the Covenant and ILO Convention No 87 concerning Freedom of Association and Protection of the Right to Organise (1948).[9]

This position was confirmed in 2018 by the CESCR during its most recent examination of Germany's last report:

Germany (2018)

45. The Committee reiterates its previous recommendation (E/C.12/DEU/CO/5, para 20) that the State party take measures to revise the scope of the category of essential services with a view to ensuring that all those civil servants whose services cannot

[7] United Nations, General Comment No 23 (2016) on the right to just and favourable conditions of work (Article 7 of the International Covenant on Economic, Social and Cultural Rights), E/C.12/GC/23, 27 April 2016, available at: www.tbinternet.ohchr.org/layouts/treatybodyexternal/Download. aspx?symbolno =E%2fC.12%2fGC%23&Lang=en.

[8] See, eg, UN, Sessional Working Group on the Implementation of the International Covenant on Economic, Social and Cultural Rights, E/1980/WG.L/SR.20, 30 April 1980.

[9] UN Doc E/C.12/DEU/CO/5, 12 July 2011.

reasonably be deemed as essential are entitled to their right to strike in accordance with article 8 of the Covenant and with the International Labour Organization (ILO) Freedom of Association and Protection of the Right to Organise Convention, 1948 (No 87).[10]

Indeed, the CESCR's observations post-2012 make clear that the right to strike has not been called into question by the UN system as a whole, despite the Employers' Group's insistence at the ILO to the contrary. The CESCR accepts that the right to strike is protected by Convention 87.

Estonia (2019)

26. Despite the explanation given by the delegation, the Committee remains concerned that article 59 of the Civil Service Act does not allow civil servants to exercise their right to strike or to take part in other collective pressure actions that interfere with the performance of functions of the recruiting authority or of other authorities, as set out in the Act (art 8).

27. The Committee recommends that the State party review the Civil Service Act with a view to allowing civil servants who do not provide essential services to exercise their right to strike in accordance with article 8 of the Covenant and with the International Labour Organization Freedom of Association and Protection of the Right to Organise Convention, 1948 (No 87).[11]

Spain (2018)

28. The Committee is concerned that the changes made during the 2012 labour reform could negatively influence enjoyment of the right to bargain collectively. It is also concerned by information it has received about the over-zealous application of article 315(3) of the Criminal Code, which has resulted in the criminal prosecution of workers who have participated in strikes (art 8).

29. The Committee recommends that the State party ensure the effectiveness of collective bargaining and of the right to union representation, both in law and in practice, in conformity with article 8 of the Covenant and with the provisions of the International Labour Organization (ILO) Freedom of Association and Protection of the Right to Organise Convention, 1948 (No 87) and Right to Organise and Collective Bargaining Convention, 1949 (No 98). It also urges the State party to consider the further revision or derogation of article 315(3) of the Criminal Code in order to prevent the criminal prosecution of workers who have participated in strikes.[12]

Mexico (2018)

35. While the Committee takes note of the legislative and constitutional reforms relating to employment that were adopted in February 2017 with a view to enhancing the protection of trade union rights, it is concerned by reports of restrictions that, in practice, may affect the exercise of these rights, such as the right to strike and collective

---

[10] CESCR, Concluding Observations (on the Sixth periodic report of Germany) held on 25 September 2018 adopted at its 58th meeting, held on 12 October 2018 (E/C.12/DEU/CO/6, 27 November 2018) para 45.

[11] CESCR, Concluding Observations, Estonia (2019), E/C.12/EST/CO/3, 27 March 2019; this example is all the more important as the HRC has explicitly referred to it, see n 32 below).

[12] CESCR, Concluding Observations, Spain (2018), E/C.12/ESP/CO/6.

bargaining. In addition, it is concerned by allegations of the commission of acts of violence against trade union leaders (art 8).

36. The Committee recommends that the State party adopt effective measures to eliminate, in practice, restrictions that hinder the effective exercise of trade union rights by all workers, in accordance with article 8 of the Covenant and with the ILO Freedom of Association and Protection of the Right to Organise Convention, 1948 (No 87), and the ILO Right to Organise and Collective Bargaining Convention, 1949 (No 98). In addition, it urges the State party to establish effective mechanisms for the protection of union rights, including by carrying out effective investigations into all complaints brought to its attention and paying adequate compensation to the workers concerned.[13]

The Concluding Observations for many other countries, including Albania,[14] Cabo Verde,[15] Colombia,[16] Korea[17] and Thailand,[18] could be cited for the same proposition. Further, the CESCR regularly goes beyond noting that there is or is not a national law on the subject, as a strict reading of the Covenant would suggest, often indicating what the content of that law should be, as the examples above illustrate.

Of note, the Committee has incorporated jurisprudence from the ILO supervisory system in interpreting Article 8. Though no mention of essential services is included in the Covenant, the Committee has drawn on the principles developed by the ILO Committee of Experts to exclude essential services from the right to strike. See, for example, the following extract from the proceedings of the ECOSOC Working Group at its third session in 1989:[19]

Trinidad and Tobago

Article 8: Trade union rights

---

[13] CESCR, Concluding Observations, Mexico (2018), E/C.12/MEX/CO/5–6.

[14] CESCR, Concluding Observations, Albania (2013), E/C.12/ALB/CO/2-3) ('ensure that the prohibition against striking for civil servants does not exceed the ILO definition of essential services').

[15] CESCR, Concluding Observations, Cabo Verde (2018), E/C.12/CPV/CO/1, para 37 ('While acknowledging the need to maintain minimum essential services, the Committee recommends that the State party ensure that the right to strike is protected and that restrictions on the right to strike for certain sectors of work are interpreted in the strict sense, in line with the ILO principles concerning the right to strike').

[16] CESCR, Concluding Observations, Colombia (2017), E/C.12/COL/CO/6, para 40 ('The Committee urges the State party to review its legislation on trade union rights and bring it into line … with the ILO Freedom of Association and Protection of the Right to Organise Convention, 1948 (No 87), and the ILO Right to Organise and Collective Bargaining Convention, 1949 (No 98)').

[17] CESCR, Concluding Observations, Republic of Korea (2009), E/C.12/KOR/CO/3 (CESCR, 2009) ('legislation on civil service be amended with a view to lifting the restrictions imposed on the right of civil servants to join a trade union and to strike in conformity with the comments made by the Committee of Experts of the International Labour Organization (ILO) in 2001, on the Convention concerning Freedom of Association and Protection of the Right to Organise (Convention No 87')).

[18] CESCR, Concluding Observations, Thailand (2015), E/C.12/THA/CO/1 (States must 'ensure that public sector employees who do not provide essential services are entitled to their right to strike in line with the Covenant and relevant ILO standards').

[19] Report on the Third Session (6–24 February 1989) UN Doc E/1989/22 and E/C.12/1989/5. In the same report, see also the exchange concerning Canada in paragraph 109. At this point the Working

289. Members of the Committee wished to know to which extent the right to strike was afforded to trade unions in the public and private sectors.

290. Referring to the provision according to which strikes in essential public services could be prohibited, members wished to know who decided whether a service was essential, and what procedures were used in that respect.

In a number of other observations, the CESCR has developed detailed jurisprudence on the scope of Article 8, drawing largely from the ILO Committee of Experts, on subjects ranging from the role of mediation in dispute settlement,[20] recourse to compulsory arbitration,[21] the use of requisition orders[22] and the appropriateness of sanctions under criminal,[23] civil[24] and labour[25] law.

In conclusion, in its case law the CESCR refers to and is very much inspired by the ILO's interpretation of the right to strike. This approach enhances the ILO understanding of Convention 87 as protecting the right to strike and thus forms an important element of 'subsequent practice' in relation to Article 31(3)(b) of the Vienna Convention on the Law of Treaties.

B. International Covenant on Civil and Political Rights

Article 22 of the Covenant on Civil and Political Rights covers some of the same ground as the ICESCR but is less extensive. In particular, it does not spell out the right to strike:

1. Everyone shall have the right to freedom of association with others, including the right to form and join trade unions for the protection of his interests.

Group had not yet evolved the practice of drawing conclusions from the information submitted, as was the case later; the assumptions it had reached concerning the contents of the rights are evident from the questions posed.

[20] CESCR, Concluding Observations, Albania (2013), E/C.12/ALB/CO/2–3.

[21] See, eg, CESCR, Concluding Observations, Iceland (2012), E/C.12/ISL/CO/4 ('The Committee recommends that the State party take measures ... to ensure that compulsory arbitration is avoided'); see also, CESCR, Concluding Observations, Russian Federation (2011), E/C.12/RUS/CO/5 ('The Committee also calls on the State party to ensure that compulsory arbitration is restricted to what are known as essential services').

[22] See, eg, CESCR, Concluding Observations, Central African Republic (2018), E/C.12/CAF/CO/1, para 32. ('The Committee ... recommends that the State party amend Order No 81/028 to restrict the powers of requisition in the event of strikes exclusively to occasions where essential services need to be maintained for the population').

[23] See, eg, Spain (n 12 above).

[24] See, eg, CESCR, Concluding Observations, Lebanon (2016), E/C.12/LBN/CO/2, para 39. ('The Committee recommends that the State party bring its laws and regulations on the right to strike into conformity with international standards, including by ... subjecting cases involving claims for reparation for damages resulting from strike-related demonstrations only to civil liability law and thereby dissociating the reparation for damages from the exercise of the right to strike').

[25] See, eg, CESCR, Concluding Observations, Argentina (2011), E/C.12/ARG/CO/3 ('The Committee also reminds the State party that reprisals such as the loss of employment for the participation in protests and strikes carried out in conformity with law must be prohibited and that re-dress must be granted to the victims of abuse').

2. No restrictions may be placed on the exercise of this right other than those which are prescribed by law and which are necessary in a democratic society in the interests of national security or public safety, public order (ordre public), the protection of public health or morals or the protection of the rights and freedoms of others. This article shall not prevent the imposition of lawful restrictions on members of the armed forces and of the police in their exercise of this right.

3. Nothing in this article shall authorize States Parties to the International Labour Organisation Convention of 1948 concerning Freedom of Association and Protection of the Right to Organize to take legislative measures which would prejudice, or to apply the law in such a manner as to prejudice, the guarantees provided for in that Convention.

The Human Rights Committee (HRC),[26] which supervises the implementation of this Covenant, applies the same basic methodology as the Committee on Economic, Social and Cultural Rights (CESCR). However, the HRC examines the protection of the right to freedom of association mostly in relation to non-governmental organisations and political parties, and for the most part does not explore the workers' rights aspect of the right to freedom of association, preferring to leave this to the ICESCR. There are nevertheless exceptions.

Originally the HRC did not consider that the ICCPR protected the right to strike; however, since 1999, it has done so, and monitors States' protection of this right.[27] As with the CESCR, the HRC's views on the right to strike have been unaffected by the Employers' Group's 2012 challenge at the ILO. Indeed, the HRC has reaffirmed the right several times since then, directing States to guarantee the right to strike by undertaking legal reforms.

Kazakhstan (2016)

53. The Committee is also concerned about the broad grounds for the suspension or dissolution of political parties. It is further concerned that the restrictive legal framework regulating strikes and the mandatory affiliation of trade unions to regional or sectorial federations under the 2014 Act on Trade Unions may adversely affect the right to freedom of association under the Covenant.

54. The State party should bring its regulations and practice governing the registration and functioning of political parties and non-governmental organizations, as well as the legal frameworks **regulating strikes** and trade unions, into full compliance with the provisions of articles 19, 22 and 25 of the Covenant.[28]

Dominican Republic (2017)

32. The State party should adopt measures to safeguard workers' freedom of association in practice, including the right to organize, the right to collective bargaining and the **right to strike**.[29]

---

[26] Officially, the abbreviation is CCPR (Committee on Civil and Political Rights).

[27] See P Macklem, 'The Right to Bargain Collectively in International Law: Workers' Right, Human Right, International Right?' in P Alston (ed), *Labour Rights as Human Rights* (Oxford, Oxford University Press, 2005).

[28] CCPR, Concluding Observations, Kazakhstan (2016), CCPR/C/KAZ/CO/2.

[29] CCPR, Concluding Observations, Dominican Republic (2018), CCPR/C/DOM/CO/6, para 32.

Belarus (2018)

55. The State party should revise relevant laws, regulations and practices with a view to bringing them into full compliance with the provisions of articles 22 and 25 of the Covenant, including by:

(d) Addressing the obstacles to the registration and operation of trade unions, **lifting the undue limitations on the right to strike,** investigating all reports of interference in the activities of trade unions and of the retaliatory treatment of trade CCPR/C/BLR/ CO/5 13 union activists, and revising the procedures governing collective bargaining with a view to ensuring compliance with the Covenant.[30]

Guinea (2018)

46. The State party should: (a) ensure that all restrictions on peaceful demonstrations that are not strictly necessary and proportionate in the light of the provisions of article 21 of the Covenant are lifted; (b) revise its legal framework in order to effectively protect the right to freedom of association, including the right to organize and **the right to strike,** and refrain in practice from any act of intimidation against trade union movements and members.[31]

The most recent example is the new 'Concluding Observations' concerning Estonia:

Estonia (2019)

31. While welcoming the significantly lower number of civil servants affected by a prohibition of strike action following the amendments to the Civil Service Act in 2013, the Committee echoes the concern of the Committee on Economic, Social and Cultural Rights regarding the strike ban on civil servants under the Act (E/C.12/EST/ CO/3, para 26). The Committee is also concerned about the requirements set forth in the Collective Labour Dispute Resolution Act that may adversely affect the meaningful exercise of the right to strike in practice, inter alia by limiting the duration of a warning strike to one hour as opposed to three days for sympathy strikes (art 22).

32. The Committee reiterates the recommendation made by the Committee on Economic, Social and Cultural Rights (E/C.12/EST/CO/3, para 27) that the Civil Service Act be reviewed with a view to allowing civil servants who do not provide essential services to exercise **their right to strike.** The State party should refrain from imposing any undue limitations on the right to strike and should ensure that the Collective Labour Dispute Resolution Act is in full conformity with article 22 of the Covenant.[32]

---

[30] CCPR, Concluding Observations, Belarus (2018), CCPR/C/BLR/CO/5, para 55 d).

[31] CCPR, Concluding Observations, Guinea (2018), CCPR/C/GIN/CO/3, para 46 (b) (authors' translation) ('L'État partie devrait : (a) veiller à lever toutes les restrictions aux manifestations pacifiques qui ne sont pas strictement nécessaires et proportionnelles au regard des dispositions de l'article 21 du Pacte ; (b) réviser son cadre légal afin de protéger efficacement le droit à la liberté d'association, *y compris le droit syndical et le droit de grève,* et s'abstenir en pratique de tout acte d'intimidation à l'encontre des mouvements et membres de syndicats').

[32] Human Rights Committee, Estonia (2019), CCPR/C/EST/CO/4, 18 April 2019; for the CESCR, Concluding Observations on Estonia (2019) to which the HRC refers, see (n 11 above).

From a methodological point of view, it is remarkable that the HRC directly refers to the CESCR's jurisprudence. In terms of content, this example is important as it confirms not only with the right to strike as such but also in respect of civil servants. Moreover, it criticises undue restrictions to the right to strike in relation to 'warning' (1 hour) or 'sympathy' (3 days) strikes.

Thus, the HRC has developed its own understanding that, even in the absence of a stated right to strike in this Covenant, the right nevertheless exists as an inherent part of the right to freedom of association, and that it is the Committee's obligation to examine not only the existence of that right but also the conditions under which it is exercised.

To leave no doubts, on 23 October 2019, both the CESCR and the HRC issued a joint statement on the right to freedom of association on the occasion of the ILO Centenary. In the brief statement, the two commissions made a point to reassert the existence of the right to strike as a corollary of the right to freedom of association. In particular, they found,

> Freedom of association, along with the right of peaceful assembly, also informs the right of individuals to participate in decision making within their workplaces and communities in order to achieve the protection of their interests. The committees recall that the right to strike is corollary to the effective exercise of the freedom to form and join trade unions. Both committees have sought to protect the right to strike in their review of the implementation of the ICESCR and the ICCPR by the States parties.[33]

II. Council of Europe Instruments

A. The European Convention on Human Rights

The right to strike is not expressly protected by the European Convention on Human Rights (ECHR).[34] However, ECHR, Article 11 provides that:

> 11(1) Everyone has the right to freedom of peaceful assembly and to freedom of association with others, including the right to form and to join trade unions for the protection of his interests.

> 11(2) No restrictions shall be placed on the exercise of these rights other than such as are prescribed by law and are necessary in a democratic society in the interests of national security or public safety, for the prevention of disorder or crime, for the protection of health or morals or for the protection of the rights and freedoms of others. This article

---

[33] Joint statement by the Committee on Economic, Social and Cultural Rights and the Human Rights Committee, E/C.12/2019/3-CCPR/C/2019/1, 23 October 2019, available at https://www.ohchr.org/Documents/HRBodies/CESCR_CCPR_Joint_STM.pdf.

[34] See KD Ewing and J Hendy, 'The Dramatic Implications of Demir and Baykara' (2010) 39 *Industrial Law Journal* 2; see more generally, F Dorssemont, K Lörcher and L Schömann, *The European Convention on Human Rights and the Employment Relation* (Oxford, Hart Publishing, 2013).

shall not prevent the imposition of lawful restrictions on the exercise of these rights by members of the armed forces, of the police or of the administration of the State.

Over the last 50 years, Article 11 has been interpreted to protect a right to strike, from an initially narrow view to a quite robust view in recent years.

i. A Narrow Perspective

In a series of cases decided in the 1970s, the European Court of Human Rights (ECtHR) took the view that Article 11 did not require Member States of the Council of Europe to protect any particular form of trade union action.[35] The ECtHR expressed and then repeated the mantra that Article 11 simply imposed a duty on Member States to have in place mechanisms to enable trade unions to represent their members, but did not guarantee any particular means by which this was to be achieved.

Thus, the failure of a Member State to provide a specific mechanism (such as permitting a right to strike) for unions to be heard in order to protect their members' interests would not breach Article 11(1) if other means were permitted by which the union could be heard. Part of the justification for this was the existence of the European Social Charter (ESC) 1961, in relation to which States are free to select which paragraphs of which Articles they are prepared to accept. Thus, it is open to a State to refuse to accept (by way of example) the obligations relating to the right to organise, the right to bargain or the right to strike (Articles 5 and 6). According to the tortured reasoning of the ECtHR, if Article 11 of the Convention was to be read to include these rights, it would mean that in 1961 the Council of Europe would have taken a step backwards by creating a Charter in which such rights were optional.[36]

ii. Evolution of the Jurisprudence

In *UNISON v United Kingdom*,[37] the ECtHR was beginning to soften its position on the right to strike. While it held that there was no violation of Article 11, the ECtHR appeared to accept that the right to strike as such was protected by Article 11(1), though the impugned restrictions imposed by national law in this case were found to have been justified under Article 11(2).[38] The same year,

---

[35] *National Union of Belgian Police v Belgium* App No 4464/70 (27 October 1975) 1 EHRR 578; *Swedish Engine Drivers v Sweden* App No 5614/72 (6 February 1976) 1 EHRR 617; *Schmidt and Dahlstrom v Sweden* App No 5589/72 (6 February 1976) 1 EHRR 632.

[36] See *Belgian Police* (n 34 above) para 38; *Swedish Engine Drivers* (n 34 above) para 39; and *Schmidt* (n 34 above) para 34.

[37] *UNISON v United Kingdom* [2002] IRLR 497.

[38] Though likewise the decision was a setback for the trade unions, a similar softening may be seen in *Federation of Offshore Workers Trade Unions v Norway* App No 38190/97 (27 June 2002) (ban on further strike in offshore oil industry justified by reason of economic catastrophe if strike continued).

in *Wilson, Palmer and others v UK*,[39] concerning discrimination against trade union members who refused to surrender trade union representation, the ECtHR held:

> [T]he essence of a voluntary system of collective bargaining is that it must be possible for a trade union which is not recognised by an employer to take steps including, if necessary, organising industrial action, with a view to persuading the employer to enter into collective bargaining with it on those issues which the union believes are important for its members' interests (para 46).

This evolution was brought to a high point in *Demir and Baykara v Turkey*,[40] a case concerning the annulment of a collective agreement in Turkey. While not addressing the right to strike, the case is very relevant. Unanimously, the Grand Chamber ruled that there had been a breach of Article 11, expressly repudiating the jurisprudence of the 1970s and emphasising that 'the Convention is a living instrument which must be interpreted in the light of present-day conditions, and in accordance with developments in international law, so as to reflect the increasingly high standard being required in the area of the protection of human rights'.[41] In holding that the right to bargain collectively was now one of the *essential elements* of the right to freedom of association, the Court took into account a wide range of international treaties (including ILO Convention 98, the ESC, and the EU Charter of Fundamental Rights), as well as the constitutional and labour law and practice of the Member States of the Council of Europe.[42]

Taking these different factors into account, the ECtHR concluded that:

> The absence of the legislation necessary to give effect to the provisions of the International Labour Conventions already ratified by Turkey, and the Court of Cassation judgment of 6 December 1995 based on that absence, with the resulting *de facto* annulment *ex tunc* of the collective agreement in question, constituted interference with the applicants' trade-union freedom as protected by Article 11 of the Convention.[43]

As a result, the question for the respondent government was whether the restrictions could be justified under ECHR, Article 11(2), a claim that was dismissed by the Court. In response to this latter question the Court said:

> There is no evidence in the case file to show that the applicants' union represented 'public servants engaged in the administration of the State', that is to say, according to the interpretation of the ILO Committee of Experts, officials whose activities are specific to the administration of the State and who qualify for the exception provided for in Article 6 of ILO Convention No 98.[44]

---

[39] *Wilson, Palmer, and others v UK* App No 30668/96 (30 January 2002) 35 EHRR 20.

[40] *Demir and Baykara v Turkey* [2008] ECHR 1345. See K Lörcher, 'The New Social Dimension in the Jurisprudence of the European Court of Human Rights (ECtHR): The *Demir and Baykara* Judgment, its Methodology and Follow-up' in F Dorssemont, K Lörcher and I Schömann, *The European Convention on Human Rights and the Employment Relation* (Oxford, Hart Publishing, 2013).

[41] *Demir and Baykara v Turkey* (n 39 above) para 146.

[42] ibid, paras 147–54.

[43] ibid, para 157.

[44] ibid, para 166.

This passage is significant because it reveals that ILO conventions are important in informing not only the content of ECHR, Article 11, but also the circumstances in which restrictions may be imposed. *Demir and Baykara* is important not just for its reliance on ILO conventions (and the ESC) but also for its deployment of the jurisprudence of the Committee of Experts and the Committee on Freedom of Association (CFA) (as well as the European Committee of Social Rights). The arguments that led the ECtHR to conclude that the right to collective bargaining is protected by ECHR, Article 11, appear to apply with equal force to right to collective action – namely that Article 11 is a living instrument, that other international treaties inform the content of the ECHR, and that the Convention must reflect the rising standards of protection.

iii. The ECtHR's Modern Jurisprudence on the Right to Strike

It is not surprising that since *Demir and Baykara* the ECtHR has more fully recognised and developed the right to strike. The evolution of the Court's treatment of the right to strike has not been uniform, but there is undoubtedly an observable trend towards the right to strike becoming, in all but name, an *essential element* of Article 11(1) but with limitations permitted in particular circumstances by Article 11(2).

Enerji Yapi-Yol Sen v Turkey[45] concerned a circular from the Prime Minister's Public-Service Staff Directorate prohibiting public sector employees from taking part in a national one-day strike organised by the Federation of Public Sector Trade Unions 'to secure the right to a collective bargaining agreement'. The first question was whether such conduct of the State violated the Convention rights of the union, the Court taking the view that:

> The terms of the Convention require that the law should allow trade unions, in any manner not contrary to Article 11, to act in defence of their members' interests [reference made to *Schmidt and Dahlström*; *Belgian police*; *Swedish Engine Drivers*]. Strike action, which enables a trade union to make its voice heard, constitutes an important aspect in the protection of trade union members' interests (*Schmidt and Dahlström*, cited above, § 36). The Court also observed that the right to strike is recognised by the International Labour Organisation's (ILO) supervisory bodies as an indissociable corollary of the right of trade union association that is protected by ILO Convention C87 on trade union freedom and the protection of trade union rights (for the Court's consideration of elements of international law other than the Convention, see *Demir and Baykara*, cited above). It recalled that the European Social Charter also recognised the right to strike as a means of ensuring the effective exercise of the right to collective bargaining. As such, the Court rejected the Government's preliminary objection [that the trade union was not a victim].[46]

---

[45] *Enerji Yapi-Yol Sen v Turkey* App No 68959/01 (21 April 2009).
[46] ibid, para 24 (unofficial translation).

The reference to *Demir and Baykara* as support for reliance on the ILO and the ESC to establish strike action as a corollary to the essential right to collective bargaining protected by Article 11 strongly suggested that the Court was accepting that the right to strike is equally 'essential'. The cited text also makes clear that the Court accepted the ILO position that the right to strike is 'an indissociable corollary of the right of trade union association'. Again, there was no discernible disharmony between the international treaties (of which Convention 87 was one) and the law and practice of the Member States as to the existence of the right to strike. It was not necessary therefore for the ECtHR to consider whether the other means by which the union might be heard on behalf of its members were sufficient: breach of the right to strike alone was a breach of Article 11(1).

As seen in the cases below, the ECtHR appears to be more generous in its recognition of the need to protect the right to strike in cases involving individual victims penalised in various ways because of their engagement in collective action.

iv. *The Turkish Cases*

In *Dilek et al v Turkey*[47] public employees staffing roadside toll booths struck for three hours during a working day to join a demonstration organised by their union to protest against their conditions of work. The government sued them and was awarded damages and interest representing the loss of revenue for the hours during which traffic passed through without paying the tolls. The ECtHR held that there was an infringement of Article 11.[48] In relation to Article 11(2), the Court found that though the penalty was prescribed by law[49] and pursued a legitimate goal,[50] the imposition of civil liability on the applicants was not necessary in a democratic society.[51]

Over a short period of time, the ECtHR issued five further judgments against Turkey concerning the right to strike.

In *Saime Özcan v Turkey*[52] and *Urcan v Turkey*,[53] secondary school teachers in the public sector who took part in a national strike day aimed at improving terms and conditions of employment were prosecuted for having abandoned their places of work and sentenced to imprisonment, commuted to a substantial fine. In the latter case, the conviction was subsequently set aside. Both were barred from teaching for significant periods. The ECtHR held that such penalisation of the exercise of the right to strike was a breach of Article 11(1), unjustifiable under Article 11(2).

---

[47] On 17 July 2007 the judgment was under the name of *Satlimiş v Turkey* and the final version was dated 30 January 2008. This was rectified on 28 April 2008 when the name was corrected to *Dilek v Turkey* App Nos 74611/02, 26876/02, and 27628/02.

[48] *Dilek* (n 46 above) para 74.

[49] ibid para 69.

[50] ibid, para 70.

[51] ibid, para 73.

[52] *Saime Özcan v Turkey* App No 22943/04 (15 September 2009), judgment in French only.

[53] *Urcan v Turkey* App No 23018/04 etc (17 July 2008), definitive judgment 17 October 2008.

This case was followed by the trilogy of *Karacay v Turkey*,[54] *Kaya and Seyhan v Turkey*[55] and *Çerikçi v Turkey*,[56] which concerned public servants who had participated in days of strike action called by their union. Each was subjected to a disciplinary inquiry (a process governed, in the public service, by law) and subsequently disciplined for leaving their workplaces without authority. Each was given a written warning 'to be more attentive to the accomplishment of his/her functions and in his/her behaviour'.[57] The Court held that, minimal as the penalty was, this constituted a breach of their right of freedom of association under Article 11(1).[58] This emphasises once again that a restriction on the right to strike will infringe Article 11(1) and can only be justified by reference to Article 11(2) (which was not done in these cases).

This in itself is a remarkable conclusion with wide implications. For example, the right to strike was protected notwithstanding that the strikes were not directly related to collective bargaining.[59] The Court thus recognised by implication that the right to strike is not a derivative of the right to bargain collectively but a free-standing right deriving from trade union membership 'for the protection of [one's] interests'. In holding that a restriction on the right to strike could only be warranted by reference to Article 11(2) the Court rejected the submission of the Turkish government that, for failing to do their jobs and absenting themselves from work without informing their employer and without justification, a warning was necessary in response to a pressing social need and was proportionate.[60] The ECtHR held that, 'The penalty in question, however minimal it may have been, is likely to dissuade trade union members from legitimately participating in strike days or in actions to defend the interests of their members'.[61]

There was no pressing social need for a disciplinary sanction and thus the warning was not necessary in a democratic society.[62]

---

[54] *Karacay v Turkey* App No 6615/03 (27 March 2007), definitive version of the judgment on 27 June 2007.

[55] *Kaya and Seyhan v Turkey* App No 30946/04 (15 September 2009).

[56] *Çerikçi v Turkey* App No 33322/07 (13 October 2010).

[57] *Kaya and Seyhan* (n 54 above) para 12. It appears that subsequently an amnesty was granted in respect of certain disciplinary sanctions on public servants but not, it seems, in relation to warnings. The applicants were thus 'victims': para 22.

[58] ibid, para 24.

[59] In *Karaçay v Turkey* the object of a national day of strike action was to defend the purchasing power of public servants; in *Çerikçi v Turkey* the activity was participation in a May Day rally; in *Kaya and Seyhan v Turkey* the national day of strike action was to protest against a proposed law on the organisation of the public service then before Parliament. For a discussion of the right to strike for the protection of the interests of workers beyond merely furtherance of collective bargaining see KD Ewing and J Hendy, *Days of Action, The Legality of Protest Strikes against Government Cuts* (Liverpool, Institute of Employment Rights, 2011).

[60] *Kaya and Seyhan* (n 54 above) para 27.

[61] ibid para 30 (authors' translation from the original French).

[62] ibid, para 31.

v. *The Jurisprudence Progresses*

The 2009 judgment of the ECtHR in *Danilenkov v Russia*[63] concerned 32 dockers, members of a small union at Kaliningrad docks, who had taken industrial action. Following the strike, the employer discriminated against the members so that they were assigned less work, received reduced income, and were subject to discriminatory selection for redundancy. Domestic criminal proceedings succeeded but failed to compensate for the losses suffered, so an application was made to the ECtHR, relying principally on Article 14 rather than Article 11 of the Convention.[64] The ECtHR held that it was a violation of Article 11 to discriminate against the members of a union which had taken strike action, relying heavily on the ESC (including the jurisprudence of the European Committee of Social Rights) and ILO Conventions 87 and 98 (including the *Digest of Decisions* of the ILO Freedom of Association Committee and a decision involving the Dockers' Union of Russia and the Russian Federation), in upholding the complaint. In so doing the Court said that

> the totality of the measures implemented to safeguard the guarantees of Article 11 should include protection against discrimination on the ground of trade union membership which, according to the Freedom of Association Committee, constitutes one of the most serious violations of freedom of association capable to jeopardize the very existence of a trade union (see paragraph 107 above).[65]

The Court continued by saying that it was

> crucially important that individuals affected by discriminatory treatment should be provided with an opportunity to challenge it and to have the right to take legal action to obtain damages and other relief. Therefore, the States are required under Articles 11 and 14 of the Convention to set up a judicial system that would ensure real and effective protection against the anti-union discrimination.[66]

Further to the endorsements of the right to strike by individuals is *Trofimchuk v Ukraine*.[67] There, the applicant was dismissed from employment as a boiler engine operator in a municipal heating supply plant on the grounds that she had failed to comply with certain of her safety duties and that she took two hours of unauthorised absence in order to join a peaceful picket over wages unpaid by her previous municipal employer from whom the plant had been taken over by her current municipal employer. The absence caused some disruption in that a colleague on an earlier shift had to work two extra hours to cover her absence. The ECtHR held that dismissal partly on the ground of unauthorised absence

---

[63] *Danilenkov v Russia* App No 67336/01 (30 July 2009).

[64] Article 14 provides that 'The enjoyment of the rights and freedoms set forth in [the] Convention shall be secured without discrimination on any ground such as sex, race, colour, language, religion, political or other opinion, national or social origin, association with a national minority, property, birth or other status'.

[65] *Danilenkov* (n 62 above) para 123.

[66] ibid, para 124.

[67] *Trofimchuk v Ukraine* App No 4241/03 (28 January 2011).

while participating in the Article 11 protected activity of peaceful picketing was a restriction of her right of peaceful assembly and must be justified by reference to Article 11(2).[68] On the facts of the case there was such justification.[69]

In *RMT v UK*[70] the direction of the Court's decisions was upheld regarding the protection of the right to strike under Article 11(1) but reversed in relation to the extent of the restriction permitted by Article 11(2). In that case, the ECtHR found that the right to strike, indeed the right to solidarity action (ie, industrial action against an employer which is not a direct party to the dispute), was protected by Article 11(1) of the European Convention.[71] The judgment, like that in *Demir and Baykara*, contains an extensive review of the ILO Committee of Experts' and CFA materials relevant to the right to strike.[72] This enabled the Court to conclude that 'secondary action is recognised and protected as part of trade union freedom under ILO Convention No 87 and the European Social Charter'.[73]

With regard to the import of ILO Convention 87 on the Court's deliberations, the UK government (echoing the Employers' Group at the ILO) had argued that the ILO Committee of Experts was 'not formally competent to give authoritative interpretations' and that the Committee had recognised that 'its opinions and recommendations ... are not binding outside the ILO unless an international instrument expressly establishes them as such or the supreme court of a country so decides of its own volition'.[74] The Court was unmoved by this argument and refused to reconsider what it regarded as the Committee's 'role as a

---

[68] ibid, para 39.

[69] Ukrainian law prescribed a right to strike with immunity against disciplinary action for exercising it. The applicant had not followed the apparently straightforward procedure required as a condition for exercise of this right. The ECtHR held that the dismissal was prescribed by law and pursued the legitimate aim of protecting the rights of others (the employer). The ECtHR did not refer to necessity in a democratic society but held that, since the applicant had not followed the specified procedure to make her action lawful and protected and had not given notice to her supervisor of her intended absence and its duration so as to prevent 'serious disruption to workplace processes', she had failed to take 'all necessary steps to ensure that she exercised her freedom of peaceful assembly in accordance with the due respect to the rights and interests of her employer' (para 46). In those circumstances the dismissal was held not to be disproportionate (para 4). The basis of the decision may be thought to lie in the ease with which Ms Trofimchuk could, under Ukrainian law, have regularised and protected her strike action from all disciplinary consequences and her failure to do so (without suggesting that she had been prevented from so doing). Furthermore, 'the applicant did not challenge the conformity of the procedure made available in domestic law to the requirements of Article 11'. The procedure appears on the face of it to be straightforward and informal (see para 29) and would not seem sufficiently restrictive or oppressive to represent lack of conformity to Article 11 had Ms Trofimchuk elected to make that challenge – perhaps the reason why she did not.

[70] *RMT v UK* App No 31045/10 (8 April 2014).

[71] The RMT Union wished to call out on strike its members employed by a main contractor in railway maintenance and renewal in support of a strike by a small number of members employed by a smaller contractor which had been hived off from the main contractor. The union's purpose was to increase the industrial pressure on the small contractor to resist cuts in terms and conditions which were to follow the hiving off. UK law precluded such secondary industrial action. The RMT application to the ECtHR challenged that prohibition.

[72] See Demir (n 39 above) paras 27–33, likewise the review of the European Committee on Social Rights case law, at paras 34–37.

[73] *RMT* (n 69 above) para 76.

[74] ibid, para 96.

point of reference and guidance for the interpretation of certain provisions of the Convention'.[75] The Court was also unconcerned by the disagreement on the existence of the right to strike in 2012, which the UK government had brought to its attention. The Court explained that 'the disagreement originated with and was confined to the employer group' and that the governments had affirmed that the right to strike was 'well established and widely accepted as a fundamental right'.[76]

It is significant that in reaching this position, the Court has been fully aware of its obligations under the Vienna Convention. The Court applied Article 31(3)(c) of the Vienna Convention and concluded that:

> 76. [T]he Court would recall that, as provided in art 31(1) of the Vienna Convention on the Law of Treaties, the provisions of a Treaty are to be interpreted in accordance with their ordinary meaning, in their context and in the light of its object and purpose. Furthermore, it has often stated that the Convention cannot be interpreted in a vacuum but must be interpreted in harmony with the general principles of international law. Account should be taken, as indicated in art 31(3)(c) of the Vienna Convention of 'any relevant rules of international law applicable in relations between the parties', and in particular the rules concerning the international protection of human rights. In this regard, it is clear from the passages set out above that secondary action is recognised and protected as part of trade union freedom under ILO Convention No 87 and the European Social Charter ... For now it suffices to refer to the following passage from the *Demir* judgment:
>
> > 'The Court, in defining the meaning of terms and notions in the text of the Convention, can and must take into account elements of international law other than the Convention, the interpretation of such elements by competent organs, and the practice of European States reflecting their common values'.
>
> It would be inconsistent with this method for the Court to adopt in relation to Article 11 an interpretation of the scope of freedom of association of trade unions that is much narrower than that which prevails in international law. In addition, such an understanding of trade union freedom finds further support in the practice of many European States that have long accepted secondary strikes as a lawful form of trade union action.
>
> 77. It may well be that, by its nature, secondary industrial action constitutes an accessory rather than a core aspect of trade union freedom, a point to which the Court will revert in the next stage of its analysis. Nonetheless, the taking of secondary industrial action by a trade union, including strike action, against one employer in order to further a dispute in which the union's members are engaged with another employer must be regarded as part of trade union activity covered by Article 11.
>
> 78. The Court therefore concludes that the applicant's wish to organise secondary action in support of the [primary employer's] employees must be seen as a wish to exercise, free of a restriction imposed by national law, its right to freedom of association within the meaning of Article 11 § 1 of the Convention. It follows that the statutory ban on

---

[75] ibid, paras 96–97, 97. The ECtHR equally brushed aside criticism of the European Committee on Social Rights: see paras 94–95.

[76] ibid, para 97.

secondary action as it operated in the example relied on by the applicant constitutes an interference with the applicant's rights under this provision.

As to the right to strike in general, the Court reviewed its case law on the right to strike and held:

> More generally, what the above-mentioned cases illustrate is that strike action is clearly protected by Article 11. The Court therefore does not discern any need in the present case to determine whether the taking of industrial action should now be accorded the status of an essential element of the Article 11 guarantee.[77]

However, the ban on secondary action was, on the facts of the case, held to be justified under Article 11(2).[78] That conclusion has been the subject of heavy academic criticism,[79] among them that the Court, in this and several other meritorious UK cases, was anxious to avoid decisions adverse to the United Kingdom at a time when the government (consistent with its policy of leaving the European Union (EU)) was committed to denouncing the European Convention.[80] Certainly, the holding in *RMT v UK* that the blanket ban in secondary action justified under Article 11(2) is in marked contrast to the series of expansive decisions upholding trade union rights and, in particular, the right to strike.

[77] ibid, para 84.

[78] ibid. paras 79–105. The Court emphasised that the margin of appreciation was wide in the context of industrial and economic policies of the State. However, it noted factors counting in favour of the RMT. One was the practice across European states, illustrating that the United Kingdom was one of a small group of European countries which adopted an outright ban on secondary strikes, at the far end of the spectrum. Another was the repeated criticisms of the UK's prohibition of sympathy action by the ILO Committee of Experts and by the decisions of the European Committee on Social Rights on the Social Charter. The Court also referred to how a ban on secondary action could in some contexts, such as an outsourced workforce, severely hamper trade unions' efforts to protect their members. But having decided that the interference with freedom of association in the small contractor was not especially far-reaching, and in light of the breadth of the margin of appreciation in this area, the Court decided that the cogent arguments adduced by the RMT on trade union solidarity and efficacy were not sufficient to persuade it that the ban was disproportionate. The case leaves open the possibility that in other circumstances restrictions (including the ban on secondary action) will not be justifiable under Article 11(2). It is likely that some commentators will conclude that the judgment represents nothing short of an appeasement by the ECtHR of the UK government's threats to withdraw from the European Convention and its repeated attacks on the ECtHR so evident in the UK stance at the 2013 Committee of Ministers meeting in Brighton which lead to the Brighton Declaration and the subsequent inclusion of the references to 'margin of appreciation' and 'subsidiarity' in the Preamble to the Convention. Certainly, parts of the judgment could be seen in that way and there is no doubt that the judges of the ECtHR have been eager to reassure the UK government, British judges and elements of the English media that little or no threat is posed to the autonomy of the British legal system by the ECtHR or the Convention. The official visit by the President and Vice-Presidents of the ECtHR to the British judges in March 2014 (with the President giving a lecture at University College, London on 'the Margin of Appreciation') and the recent article by the former President (N Bratza, 'Living Instrument or Dead Letter – The Future of the European Convention on Human rights' (2014) *European Human Rights Law Review* 116) might be thought to be illustrative of the Court's concern to reassure. The cynical commentator might say that the judgment is a timely demonstration of that reassurance. Whether the trade union movement in the United Kingdom or in Europe will view the Court's treatment of the right to strike in the case as reassuring is doubtful.

[79] A Bogg and KD Ewing, 'The Implications of the RMT Case' (2014) 43 *Industrial Law Journal* 221.

[80] KD Ewing and J Hendy, 'Article 11(3) of the European Convention on Human Rights' [2017] *European Human Rights Law Review* 356.

vi. *The Question of Scope: A Right of 'Everyone' or a Right of 'Workers'?*

One issue that has arisen is the extent to which the trade union rights protected by Article 11(1) are the rights of 'everyone' as the Article expressly provides, or whether they are confined to 'workers', and, if so, what the definition of 'workers' might be. A crucial stepping stone in the Court's jurisprudence on Article 11 is the Grand Chamber case of *Sindicatul 'Păstorul cel Bun' v Romania*.[81] There, the relationship between priests and their bishop was based on a religious vow, they had no contracts and their pay came from the State not the bishopric. Those features did not, the Grand Chamber held, preclude the priests being 'workers' for the purpose of exercising their right to form a trade union pursuant to Article 11. Importantly, the Court applied a determination as to whether the priests had sufficient features of an 'employment relationship' to rank as workers entitled to the trade union rights of Article 11. This test was by application of ILO Recommendation 198 and the indicia there set out in addition to the presumption in ILO Convention 87 that workers 'without distinction' had entitlement to the rights there. Plainly, the rationale of this decision would apply to the right to strike.

There seems little to quibble about in that broad definition of those entitled to Article 11 trade union rights, yet in *Manole and 'Romanian Farmers Direct' v Romania*[82] self-employed farmers who were refused permission to register a trade union were held to have their Article 11(1) rights infringed, though the infringement was justified under Article 11(2).[83] And in *Vörður Ólafsson v Iceland*,[84] the Court expressly considered an employer's challenge to the legitimacy of a compulsory subscription to an employers' association was an issue of 'trade union

---

[81] *Sindicatul 'Păstorul cel Bun' v Romania* App No 2330/09 (9 July 2013); (2014) 58 EHRR 10, [2014] IRLR 49. The UK courts have recently grappled with the import of this case: *R (Independent Workers' Union of Great Britain) v CAC and RooFoods Ltd t/a Deliveroo* [2018] EWHC 1939 (Admin), [2018] IRLR 911; and *R (Independent Workers' Union of Great Britain) v CAC, Cordant Security Ltd, University of London, Secretary of State for BEIS* [2019] EWHC 728 (Admin).

[82] *Manole and 'Romanian Farmers Direct' v Romania* App No 46551/06 (16 June 2015).

[83] The self-employed farmers (who may have employed farmworkers [see para 50]) wished to defend the interests of themselves and *'persons providing services for farmers, including transport facilities'* (para 8). They wished to organise local centres to provide *'legal information, accountancy advice and judicial assistance to individual farmers'* (ibid) in order to improve farm production from self-sufficiency to a level where produce could be marketed (ibid). They were concerned to express farmers' views on government agricultural and tax policies (paras 50 and 51). In effect, they wished to form a trade association and were held to be free to do so; such an association was quite capable of advancing their aims (paras 72 and 73). What the ECtHR held they could permissibly be restricted from doing under Article 11(2) was to form a trade union, though they were permitted to join any extant union (para 13). It is clear from the judgment that the farmers were not seeking to carry out the fundamental purpose of a trade union, namely collective bargaining with persons or bodies in the position of employers over terms and conditions of work, a right conferred on Romanian trade unions (see paras 48, 53, and 59). The Court was content to preserve the difference in Romanian law between a trade union and a trade association (para 65).

[84] *Vörður Ólafsson v Iceland* App No 20161/06.

freedom'.[85] It may be concluded therefore that the right to strike is not confined only to 'workers', however defined.

A broad approach is supported by *Matelly v France*.[86] Article 11(1) explicitly states that the rights contained therein apply to '*everyone*'. The only exceptions are the categories of worker specified in the last sentence of Article 11(2): 'This Article shall not prevent the imposition of lawful restrictions on the exercise of these rights by members of the armed forces, of the police or of the administration of the State'. Yet even in relation to these identified subcategories, the ECtHR has held that the essence of the trade union rights of Article 11 may not be impaired. In *Demir and Baykara v Turkey* the Grand Chamber had held:

> 97. In this connection, the Court considers that the restrictions imposed on the three groups mentioned in art 11 are to be construed strictly and should therefore be confined to the 'exercise' of the rights in question. These restrictions must not impair the very essence of the right to organise.

These propositions were reiterated by the ECtHR in *Matelly v France* in which members of the military were prohibited by law from joining an occupational association with apparent trade union characteristics. The ECtHR held, in partic-ular, that the special protections put in place by the French State to protect the interests of military personnel were no substitute for the right to form and to join trade unions.[87] It held:

> 75. Although freedom of military association may be subject to legitimate restrictions, a prohibition pure and simple on forming or joining a trade union encroaches on the very essence of this liberty, a restriction prohibited by the Convention.

The Court has held that 'only convincing and compelling reasons' can justify restrictions on such parties' freedom of association.[88] The relevance of *Matelly* (which chimes with jurisprudence to the same effect in the ECSR – see below) is that, given that the ECtHR holds that it is not permissible, in relation to the categories of worker identified for restriction in Article 11(2), to impair or prohibit the essence of the trade union freedoms protected by Article 11(1), still more it must be impermissible to prohibit a protected element of Article 11(1) in rela-tion to a class of applicant in relation to which the Article has not expressed any permitted restriction.

---

[85] Para 75. The employer relied on ECtHR jurisprudence on trade unions (see paras 22–25, 29, 31, 57 and 61); as did the government (see paras 37, 38, 66 and 68). The Court also applied that jurisprudence in its assessment that there was an interference with the applicant's Article 11(1) rights (paras 45–46, and 50–51), [53]).

[86] *Matelly v France* App No 10609/10 (2 October 2014). See also the sister case of *ADEFROMIL v France* App No 32191/09, judgment handed down on the same date.

[87] Para 70. This decision follows *Rekvényi v Hungary* App No 25390/94 (20 May 1999) (2000) 30 EHRR 519, para 59 where the ECtHR held that police officers are entitled to the right of freedom of association, though subject to legitimate restriction imposed by national law.

[88] *Tüm Haber Sen v Turkey* App No 28602/95 (21 February 2006) (2008) 46 EHRR 19, para 35.

vii. Recent Judgments on the Right to Strike

Recent right to strike cases have all recognised that the right to strike is protected by Article 11(1) but have differed in the results by application of Article 11(2). For example, the right to strike was denied to armed police officers without infringement of Article 11 in *Junta Rectora del Ertzainen Nazional Elkartasuna v Spain*.[89] The fact that those concerned were armed police officers engaged in the protection of the State, well within the express exemption of Article 11(2), explains the rationale of the case and does not detract from the ECtHR's more recent approach to the right to strike.

In *Svenska Transportarbetareförbundet and Seko v Sweden*,[90] the conflict between the *Viking* and *Laval* line of cases in the EU and Article 11 of the ECHR arose. Swedish trade unions had refused to load or handle the mooring lines of a Norwegian owned ship flagged in Panama which had docked in Sweden, unless and until the owners entered an International Transport Workers Federation (ITF)-approved collective agreement which paid ITF wage rates to the Polish officers and Russian crew. The owner made the agreement but later reneged on it and sued the unions in the Swedish Labour Court. The latter referred the case to the Court of Justice of the European Union (CJEU). The CJEU held that the industrial action might infringe the Norwegian company's freedom, under the EU Treaty, to provide services to another State. On that basis the Swedish Labour Court held that the proportionality of the industrial action therefore had to be examined. It concluded that the wage rates in the collective agreement were excessive and therefore the industrial action illegitimately interfered with the Norwegian shipowner's freedom to provide services. Substantial damages were awarded. The Swedish unions applied to the ECtHR claiming a violation of their right to strike and to bargain collectively protected by Article 11. The ECtHR decided that the application was manifestly inadmissible in failing to meet the admissibility criteria set out in Articles 34 and 35 of the ECHR but failed to explain why.[91] It is impossible to consider that this case adds or subtracts from the jurisprudence of the ECtHR on the right to strike.[92]

In *Trade Union in the Factory '4th November' v Macedonia*[93] a strike was declared unlawful because it had been called in breach of the legislative requirements for a compulsory period of conciliation. This was not disproportionate, and the declaration was not therefore a violation of Article 11. The Court reiterated that 'having regard to its case-law', 'strike action is protected under Article 11 of

---

[89] *Junta Rectora del Ertzainen Nazional Elkartasuna v Spain* App No 45892/09 (21 April 2015).
[90] *Svenska Transportarbetareförbundet and Seko v Sweden* App No 29999/16 (1 December 2016).
[91] This is discussed in KD Ewing and J Hendy, 'The Strasbourg Court Treats Trade Unionists with Contempt: *Svenska Transportarbetareförbundet and Seko v Sweden*' (2017) 46 *Industrial Law Journal* 435.
[92] The issue will be raised again in *Norsk Transportforbund v Norway*, a pending application in the ECtHR. Discussed in J Hendy and T Novitz, 'The Holship Case' (2018) 47 *Industrial Law Journal* 315.
[93] *Trade Union in the Factory '4th November' v Macedonia* App No 15557/10 (8 September 2015).

the Convention.'[94] A requirement of a limited period of attempted conciliation before strike action would not appear to be inconsistent with the approach of the ILO bodies, though their jurisprudence was not cited.

This case may be compared with *Association of Academics v Iceland*.[95] There the Court, consistently with the '*4th November*' case, held that the imposition of mandatory arbitration after many days of strike action and 24 meetings endeavouring to reach a collective agreement between health workers and the State was not a violation of Article 11. The Court reviewed many of its earlier cases[96] and reiterated some broad principles established in the cases so far discussed:

24. So far the Court has not found that the taking of industrial action should be accorded the status of an essential element of the Article 11 guarantee (see *National Union of Rail, Maritime and Transport Workers v the United Kingdom*, no 31045/10, § 84, 8 April 2014), but it is clear that strike action is protected by Article 11 as it is considered to be a part of trade union activity (ibid, § 77). Yet the fact that the process of collective bargaining and industrial action, including strike actions against the employer of the union members who were the subject of the dispute, does not lead to the outcome desired by the union and its members does not mean that the exercise of their Article 11 rights is illusory. The right to collective bargaining has not been interpreted as including a 'right' to a collective agreement. Nor does the right to strike imply a right to prevail. As the Court has often stated, the Convention requires that under national law trade unions should be able, in conditions not at variance with Article 11, to strive for the protection of their members' interests (ibid, § 85).

25. To be compatible with paragraph 2 of Article 11, the interference must be shown to be 'prescribed by law', to pursue a legitimate aim, and to be 'necessary in a democratic society' to achieve those aims (see, among many others, ibid, § 78). To be considered necessary in a democratic society, it must be shown that an interference with a right protected by Article 11 corresponded to a 'pressing social need', that the reasons given by the national authorities to justify it were relevant and sufficient and that the interference was proportionate to the legitimate aim pursued (see, ibid, § 83). Regard must be had to the fair balance to be struck between the competing interest of the individual and of the community as a whole. Since achieving a proper balance between the interest of labour and management involves the sensitive character of social and political issues, the Contracting State must be afforded a margin of appreciation as to how trade union freedom and protection of the occupational interest of union members may be secured, given the high degree of divergence between the domestic systems in this field. The breadth of the margin will still depend on the factors that the Court, in its case-law, has identified as relevant, including the nature and extent of the restriction on the trade union right at issue, the object pursued by the contested restriction and the competing rights and interests of other individuals in society who are liable to suffer as a result of the unrestricted exercise of that right. The degree of common ground between member States of the Council of Europe in relation to the issue arising in the case may also

---

[94] Para 36.
[95] *Association of Academics v Iceland* App No 2451/16 (15 May 2018) (2018) 67 EHRR SE4.
[96] Para 26.

be relevant, as may any international consensus reflected in the apposite international instruments (see, ibid., § 86).

The *Association of Academics* judgment is notable for its failure to mention ILO standards relating to the right to strike, but also for its brevity and paucity of reasoning. The best view of its application of Article 11(2) is its focus on the objective of protection of the health and safety of the community, a legitimate concern when strikes in the healthcare sector arise, it therefore upheld the Icelandic legislation which imposed arbitral resolution of the dispute in question.

Three ECtHR cases since *RMT v UK* have notably upheld the right to strike.

In *Hrvatski Liječnički Sindikat v Croatia*, an injunction had been granted to restrain a strike by doctors seeking to enforce a collective agreement. The ECtHR described the right to strike as the 'most powerful instrument of trade union to protect the occupational interests of their members'.[97] It dismissed the government's justification for the injunction on grounds of technical irregularities in the collective agreement as not proportionate to the legitimate aim.

In *Veniamin Tymoshenko v Ukraine*, an injunction had been granted to restrain a strike by airline cabin crew in pursuit of improved terms and conditions of employment.[98] The ECtHR held that 'strike action is clearly protected by art 11'[99] and the injunction could not be justified by reference to Article 11(2).[100] It cited the jurisprudence of the ILO Committee of Experts and the CFA, and that of the European Committee on Social Rights of the European Social Charter.[101] It held that the injunction could not be justified by reference to Article 11(2).[102]

The third positive (indeed most positive) strike case is that of *Ognevenko v Russia*.[103] This case concerns the protection of an individual striker, namely a train driver, who was dismissed for participating in strike action in railway transport which was wrongly deemed an 'essential service' by Russian legislation. This is only a 'Chamber' judgment, as in the three other most recent cases. However, it is significant insofar as it harks back to the desire to protect individual workers in the earlier Turkish cases, from prosecution but also disciplinary proceedings in the workplace. Indeed, the case is notable in a number of respects.

Decided only a few months after *Association of Academics v Iceland*,[104] it takes a very different view perhaps influenced by a concern not with the collective rights of a trade union, but the right to strike of an individual worker. In so doing,

---

[97] *Hrvatski Liječnički Sindikat v Croatia* App No.36701/09 (27 November 2014) para 59. This case is discussed in Ewing and Hendy, 'The Strasbourg Court Treats Trade Unionists with Contempt' (n 90 above).

[98] *Veniamin Tymoshenko v Ukraine* App No 48408/12 (2 January 2015).

[99] Para 78.

[100] Because the legislation on which the injunction was based was not sufficiently clear and foreseeable to be 'prescribed by law': see [79]–[86].

[101] Paras 33–49.

[102] Because the legislation on which the injunction was based was not sufficiently clear and foreseeable to be 'prescribed by law': see paras 79–86.

[103] *Ognevenko v Russia* App No 44873/09 (20 November 2018).

[104] App No 2451/16 (15 May 2018) (2018) 67 EHRR SE4.

reference is made to ICESCR, Article 8, but more significantly (and at length) 'ILO principles concerning the right to strike' derived from the fifth revision of the CFA *Digest of Decisions* and CFA case law regarding Russia.[105] The reiteration of the CFA findings by the CEACR is also given explicit attention, namely

> that the right to strike may be restricted only in respect of public servants exercising authority in the name of the State and in essential services in the strict sense of the term – that is to say services the interruption of which would endanger the life, personal safety or health of the whole or part of the population.

(This was the basis on which *Association of Academics* was ultimately – if problematically – decided).[106] Further, the ECtHR referred to the reminder issued by the CEACR to Russia that 'railway transport did not constitute an essential service in the strict sense of the term', and that the CEACR 'continues to request Russia to ensure that railway workers can exercise the right to strike'.[107]

Secondly, the Chamber of the Court in *Ognevenko* is less coy than the entirely differently constituted Chamber in *Association of Academics* regarding the status of the right to strike. There is a return to the Croatian emphasis on the right to strike as 'one of the most important means' … 'to be used to secure a trade union's freedom to protect the occupational interests of its members'.[108] Moreover, it is acknowledged that 'the Court has held on several occasions that strike action is protected by Article 11'.[109] While the right to strike is not absolute, exceptions must be 'construed strictly' and 'therefore be confined to the "exercise" and must not impair the very essence of the right to organise'.[110] In this case, the requirements of Article 11(2) were not met and there had been a disproportionate restriction of Ognevenko's right to freedom of association, leading to award of pecuniary and non-pecuniary damages as well as a sum for costs and expenses incurred before the Court. Despite the lengthy dissenting opinion of the Russian Judge Dedov, which requested a greater margin of appreciation for his home State, *Ognevenko* returns to recognition of the significance of ILO standards for the analysis of the ECtHR of compliance with Article 11.[111]

Finally, in relation to the ECtHR and the right to strike, it is common knowledge that in national litigation employers erect their own commercial interests as a counterweight to the trade union (and workers') right to strike in the proportionality exercise to be conducted under Article 11(2). In that connection, it is to be observed that Article 11(2) does not provide for every countervailing interest to

---

[105] See App No 44873/09, 20 November 2018, paras 19–21.
[106] ibid, para 22.
[107] ibid, para 23.
[108] ibid, para 56.
[109] ibid, para 57.
[110] ibid, paras 58–59.
[111] See T Novitz, 'Dispatch No 15 – Iceland and Russia – "To Protect the Right to Strike or Not? The Question before the European Court of Human Rights in App No 2451/16 Association of Academics v Iceland and App No 44873/09 Ognevenko v Russia"' (2019) *Comparative Labor Law & Policy Journal*, available at: cllpj.law.illinois.edu/dispatches.

be weighed in the balance but only those which are specified and which are necessary in a democratic society including those for the 'protection of the rights and freedoms of others'. Not every asserted commercial interest of the employer ranks as a 'right or freedom'. Where one party has a right protected by the ECHR and the other does not, then only 'indisputable imperatives' can justify interference with enjoyment of the Convention right. So it was held in *Chassagnou v France*:

> 113. In the present case the only aim invoked by the Government to justify the interference complained of was 'protection of the rights and freedoms of others'. Where these 'rights and freedoms' are themselves among those guaranteed by the Convention or its Protocols, it must be accepted that the need to protect them may lead States to restrict other rights or freedoms likewise set forth in the Convention. It is precisely this constant search for a balance between the fundamental rights of each individual which constitutes the foundation of a 'democratic society'. The balancing of individual interests that may well be contradictory is a difficult matter, and Contracting States must have a broad margin of appreciation in this respect, since the national authorities are in principle better placed than the European Court to assess whether or not there is a 'pressing social need' capable of justifying interference with one of the rights guaranteed by the Convention.

> It is a different matter where restrictions are imposed on a right or freedom guaranteed by the Convention in order to protect 'rights and freedoms' not, as such, enunciated therein. In such a case only indisputable imperatives can justify interference with enjoyment of a Convention right.

> In the present case the Government pleaded the need to protect or encourage democratic participation in hunting. Even supposing that French law enshrines a 'right' or 'freedom' to hunt, the Court notes, like the Bordeaux Administrative Court, that such a right or freedom is not one of those set forth in the Convention, which does, however, expressly guarantee the freedom of association.[112]

B. The European Social Charter

As a complementary instrument to the ECHR, the European Social Charter (ESC – CETS No 35) was adopted in 1961 and revised in 1996 as the 'Revised European Social Charter' (RESC – CETS No 163).[113] Both instruments contain an explicit guarantee of the right to collective action, including to strike, in the same wording:

Article 6 – The right to bargain collectively

With a view to ensuring the effective exercise of the right to bargain collectively, the Parties undertake: ...

---

[112] *Chassagnou v France* (2000) 29 EHRR 615 (a case in which landowners challenged the compulsion to join an association of hunters) para 113.

[113] Out of the 47 Council of Europe Member States only four have ratified neither the ESC nor the RESC (Liechtenstein, Monaco, San Marino and Switzerland). See generally, N Bruun, K Lörcher, I Schömann and S Clauwaert (eds), *The European Social Charter and the Employment Relation* (Oxford, Hart Publishing, 2017).

and recognise:

4. the right of workers and employers to collective action in cases of conflicts of interest, including the right to strike, subject to obligations that might arise out of collective agreements previously entered into.

This right has become one of the most important elements in the collective rights protection from the human rights perspective. It is, however, not without limits, with the ESC, Article 31(1), RESC, Appendix G(1) providing that:

The rights and principles set forth in Part I when effectively realised, and their effective exercise as provided for in Part II, shall not be subject to any restrictions or limitations not specified in those parts, except such as are prescribed by law and are necessary in a democratic society for the protection of the rights and freedoms of others or for the protection of public interest, national security, public health, or morals.

Before considering the substance of Article 6(4), it should be recognised that the ESC was the first treaty explicitly to 'recognise' the 'right to strike'.[114] Moreover, in the context of the Charter, this right is important because of the formulation whereby States undertake to 'recognise' the right to strike in contrast to more diluted formulations in relation to other Charter rights. Indeed, this formulation of the right was thought to be especially significant by the Hoge Raad, by which Article 6(4) was incorporated into domestic law to form the basis of the right to strike in the Netherlands. The Hoge Raad took this step, in view of the wording of the Charter and the undertaking of the Dutch government to 'recognise' the right to strike in Article 6(4), in contrast to more equivocal wording used in relation to other rights.[115]

i. Principles Relating to the Right to Strike

The European Committee of Social Rights (ECSR), which supervises the implementation of the Charter's provisions, publishes 'Conclusions' in respect of its (cyclical) reporting system,[116] and 'Decisions' from the complaints procedure – based on an Additional Protocol Providing for a System of Collective Complaints (CCPP – CETS No 158).[117] This Committee has developed an extensive case law

---

[114] See ESC, *Conclusions I*, 34; but at that time there was already an established case law in the ILO concerning the right to strike, and ILO Convention 87 as well as the Declaration of Philadelphia existed.

[115] 'NV Dutch Railways v Transport Unions FNV, FSV and CNV' (1986) 6 *International Labour Law Reports* 3.

[116] The most recent 'Conclusions' on Article 6(4) ESC were adopted on 24 January 2019 (for the reference period dating from 1 January 2013 to 31 December 2016) as '*Conclusions 2018*' in relation to those States having ratified the Revised European Social Charter and '*Conclusions XXI-3 (2018)*' in relation to the States being only bound by the (original) 1961 ESC.

[117] 15 Council of Europe Member States have agreed to be bound under the Protocol. They are: Belgium, Bulgaria, Croatia, Cyprus, Czech Republic, Finland, France, Greece, Ireland, Italy, Netherlands, Norway, Portugal, Slovenia and Sweden. See: www.coe.int/en/web/conventions/full-list/-/conventions/treaty/158/signatures?p_auth=oPbZjf8n.

on the right to strike.[118] In a recent substantive decision[119] on the right to strike based on a complaint filed by Swedish trade unions,[120] the ECSR made several general statements by referring to the Charter itself:

> From a general point of view, the Committee considers that the exercise of the right to bargain collectively and the right to collective action, guaranteed by Article 6§§2 and 4 of the Charter, represents an essential basis for the fulfilment of other fundamental rights guaranteed by the Charter.[121]

More importantly, the ECSR also referred to international standards such as ILO Convention 87:

> In addition, the Committee notes that the right to *collective* bargaining and *action* receives constitutional recognition at national level in the vast majority of the Council of Europe's member States, as well as in a significant number of binding legal instruments at the United Nations and EU level. In this respect, reference is made *inter alia* to Article 8 of the International Covenant on Economic, Social and Cultural Rights (see paragraph 37 above), the relevant provisions of the *ILO conventions Nos 87,* 98 and 154 (see paragraph 38 above)[122] as well as the EU Charter of Fundamental Rights, Directive 2006/123/EC on services in the internal market (cf Article 1§7) and the Directive 2008/104/EC on temporary agency work – recital 19 (see paragraph 36 above).[123]

Finally, the ECSR has emphasised in strong terms 'the fundamental right of workers and trade unions to engage in collective action for the protection of economic and social interests of the workers', noting in the Swedish case that:

> In this context, within the system of values, principles and fundamental rights embodied in the Charter, the right to collective bargaining and collective action is essential in ensuring the autonomy of trade unions and protecting the employment conditions of workers: if the substance of this right is to be respected, trade unions must be allowed to strive for the improvement of existing living and working conditions of workers, and its scope should not be limited by legislation to the attainment of minimum conditions.[124]

---

[118] The most important elements of its case-law are summarised in a 'Digest' (Council of Europe, *Digest of The Case Law of The European Committee of Social Rights*, December 2018, available at: www. rm.coe.int/digest-2018-parts-i-ii-iii-iv-en/1680939f80; for Article 6 para 4 see, 101 ff). Collective complaints are reported on the Council of Europe's website.

[119] The ESC did publish a decision in 2018 in response to a complaint filed by a Croatian union in which it alleged the violation of, inter alia, 6(4). However, the ESC held that the information submitted by the complainant regarding the imposition of a back to work order of doctors during a strike was insufficient to allow the ESC to determine whether a violation of the Charter had occurred. See Complaint No 116/2015, *Matica Hrvatskih Sindikata v Croatia*, ECSR Decision (27 August 2018).

[120] Complaint No 85/2012, *LO and TCO v Sweden*, ECSR Decision (3 July 2013). And see, Resolution CM/ResChS (2014) 1 adopted by the Council of Ministers, 5 February 2014.

[121] ibid para 109 (which is the opening paragraph of the aforementioned Resolution).

[122] ILO Convention 87 was ratified by Sweden on 25 November 1949.

[123] Complaint No 85/2012, *LO and TCO v Sweden* (n 119 above) para 110 (emphasis added).

[124] ibid, para 120.

ii. Scope of the Right to Strike

The right to strike protected by the Charter is not unlimited. However, the Committee has narrowly construed the scope of restrictions permitted by Article 31 (ESC) and Appendix G (RESC),[125] emphasising that:

> The Committee considers that in accordance to the Appendix to the Charter relating to Article 6§4 '[E]ach Party may, insofar as it is concerned, regulate the exercise of the right to strike by law, provided that any further restriction that this might place on the right can be justified under the terms of Article G'. This means that even though the right of trade unions to collective action is not an absolute one. Nevertheless, a restriction to this right can be considered in conformity with Article 6(4) of the Charter only if, as set forth by Article G, the restriction: a) is prescribed by law; b) pursues a legitimate purpose – ie, the protection of rights and freedoms of others, of public interest, national security, public health or morals – and, c) is necessary in a democratic society for the pursuance of these purposes, ie, the restriction has to be proportionate to the legitimate aim pursued.[126]

It is not possible to give a full overview on all aspects of the right to strike guaranteed by Article 6(4). However, some key elements are described here in more detail.

a. Conditions to Call a Strike

The Charter protects action of a wide and varied kind, and so far as the parties are concerned, the right to strike ought not to be confined to representative or most representative trade unions. Moreover, the percentage of workers required to call a strike must not be too high[127] nor would it be compatible with Article 6(4) if a decision to call a strike would have to be endorsed by the executive committee of a trade union.[128]

b. Subject Matter

The Committee has recognised the fundamental right of workers and trade unions to engage in collective action for the protection of economic and social interests of workers. In the *Swedish LO/TCO* case referred to above the Committee considered that:

> [N]ational legislation which prevents *a priori* the exercise of the right to collective action, or permits the exercise of this right only in so far as it is necessary to obtain

---

[125] Complaint No 32/2005, *ETUC/CITUB/Podkrepa v Bulgaria*, ECSR Decision (16 October 2006).
[126] Complaint No 85/2012, *LO and TCO v Sweden* (n 119 above) para 118.
[127] See, eg, *Conclusions 2018*, Armenia, Russian Federation, or Romania in relation to the conditions of 'representativeness criteria and if the strike is approved by at least half of the respective trade union's members'.
[128] See, eg, *Conclusions 2018*, Cyprus.

given minimum working standards would not be in conformity with Article 6§4 of the Charter, as it would infringe the fundamental right of workers and trade unions to engage in collective action for the protection of economic and social interests of the workers.[129]

Accordingly, prohibiting strikes not aimed at concluding a collective agreement is not in conformity with the right to strike.[130] Nevertheless, the Committee has pointed out that the protection in Article 6(4) applies only to 'conflicts of interest'.[131] According to the Committee,

> it follows that it cannot be invoked in cases of conflicts of right, ie, in particular in cases of disputes concerning the existence, validity or interpretation of a collective agreement, or its violation, eg, through action taken during its currency with a view to the revision of its contents.[132]

c. The Personal Scope

So far as participants are concerned, any employee concerned, irrespective of whether he is a member of the trade union having called the strike or not, has the right to participate in the strike.[133] A general ban on the right to strike, even in essential sectors, is not permissible since it cannot be regarded as necessary in a democratic society. Accordingly, only civil servants 'exercising authority in the name of the State' may be excluded.[134]

In the important *Eurocop* decision, the ECSR recognised the right to strike even for members of the police forces in the sense that the 'right to strike affects one of the essential elements of the right to collective bargaining, as provided for in Article 6 of the Charter, and without which the content of this right

---

[129] Complaint No 85/2012, *LO and TCO v Sweden* (n 119 above) para 120.

[130] ECSR, *Conclusions IV, Germany*: 'It does not, however, seem possible to accept that there should be no other type of collective bargaining in labour relations other than that aimed at concluding a collective agreement. There are many circumstances which, apart from any collective agreement, call for "collective bargaining", such as when dismissals have been announced or are contemplated by a firm and a group of employees seeks to prevent them or to serve the re-engagement of those dismissed. Any bargaining between one or more employers and a body of employees (whether "de jure" or "de facto") aimed at solving a problem of common interest, whatever its nature may be, should be regarded as "collective bargaining within the meaning of Article 6"' (p 50). This criticism has recently been confirmed by *Conclusions XXI-3* concerning Germany: The 'prohibition on all strikes not aimed at achieving a collective agreement constitutes an excessive restriction on the right to strike'.

[131] T Jaspers, 'The Right to Collective Action in European Law' in F Dorssemont, T Jasper and A Van Hoek (eds), *Cross-Border Collective Actions in Europe: A Legal Challenge* (Antwerp, Intersentia, 2007) 56.

[132] Complaint No 85/2012, *LO and TCO v Sweden* (n 119 above) para 117.

[133] See Council of Europe, *Digest of The Case Law of The European Committee of Social Rights* (n 117 above) 103 ('Group entitled to call a collective action').

[134] In its recent *Conclusions 2018* and *XXI-3*, the ECSR has found, eg, Azerbaijan, Denmark, Estonia, Germany and Ukraine in non-conformity in this respect.

becomes void of its very substance and is therefore deprived of its effectiveness' (paragraph 212) and that only 'compelling reasons' (paragraph 211) could justify such an approach:[135]

> 209. The Committee however observes that, in spite of the specific internal organisation of the police force and the 'integral role' of the Gardaí in national security mentioned above, the reasons provided by the Government do no demonstrate the existence of a concrete pressing social need. Indeed, the Government has not justified that the legitimate purpose of maintaining national security may not be achieved by establishing restrictions on the exercise of the right to strike (such as requirements relating to the mode and form of industrial action) rather than by imposing an absolute prohibition.

> 210. From this point of view, Section 8 of the Industrial Relations Act not only amounts to a restriction but to a complete abolition of the right to strike. In this regard, the Committee has held that '[...] national legislation which prevents a priori the exercise of the right to collective action, or permits the exercise of this right only in so far as it is necessary to obtain given minimum working standards would not be in conformity with Article 6§4 of the Charter, as it would infringe the fundamental right of workers and trade unions to engage in collective action for the protection of economic and social interests of the workers. In this context, within the system of values, principles and fundamental rights embodied in the Charter, the right to collective bargaining and collective action is essential in ensuring the autonomy of trade unions and protecting the employment conditions of workers' (Swedish Trade Union Confederation (LO) and Swedish Confederation of Professional Employees (TCO) v Sweden, Complaint No 85/2012; decision on the admissibility and merits of 3 July 2013, §120).

> 211. Since this applies in respect of restrictions on the exercise of the right to strike for the purpose of improving conditions of work beyond a given minimum level, it a fortiori applies also for every absolute prohibition of the right to strike established a priori by law. In other words, the Committee holds that restrictions on human rights must be interpreted narrowly. As a consequence, in the context of the regulation of the collective bargaining rights of police officers, states must demonstrate compelling reasons as to why an absolute prohibition on the right to strike is justified in the specific national context in question, as distinct from the imposition of restrictions as to the mode and form of such strike action.

> 212. Thus, in this case, the margin of appreciation of the state party is restricted, because the abolition of the right to strike affects one of the essential elements of the right to collective bargaining, as provided for in Article 6 of the Charter, and without which the content of this right becomes void of its very substance and is therefore deprived of its effectiveness.

> 213. In the situation at issue in this complaint, the Government as previously noted has not presented such a compelling justification for the imposition of the absolute prohibition on the right to strike set out in Section 8 of the 1990 Industrial Relations Act.

---

[135] Complaint No 83/2012, *European Confederation of Police (EuroCOP) v Ireland*, ECSR Decision (2 December 2013) paras 207–13.

As a result, the Committee considers that this statutory provision is not proportionate to the legitimate aim pursued and, accordingly, is not necessary in a democratic society.[136]

On the other hand, the ECSR denied the members of the armed forces the right to strike in *European Organisation of Military Associations (EUROMIL) v Ireland*.[137] This decision aligns the jurisprudence of the ECSR with that of the ECtHR in *Matelly v France*, discussed above.

Finally, in *ICTU v Ireland*[138] it was held that the exclusion of the self-employed from the right to bargain collectively under EU competition law (which was applied in Ireland by Irish legislation) breached Article 6(2) of the ESC. The significance of the decision here is that the right to strike must equally extend to the self-employed under the ESC. This case will no doubt have significant import with the limited yet increasing employment of workers through online platforms.

d. The Methods and Consequences of a Strike

The Committee has said that as to methods adopted in the course of a dispute, 'Article 6§4 encompasses other types of action taken by employees or trade unions, including *blockades* or *picketing*'.[139] Concerning the consequences of a strike there must be – according to the Committee – sufficient protection of workers against dismissal when taking industrial action.[140]

III. The Right to Strike and the European Union

Ostensibly, regulation of the right to strike does not come within the legislative competence of the European Union (EU). This is a long-standing exclusion, first made explicit in the Social Protocol to the Maastricht Treaty on European

---

[136] This has been confirmed in its most recent decision in Complaint No 140/2016, *Confederazione Generale Italiana del Lavoro (CGIL) v Italy*, ECSR Decision (22 January 2019) paras 152–53 (concerning the Italian 'Guardia di Finanza' in which the Committee considered 'that the absolute prohibition of the right to strike imposed on members of the Guardia di Finanza is not proportionate to the legitimate aim pursued and, therefore, is not necessary in a democratic society' (para 152) and held 'that there is a violation of Article 6§4 of the Charter'. See: hudoc.esc.coe.int/eng?i=cc-140-2016-dmerits-en.

[137] Complaint No 112/2014, *European Organisation of Military Associations (EUROMIL) v Ireland* (12 September 2017), (2018) 66 EHRR SE12. The ECSR also held at [56]–[57] (particularly in the light of *Matelly* (n 85 above); see *EUROMIL* at [45] and [46]) that the ban on the associations from affiliating to the Irish Congress of Trade Unions was in violation of Article 5. It also held (at [90]–[96]) that the exclusion of the associations from pay discussions was a violation of Article 6(2) (the right to bargain collectively).

[138] *ICTU v Ireland* Complaint No 123/2016, ECSR Decision (12 December 2018).

[139] Complaint No 85/2012, *LO and TCO v Sweden* (n 119 above) para 117; See also Complaint No 59/200, *ETUC/CGSLB/CSC/FGTB v Belgium*, ECSR Decision (13 September 2011) para 29.

[140] See, eg, *Conclusions 2018*, United Kingdom.

Union and now set out in Article 153(5) of the Treaty on the Functioning of the European Union (TFEU). In the background, however, was the understanding that the International Labour Organization (ILO) would regulate such fundamental aspects of labour law, which would be implemented by EU Member States in accordance with their international obligations.[141]

The connection between the common market and the need for protection of workers' rights was not immediately in evidence when the predecessor of the EU, the 'European Economic Community' (EEC) was founded in 1957. Prior to establishment of the EEC, a group of ILO experts, headed by Bertil Ohlin, considered the place of social standards within a common market, which considered the adoption of particular labour standards by the new European institution unnecessary.[142] The ILO Committee recommendations were broadly accepted in the Treaty of Rome's 'White Paper', otherwise known as the 'Spaak Report', adopted by 'the Six' founding Member States in 1956.[143] This conclusion had the effect of reserving for the ILO (and the ILO's European Regional Council) the role of setting global and European-level labour standards which would then be applied domestically, rather than through the EEC as an intermediary.

Nevertheless, despite this historical reluctance to engage with industrial relations issues at the outset, the right to strike has been recognised in the EU (in its present and past incarnations, such as 'the European Community' or the 'European Economic Community') in a number of ways. First, there has been express inclusion of the right in EU human rights instruments, such as the Community Charter of the Fundamental Social Rights of Workers (CCFSRW) and the EU Charter of Fundamental Rights (CFREU),[144] both of which receive specific mention in the Treaty on European Union (TEU) and the Treaty on the Functioning of the European Union (TFEU). Both Treaties also make specific reference to the ESC, noted above, which also under Article 6(4) refers to the right to take collective action, including the right to strike. Secondly, the right to strike has been given effect through legislative instruments, such as the 'Monti' Regulation[145] relating to

---

[141] eg, then in force was the Exchange of Letters between the European Commission and the EU (1989), available at: www.ilo.org/wcmsp5/groups/public/---dgreports/---jur/documents/genericdocument/wcms_440259.pdf. For a summary of the contemporary terms of EU–ILO cooperation, see the 2001 corigendum, available at: www.ilo.org/wcmsp5/groups/public/---europe/---ro-geneva/---ilo-brussels/documents/genericdocument/wcms_169295.pdf; and also see for a summary in 2018: www.ilo.org/pardev/donors/WCMS_350516/lang--en/index.htm.

[142] See Report of a Group of Experts, *Social Aspects of European Economic Co-operation* (Geneva, ILO 1956), discussed by J Murray, *Transnational Labour Regulation: The ILO and EC Compared* (The Hague, Kluwer, 2001) 81.

[143] Outlined in P Davies, 'The Emergence of European Labour Law' in W McCarthy (ed), *Legal Intervention in Industrial Relations* (Oxford, Oxford University Press, 1992) 319.

[144] See generally, F Dorssemont, K Lörcher, S Clauwaert and M Schmitt, *The Charter of Fundamental Rights of the European Union and the Employment Relation* (Oxford, Hart Publishing, 2019).

[145] Council Regulation (EC) No 2679/98 of 7 December 1998 on the functioning of the internal market in relation to the free movement of goods among the Member States, available at: www.eur-lex.europa.eu/legal-content/EN/TXT/?uri=CELEX%3A31998R2679.

free movement of goods and the 'Services Directive'[146] regarding free movement of services. Further, the ECJ (now the Court of Justice of the European Union or CJEU) has explicitly recognised that, by virtue of international law (including ILO instruments such as ILO Convention No 87) and under European human rights law, there is a right to strike. In November 2017 the EU proclaimed a European Pillar of Social Rights,[147] in respect of 'Eurozone' Member States, which also recognises explicitly a right to collective action.

A. EU Human Rights Instruments

Article 151 of the TFEU is, in essence, a preamble to the Social Policy Title of that Treaty, which enables the EU to adopt legislation on such matters. Notably, this provision stresses that 'the Union and the Member States' have 'in mind fundamental social rights such as those set out in' the ESC 1961 and the CCFSRW 1989. Article 6(4) of the ESC protects the right to strike and provision for this entitlement is set out in 'point 13' of the CCFSRW provision.[148] The ESC and CCFSRW could then be expected to inform interpretation of the EU Treaty provisions pertaining to social policy.[149]

It might seem curious that the content of these instruments (and their specific mention in the Treaties) stands in direct contradiction to the specific exclusion of the right to strike from the remit of European social policy in the succeeding provisions of the Social Title. The reason would seem to be that the EU institutions have, since 1992, expected that all ILO standards, including the right to strike, would be protected by Member States at the national level in accordance with other international obligations, such that the EU had no need to duplicate such efforts, merely to respect them.[150]

The drafting of what is now Article 151 of the TFEU, which draws on the wording of Article 117 of the Treaty of Amsterdam of 1997, predates the adoption by EU institutions of the Charter of Fundamental Rights of the European Union 2000 (CFREU), which may explain why Article 151 makes no mention of that instrument.

---

[146] Directive 2006/123/EC of the European Parliament and of the Council of 12 December 2006 on services in the internal market, available at: www.eur-lex.europa.eu/legal-content/EN/TXT/PDF/?uri=CELEX:32006L0123&from=EN.

[147] Interinstitutional Proclamation on the European Pillar of Social Rights, OJ C 428 (13 December 2017).

[148] B Bercusson, 'The European Community's Charter of Fundamental Social Rights of Workers' (1990) 53 *Modern Law Review* 624.

[149] See L Betten, 'The EU Charter on Fundamental Rights: A Trojan Horse or a Mouse?' (2001) 17 *International Journal of Comparative Labour Law and Industrial Relations* 151, 157.

[150] See T Novitz, 'The EU and the Right to Strike: Regulation through the Back Door and its Impact on Social Dialogue' (2016) 27 *King's Law Journal* 46, 51–55.

The CFREU was agreed by the Treaty of Nice in 2000, and has since been given, by the Treaty of Lisbon in 2007, equal legal value to the EU Treaties themselves.[151] Article 12(1)[152] provides that:

> Everyone has the right to freedom of peaceful assembly and to freedom of association at all levels, in particular in political, trade union and civic matters, which implies the right of everyone to form and to join trade unions for the protection of his or her interests.

Article 28[153] provides that:

> Workers and employers, or their respective organisations, have, in accordance with Community law and national laws and practices, the right to negotiate and conclude collective agreements at the appropriate levels and; in cases of conflicts of interest, to take collective action to defend their interests, including strike action.

Article 52(3)[154] provides that:

> Insofar as this Charter contains rights which correspond to rights guaranteed by the Convention for the Protection of Human Rights and Fundamental Freedoms, the meaning and scope of those rights shall be the same as those laid down by the said Convention. This provision shall not prevent Union law providing more extensive protection.

The CFREU is remarkable for its apparent blending of economic and social with civil and political rights – the indivisibility of rights is emphasised.[155] There are links between the text of the CFREU and the ESC and CCFSRW, so that there is scope for an integrated understanding of the former as a manifestation of existing EU Treaty commitments. The *Explanations relating to the [EU] Charter of Fundamental Rights*[156] (prepared originally by the Praesidium of the Committee which drafted the EU Charter), which are to be regarded as 'a valuable tool of interpretation intended to clarify the provisions of the [EU] Charter',[157] indicate that Article 12 is based on Article 11 of the ECHR and Article 11 of the CCFSRW.

---

[151] Treaty of European Union, Article 6(2).

[152] See A Jacobs, 'Article 12 – Freedom of Assembly and of Association' in F Dorssemont, K Lörcher, S Clauwaert and M Schmitt, *The Charter of Fundamental Rights of the European Union and the Employment Relation* (Oxford, Hart Publishing, 2019).

[153] See F Dorssemont and M Rocca, 'Article 28 – Right of Collective Bargaining and Action' in F Dorssemont, K Lörcher, S Clauwaert and M Schmitt, *The Charter of Fundamental Rights of the European Union and the Employment Relation* (Oxford, Hart Publishing, 2019).

[154] See K Lörcher, 'Interpretation and Minimum Level of Protection' in F Dorssemont, K Lörcher, S Clauwaert and M Schmitt, *The Charter of Fundamental Rights of the European Union and the Employment Relation* (Oxford, Hart Publishing, 2019).

[155] J Kenner, 'Economic and Social Rights in the EU Legal Order: The Mirage of Indivisibility' in T Hervey and J Kenner (eds), *Economic and Social Rights under the EU Charter of Fundamental Rights: A Legal Perspective* (Oxford, Hart Publishing, 2003) 15.

[156] *Explanations relating to the Charter of Fundamental Rights*, 2007/C 303/02, 14 December 2007, available at: eur-lex.europa.eu/legal-content/EN/TXT/?uri=CELEX%3A32007X1214%2801%29.

[157] ibid, Preface.

Article 28 is said to be based on 'Article 6 of the European Social Charter and on the Community Charter of the Fundamental Social Rights of Workers (points 12 to 14)'. It is interesting that the *Explanations* observe that: 'The right of collective action was recognised by the European Court of Human Rights as one of the elements of trade union rights laid down by Article 11 of the ECHR'.

Thus, the primary source of the right to strike in EU law is twofold: both Article 12 and Article 28 of the EU Charter since both invoke Article 11 of the ECHR and must, by Article 52(3) of the EU Charter, be construed consistently with Article 11 of the ECHR, which as the *Explanations* observe includes the right to strike. To the extent that Article 28 of the EU Charter refers to the right to strike in accordance with EU law, this must include the right to strike to the extent permitted under Article 11 of the ECHR. The latter in turn is informed in part by ILO standards, leading the way to ILO standards percolating through the ECHR to become part of EU law.[158]

Still, the CFREU remains subject to certain limitations in terms of its effects. First, in accordance with the First Declaration to the current TEU:

> The Charter does not extend the field of application of Union law beyond the powers of the Union or establish any new power or task for the Union, or modify powers and tasks as defined by the Treaties.

This is stressed by Protocol 30 which seeks to limit its application to Poland and the United Kingdom, particularly in respect of Title IV in which protection of the right to strike and other 'solidarity' rights are situated. Rather, under Article 51(1):

> The provisions of this Charter are addressed to the institutions, bodies, offices and agencies of the Union with due regard for the principle of subsidiarity and to the Member States only when they are implementing Union law.[159]

One might expect Article 28 to prevent EU institutions acting in contravention of the right to strike (and Member States when implementing EU law), even though the instrument does not require that Member States respect the right to strike in a purely domestic context. Secondly, Article 53 of the Charter states that:

> Nothing in this Charter shall be interpreted as restricting or adversely affecting human rights and fundamental freedoms as recognised, in their respective fields of application, by Union law and international law and by international agreements to which the Union or all the Member States are party.

---

[158] *Demir and Baykara v Turkey* (n 39 above) For comment, see Ewing and Hendy, 'The Dramatic Implications of Demir and Baykara' (n 33 above); and V Mantouvalou, 'Labour Rights in the European Convention on Human Rights: An Intellectual Justification for an Integrated Approach to Interpretation' (2013) 13 *Human Rights Law Review* 529.

[159] See A Koukiadaki, 'Application (Article 51) and Limitations (Article 52(1))' in F Dorssemont, K Lörcher, S Clauwaert and M Schmitt, *The Charter of Fundamental Rights of the European Union and the Employment Relation* (Oxford, Hart Publishing, 2019).

The *Explanations* indicate that such agreements are to include instruments such as the ECHR but one might also include, by implication, the ILO Constitution and conventions.[160]

B. The Court of Justice of the European Union

There was a sizeable window between the adoption of the CFREU in 2000 and the entry into force of the Lisbon Treaty, due to which the instrument is now formally recognised in Article 6(1) of the TEU. Initially, the CJEU seemed reluctant to refer to the CFREU in preference to the ECHR.[161] However, a constitutional shift has now taken place[162] such that that the CJEU has become a 'human rights adjudicator', which refers to the ECHR and the case law of the ECtHR less than it did previously.[163]

The right to strike has now been recognised in two important decisions of the CJEU (formerly the European Court of Justice). The first of these cases is the *Viking* case,[164] in which the Court said that:

> 43. In that regard, it must be recalled that the right to take collective action, including the right to strike, is recognised both by various international instruments which the Member States have signed or cooperated in, such as the European Social Charter, signed at Turin on 18 October 1961 – to which, moreover, express reference is made in Article 136 EC – and Convention No 87 concerning Freedom of Association and Protection of the Right to Organise, adopted on 9 July 1948 by the International Labour Organisation – and by instruments developed by those Member States at Community level or in the context of the European Union, such as the Community Charter of the Fundamental Social Rights of Workers adopted at the meeting of the European Council held in Strasbourg on 9 December 1989, which is also referred to in Article 136 EC, and the Charter of Fundamental Rights of the European Union proclaimed in Nice on 7 December 2000 (OJ 2000 C 364, p 1).

> 44. Although the right to take collective action, including the right to strike, must therefore be recognised as a fundamental right which forms an integral part of the general principles of Community law the observance of which the Court ensures, the exercise of that right may none the less be subject to certain restrictions. As is reaffirmed by Article 28 of the Charter of Fundamental Rights of the European Union, those rights are to be protected in accordance with Community law and national law and practices.

Although it recognised the right to strike, the CJEU also introduced a number of contested restrictions deriving from the four business freedoms protected by

---

[160] For more details on Article 52 CFREU, see Lörcher, 'Interpretation and Minimum Level of Protection' (n 153 above).

[161] See, eg, Case C-263/02 P *Commission of the European Communities v Jégo-Quéré & Cie SA* [2004] ECR I-3425.

[162] J Fudge, 'Constitutionalizing Labour Rights in Canada and Europe: Freedom of Association, Collective Bargaining and Strikes' (2015) 68 *Current Legal Problems* 267, 269.

[163] G de Búrca, 'After the EU Charter of Fundamental Rights: The Court of Justice as a Human Rights Adjudicator' (2013) 20 *Maastrict Journal of European and Comparative Law* 2.

[164] Case C-438/05 *ITF and FSU v Viking Line ABP* [2008] IRLR 143.

the EU Treaties[165] before it could lawfully be exercised in accordance with EU law.[166] Thus, collective action such as that at issue in the *Viking* case, which sought to induce an undertaking whose registered office is in a given Member State to enter into a collective work agreement with a trade union established in that State and to apply the terms set out in that agreement to the employees of a subsidiary of that undertaking established in another Member State, constitutes a restriction (on freedom of establishment) within the meaning of the relevant Article of the EU Treaty. That restriction may, in principle, be justified by an overriding reason of public interest, such as the protection of workers, provided that it is established that the restriction is suitable for ensuring the attainment of the legitimate objective pursued and does not go beyond what is necessary to achieve that objective.

These restrictions giving precedence to business freedoms over fundamental human rights are contested in the sense that they are not consistent with ILO principles,[167] they breach the provisions of the ESC,[168] and they are difficult to reconcile with the recent strike cases by the ECtHR (even with their often generous interpretation of Article 11(2)).

---

[165] Freedom of movement of capital, freedom of movement of labour, freedom of an EU business to provide services in another EU State, and freedom to establish a business in another EU State.

[166] ibid, para 90.

[167] 'The Committee observes with *serious concern* the practical limitations on the effective exercise of the right to strike of the BALPA workers in this case. The Committee takes the view that the omnipresent threat of an action for damages that could bankrupt the union, possible now in the light of the *Viking* and *Laval* judgements, creates a situation where the rights under the Convention cannot be exercised. While taking due note of the Government's statement that it is premature at this stage to presume what the impact would have been had the court been able to render its judgement in this case given that BALPA withdrew its application, the Committee considers, to the contrary, that there was indeed a real threat to the union's existence and that the request for the injunction and the delays that would necessarily ensue throughout the legal process would likely render the action irrelevant and meaningless'. ILO Committee of Experts, *Observations 2010 (United Kingdom)* (*BALPA* case) 200; 'The Committee wishes once again to recall the serious concern it raised as to the circumstances surrounding the BALPA proposed industrial action, for which the courts granted an injunction on the basis of the Viking and Laval case law and where the company indicated that, should the work stoppage take place, it would claim damages estimated at £100 million per day. The Committee recalls in this regard that it has been raising the need to ensure fuller protection of the right of workers to exercise legitimate industrial action in practice and considers that adequate safeguards and immunities from civil liability are necessary to ensure respect for this fundamental right, which is an intrinsic corollary of the right to organize. While taking due note of the Government's observations in relation to its obligations under EU law, the Committee considers that protection of industrial action in the country within the context of the unknown impact of the ECJ judgments referred to by the Government (which gave rise to significant legal uncertainty in the BALPA case), could indeed be bolstered by ensuring effective limitations on actions for damages so that unions are not faced with threats of bankruptcy for carrying out legitimate industrial action. The Committee further considers that a full review of the issues at hand with the social partners to determine possible action to address the concerns raised would assist in demonstrating the importance attached to ensuring respect for this fundamental right. The Committee therefore once again requests the Government to review the TULRA, in full consultation with the workers' and employers' organizations concerned, with a view to ensuring that the protection of the right of workers to exercise legitimate industrial action in practice is fully effective, and to indicate any further measures taken in this regard'. ILO Committee of Experts, *Observations 2011 (United Kingdom)* (*BALPA* case) 187.

[168] See Complaint No 85/2012, *LO and TCO v Sweden* (n 119 above).

Despite the controversy surrounding the *Viking* judgment, it is nevertheless important to acknowledge that the Court, at the European level, recognised the existence of the right to strike. In the *Laval* judgment, published a week later,[169] the Court held:

> [T]he right to take collective action must therefore be recognised as a fundamental right which forms an integral part of the general principles of Community law the observance of which the Court ensures, the exercise of that right may none the less be subject to certain restrictions.[170]

Thus, the Court again reaffirmed the existence of the right to strike, but finally held that the restriction (on the business freedom) caused by the industrial action may, in principle, be justified by an overriding reason of public interest. It was found that there was no protection for action that was designed to compel a foreign service provider to comply with terms and conditions of employment more beneficial to the workers than those required by the Posted Workers' Directive of 1996.[171] Yet, the crucial point is that *Viking* and *Laval* recognise the fundamental right to strike; what is debatable are the restrictions that may legitimately be placed upon such a right under EU law.

C. EU Legislative Initiatives Relating to the Right to Strike

A key question raised by the *Viking* and *Laval* cases is how the right to strike will be treated when its exercise conflicts with EU market freedoms, such as free movement of goods, services or establishment. In certain instances, the political institutions of the EU, namely the Commission, Council and Parliament, have sought reconciliation through legislative action. While any EU legislation adopted would ultimately be subject to potential intervention by the Court, so as to ensure that it was not ultra vires, that is in breach of Treaty provisions or fundamental rights, there is an opportunity for these legislative organs to formulate a political statement which could influence the Court's view of its role and its subsequent determinations.[172]

---

[169] Case C-341/05 *Laval Un Partneri Ltd v Svenska Byggnadsarbetareförbundet* [2008] IRLR 160.

[170] ibid, para 91.

[171] Directive 96/71/EC of the European Parliament and of the Council of 16 December 1996 concerning the posting of workers in the framework of the provision of services. It is also important to note that it is not only industrial action to force standards higher than those required by the PWD that is prohibited by EU law. See: Case C-346/06 *Rüffert v Land Niedersachsen* [2008] ECR I-1989; Case C-319/06 *Commission v Luxembourg* [2008] ECR I-4323.

[172] See P Syrpis, *EU Intervention in Domestic Labour Law* (Oxford, Oxford University Press, 2007) 123, who argues that the Court, not only does, but should allow the interventions of the EU political institutions 'to colour its views of the nature of the market-making endeavour'; and subsequently P Syrpis, 'The Relationship between Primary and Secondary Law' (2015) 52 *Common Market Law Review* 461.

Since the right to strike is excluded from the legislative 'social policy' competence of EU institutions, the means by which such an entitlement could be recognised is most likely as an exception to other EU legislation. An example is the 'saving clause' in the Monti Regulation relating to free movement of goods, which 'may not be interpreted as affecting in any way the exercise of fundamental rights as recognised in Member States, including the right or freedom to strike'.[173] This is also the technique adopted in the Services Directive.

i. *The Monti I Regulation (1998)*

Monti I was an instrument adopted in response to the *Spanish Strawberries* case,[174] the Commission's response to a Spanish complaint (also supported by the United Kingdom) concerning the behaviour of French farmers. They had initiated a campaign protesting against the sale of agricultural products which originated outside France, which the French government claimed it found impossible to suppress. The French government pleaded it had no legal obligation to constrain the actions of private citizens for common market purposes. The ECJ (as it then was) took a different view, treating the French government's apparent tolerance of various violent actions as tacit approval. For example, the police had omitted to intervene when there was an attack on three trucks transporting fruit and vegetables from Spain into Southern France. This was a breach of the basic free movement of goods, since French actions were 'manifestly inadequate to ensure freedom of intra-Community trade'.[175] In initiating legislation to address future breaches, the Commission had to consider whether industrial action (such as stoppage of work or a picket), which affected the free movement of goods, would also be prohibited. The trade union movement was aware that it was not impossible for Member States to be required to adhere to EC law rather than established ILO standards, given the mass denunciation of ILO Convention No 89 of 1948 (Night Work – Women) which was found to be contrary to the principle of gender equality enshrined in the EC Equal Treatment Directive.[176] The answer came finally in the form of a Council (often known as the 'Monti Regulation' of 1998, named after the Commissioner responsible.[177]

---

[173] Council Regulation (EC) No 2679/98 (n 144 above) [1998] OJ L337/8, Article 2.

[174] Case C-265/95 *Commission v France* [1997] ECR I-6961; the analysis that follows draws on T Novitz, *International and European Protection of the Right to Strike* (Oxford, Oxford University Press, 2003) 253–55.

[175] Case C-265/95 *Commission v France* (n 173 above), Judgment, para 52.

[176] See Council Directive 76/207 of 9 February 1976 on the implementation of the principle of equal treatment for men and women as regards access to employment, vocational training and promotion, and working conditions [1976] OJ L39/40. See Case C-345/89 *Stoeckel* [1991] ECR I-4047; Case C-158/91 *Levy* [1993] ECR I-4287; and Case C-13/93 *Minne* [1994] ECR I-371. Discussed in C Kilpatrick, 'Production and Circulation of EC Nightwork Jurisprudence' (1996) 25 *Industrial Law Journal* 169.

[177] Council Regulation (EC) No 2679/98 (n 144 above) [1998] OJ L337/8, Article 2. Named after Mario Monti.

The Monti Regulation created a mechanism whereby the Commission could intervene in order to prevent obstacles to trade, but this was ultimately subject to an exception in Article 2, which states that the Commission's powers are not to

> be interpreted as affecting in any way the exercise of fundamental rights as recognised in Member States, including the right or freedom to strike. These rights may also include the right or freedom to take other actions covered by the specific provisions governing industrial relations systems in Member States.

The question, of course, is what the scope of any right or freedom to strike will be.[178] Ultimately, that has been determined by subsequent case law of the Court of Justice which makes explicit that ILO Convention 87 is a significant source of that entitlement.[179]

ii. The Services Directive (2006)

The Services Directive[180] was the subject of considerable controversy, insofar as its aims were liberalisation of EU trade in services and the dismantling of domestic laws which acted as obstructions to such trade. The fear was that domestic labour standards, which could apply to the cross-border provision of services, whether temporary or otherwise, would be viewed as a barrier to the employer's exercise of their market freedoms.

In 2002, Commissioner Bolkestein stated an ambition in the field of services to 'remove obstacles to economic activity', 'solve cross-border problems' and to 'utilise economies of scale', which led to a Commission Proposal in 2004. But this was only the beginning, for what came to be mockingly called the 'Bolkenstein' Services Directive went through several incarnations before its adoption in 2006. The European Trade Union Confederation (ETUC) was sceptical of the merits of the instrument, expressing the fear that Member States would be encouraged to lower standards, spurring 'a downward spiral in working conditions'.[181] Trade unions across Europe responded in opposition, organising extensive protests. In March 2005, ETUC reported that over 75,000 people had attended demonstrations in Brussels against the Directive, while a significant protest took place on 14 February 2006 in front of the European Parliament, just before the vote on the first reading. The Parliament responded, by seeking to follow the precedent by

---

[178] G Orlandini, 'The Free Movement of Goods as a Possible "'Community'" Limitation on Industrial Conflict' (2000) 6 *European Law Journal* 341, 351.

[179] Case C-438/05 *International Transport Workers' Federation (ITF) and Finnish Seamen's Union (FSU) v Viking Line (Viking)* [2007] ECR I-10779, para 44; Case C-341/05 *Laval un Partneri v Svenska Byggnadsarbetareförbundet (Laval)* [2007] ECR I-11767, para 91.

[180] Directive 2006/123/EC on Services in the Internal Market (n 145 above) [2006] OJ L376/36.

[181] ETUC comment on 'Draft Directive on Services in the Internal Market', available at: www.etuc.org/a/499.

the Monti Regulation, so as to exclude 'the field of labour law' from the scope of the Directive:[182]

> In particular, [the Directive] shall fully respect the right to negotiate, conclude, extend or enforce collective agreements, and the right to strike and to take industrial action according to the rules governing industrial relations in Member States ... [and] ... shall not be interpreted as affecting in any way the exercise of fundamental rights as recognised in the Member States and by the Charter of the European Union, including the right to take industrial action.[183]

This attempt at amendment was greeted by the ETUC as 'a major victory for European workers',[184] but the final text was diluted. It now reads, in Article I(7):

> This Directive does not affect the exercise of fundamental rights as recognised in the Member States and by Community law. Nor does it affect the right to negotiate, conclude and enforce collective agreements and to take industrial action in accordance with national law and practices which respect Community law.

What is notable is the insertion of the reference to 'Community law', not found in the Monti Regulation (where what was deemed significant were fundamental rights 'as recognised in Member States', obviously in accordance with their international obligations). More curiously, Article 1(7) indicates that a right to take industrial action is only a legitimate exception to a freedom to provide services insofar as this is consistent with Community law, which opens up the possibility that industrial action which the Court would deem inconsistent with Community law will be covered by the Services Directive. This wording is similar to that of Article 28 of the 2000 CFREU, which, unlike the relevant provisions of the 1989 CCFSRW, indicates that the right to strike can be circumscribed with reference to EU law.[185]

There were attempts to amend this wording in the second reading before the Parliament, so that the provision would read:

> This Directive does not affect the exercise of fundamental rights as recognized in the Member States and by the *Charter of Fundamental Rights*. Nor does it affect the right to negotiate, conclude and enforce collective agreements, *the right to strike and* to take industrial action in accordance with national law and practices.[186]

It is not clear from the records of the debates why the amendment failed, but it may have been due to the more generous wording of the Preamble to the Services Directive, which at least refers explicitly to the 'right to strike' in Recital 14, even

---

[182] Texts Adopted by Parliament, 16 February 2006, Provisional Edition, P6_TA-PROV(2006)0061, available at: www.europarl.eu.int, Amendment 9, Recital 6(d) (new).

[183] ibid, Amendments 72, 233/rev, 403, 289, 290, 292, 297 and 298, Article 1(7) and (8).

[184] W Kowalsky, 'The Services Directive: The Legislative Process Clears the First Hurdle' (2006) 12 *Transfer* 231, 246.

[185] See for this analysis, T Novitz, 'Labour Rights as Human Rights' in C Barnard (ed), *The Cambridge Yearbook of European Law*, Vol 9 (Cambridge, Cambridge University Press, 2007).

[186] Amendment 11 by Francis Wurtz et al, 8 November 2006, A6-0375/11.

though it does still contain the formula requiring 'respect' for 'Community law'. Perhaps more persuasive may have been the undertaking made by Commissioner McCreevy at the European Parliament Plenary Session on 15 November 2006, who stressed that:

> Concerning the impact of the Services Directive on labour law, the European Parliament and the Council wanted to avoid that the Services Directive affects labour law or the rights of the social partners to defend their collective interests. The Commission wants to state unambiguously that the Services Directive does indeed not affect labour law laid down in national legislation and established practices in the Member States and that it does not affect collective rights which the social partners enjoy according to national legislation and practices. The Services Directive is neutral as to the different models in the Member States regarding the role of the social partners and the organisation of how collective interests are defined according to national law and practices ... However, Community law and in particular the Treaty continue to apply in this field.[187]

This last statement indicates an abdication of political responsibility to the Court in difficult circumstances.

iii. The Draft Monti II Regulation

The draft 'Monti II Regulation'[188] proposed in the wake of the *Viking* and *Laval* litigation sought to rebalance economic and social interests by offering 'A New Strategy for the Single Market'. Both the *Viking* and *Laval* judgments had stressed the recognition by the Court of Justice of a right to strike under EU law, but in both instances priority had been given to the economic freedom of the employer.

Drafts of the Monti II Regulation were leaked before the official version was issued, but the key provision was an exception clause (or 'Monti clause'), which stated that the Regulation would not affect 'the exercise of fundamental rights as recognised in the Member States, including the right or freedom to strike or to take other action covered by the specific industrial relations systems in Member States in accordance with national law and practices'. Then followed Article 2, which stated that:

> The exercise of the freedom of establishment and the freedom to provide services enshrined in the Treaty shall respect the fundamental right to take collective action, including the right or freedom to strike, and conversely, the exercise of the fundamental right to take collective action, including the right or freedom to strike, shall respect these economic freedoms.

---

[187] Commissioner Charlie McCreevy's Statement on the Vote in the European Parliament on the Services Directive, SPEEC/06/687, European Parliament Plenary Session, Strasbourg, 15 November 2006.

[188] Proposal for a Council Regulation on the exercise of the right to take collective action within the context of the freedom of establishment and the freedom to provide services, COM(2012) 130 final (Monti II Regulation).

An earlier leaked draft had said that there would be 'no primacy' between the two, but that explicit statement was dropped from the final text.[189]

Ultimately, the Member States rejected the entire proposal. After 12 parliaments adopted 'Reasoned Opinions' objecting to the EU legislative proposal, the Commission decided to withdraw the proposal.[190] The judicial statements in *Laval* (and *Rüffert*) regarding the right to collective action, but also its scope, remained determinative. An 'Enforcement Directive' relating to posted workers has not changed the status quo.[191] However, the amended Posted Workers Directive of 2018 does now provide clear and concrete recognition of a right to strike, challenging in this respect the outcome in *Laval*.[192] Article 1(a) now states that: 'This Directive shall not in any way affect the exercise of fundamental rights as recognised in the Member States and at Union level, including the right or freedom to strike or to take other action'.

Meanwhile the full dangers of the *Viking* and *Laval* line of reasoning have become apparent in a decision of the European Free Trade Association States (EFTA) Court to which the Norwegian Supreme Court paid deference. At issue in *Holship Norge AS v Norsk Transportarbeiderforbund* was the national dock labour scheme which was established by long-standing collective agreement in order to fulfil ILO Convention 137 to give priority of dock work to registered dock workers. A strike in defence of the scheme was held to be unlawful since it conflicted with a shipowner's freedom of establishment under EFTA to use its own directly-hired labour to discharge cargo.[193] The case epitomises the conflict between EU and EFTA business freedoms and the fundamental trade union rights guaranteed by the ECHR. An application to the ECtHR has been lodged by the Norwegian union.

iv. *The European Pillar of Social Rights*

The European Pillar of Social Rights was jointly signed by the European Parliament, the Council and the Commission at the Social Summit for Fair Jobs and

---

[189] KD Ewing, 'The Draft Monti II Regulation: An Inadequate Response to Viking and Laval' (2011), available at: www.ier.org.uk/sites/ier.org.uk/files/The%20Draft%20Monti%2011%20Regulation%20 by%20Keith%20Ewing%20March%202012.pdf.

[190] See I Cooper, 'A Yellow Card for the Striker: National Parliaments and the Defeat of EU Legislation on the Right to Strike' (2015) 22 *Journal of European Public Policy* 1406, 1407 and 1421.

[191] Directive 2014/67/EU of the European Parliament and of the Council of 15 May 2014 on the enforcement of Directive 96/71/EC concerning the posting of workers in the framework of the provision of services and amending Regulation (EU) No 1024/2012 on administrative cooperation through the Internal Market Information System (IMI Regulation) (PWD Enforcement Directive) [2014] OJ L159/11.

[192] Directive 2018/957/EU of the European Parliament and of the Council of 28 June 2018 amending Directive 96/71 concerning the posting of workers in the framework of the provision of services (Amending PWD 2018).

[193] Case E-14/15 *Holship Norge AS v Norsk Transportarbeiderforbund* [2016] 4 CMLR 29 in the CJEU; HR-2016-2554-P (Case No 2014/2089), 16 December 2016 in the Norwegian Supreme Court. For a full discussion, see Hendy and Novitz (n 91 above). Had the ECtHR faced its responsibilities in *Svenska*

Growth which took place on 17 November 2017. Its aim is a 'deeper and fairer monetary union' and as such it proclaims 20 principles to be applicable to all eurozone EU States, namely those countries which have adopted the euro as their currency.[194]

Principle 8 of the Pillar concerns 'Social dialogue and involvement of workers'. This makes explicit mention of the significance of 'social partners' who are to be 'encouraged to negotiate and conclude collective agreements in matters relevant to them, while respecting their autonomy and right to collective action'. In this way, once again, the right to collective action, namely the right to strike, is given prominence by the EU political institutions. What matters now is how the Pillar is implemented in practice.

IV. The Inter-American System

A. Inter-American Instruments

Several instruments of the Inter-American Human Rights System protect the right to freedom of association, including the right of workers to strike. Indeed, the foundational instrument, the Charter of the Organization of American States (OAS), identifies the strike as a means to defend and promote workers' interests:

Article 45(2)(c)

Employers and workers, both rural and urban, have the right to associate themselves freely for the defence and promotion of their interests, including the right to collective bargaining and the workers' right to strike, and recognition of the juridical personality of associations and the protection of their freedom and independence, all in accordance with applicable laws.[195]

Adopted in 1948 with the OAS Charter, the American Declaration of the Rights and Duties of Man also recognises the right to freedom of association, although unlike the former it makes no explicit reference to the right to strike.[196]

Transportarbetareförbundet and Seko v Sweden (n 89 and text above) and dealt substantively with the case this result might have been avoided.

[194] See: www.ec.europa.eu/commission/priorities/deeper-and-fairer-economic-and-monetary-union/european-pillar-social-rights/european-pillar-social-rights-20-principles_en.

[195] The original text of the OAS Charter, adopted in April 1948, recognised at Article 29(b) that 'Work is a right and a social duty; it shall not be considered as an article of commerce; it demands respect for freedom of association and for the dignity of the worker'. The language is clearly inspired by the ILO's 1944 Declaration of Philadelphia, both with regard to the idea that labour is not a commodity and the centrality of freedom of association. The current text of the Charter was introduced in 1967 through the Protocol of Buenos Aires, the first of four sets of amendments to the Charter. The text, then numbered as Article 43(c), would appear to be influenced by ILO Conventions 87 and 98 as well as the two UN covenants. See Protocol of Amendment to the Charter of the Organization of American States, 'Protocol of Buenos Aires', OAS Treaty Series No 1-A, entered into force 12 March 1970.

[196] OAS Res XXX, adopted by the Ninth International Conference of American States (1948), OEA/Ser.L.V/II.82, doc.6 rev.1, 17 (1992).

Article 22 provides that, 'Every person has the right to associate with others to promote, exercise and protect his legitimate interests of a political, economic, religious, social, cultural, professional, labor union or other nature'.[197]

With the 1967 amendments to the OAS Charter, which incorporated economic, social and cultural rights, Member States resolved to adopt a convention on human rights. This became the 1969 American Convention on Human Rights, which also protects the right to freedom of association.[198]

Article 16

1. Everyone has the right to associate freely for ideological, religious, political, economic, labor, social, cultural, sports, or other purposes.
2. The exercise of this right shall be subject only to such restrictions established by law as may be necessary in a democratic society, in the interest of national security, public safety or public order, or to protect public health or morals or the rights and freedoms of others.
3. The provisions of this article do not bar the imposition of legal restrictions, including even deprivation of the exercise of the right of association, on members of the armed forces and the police.

In 1988, the OAS promulgated the 'Additional Protocol to the American Convention on Human Rights in the Area of Economic, Social and Cultural Rights', known as the 'Protocol of San Salvador'.[199] Articles 6–9 of the Protocol incorporate, with some modification, the same subjects covered in Articles 6–9 of the ICESCR. Article 8 of the Protocol protects trade union rights, which, like the ICESCR, includes both the right to form or join a trade union and to strike.

Article 8: Trade Union Rights

The States Parties shall ensure:

a. The right of workers to organize trade unions and to join the union of their choice for the purpose of protecting and promoting their interests. As an extension of that right, the States Parties shall permit trade unions to establish national federations or confederations, or to affiliate with those that already exist, as well as to form international trade union organizations and to affiliate with that of their choice.

---

[197] The Inter-American Commission has explained that the right to strike is a 'basic collective right' protected by both the American Declaration and the OAS Charter. See, eg, CIDH, 'La situacion de los derechos humanos en Cuba, Septimo Informe' (1983), OEA/Ser.L/V/II. 61, doc.29 rev.1 (4 de octubre 1983) 159–60. ('The right to strike and to collective bargaining, although not specifically set forth in the American Declaration on the Rights and Duties of Man, are closely linked to fundamental labor rights. In addition, the Charter of the Organization of American States declares in Article 43 that: "Employers and workers, both rural and urban, have the right to free association to defend and promote their interests, including the right of collective bargaining and the right to strike of workers". *In view of this, the Commission considers that the right to strike and to collective bargaining should be considered, implicitly, as basic collective rights*') (emphasis added).

[198] OAS Treaty Series No 36, 1144 UNTS 123, entered into force 18 July 1978, OEA/Ser.L.V/II.82, doc.6 rev.1, 25 (1992).

[199] OAS Treaty Series No 69 (1988), entered into force 16 November 1999, OEA/Ser.L/V/II 82, doc.6 rev.1, 67 (1992).

The States Parties shall also permit trade unions, federations and confederations to function freely;

b. The right to strike.

Article 1 of the Protocol requires States Parties to 'to adopt the necessary measures ... for the purpose of achieving progressively and pursuant to their internal legislations, the full observance of the rights recognized in this Protocol'. Article 2 requires them to 'adopt ... such legislative or other measures as may be necessary for making those rights a reality'. While all of the substantive Articles of the Protocol are subject to supervision through regular reporting under Article 19 of the Protocol,[200] Article 19(6) provides that violations of Article 8(a) may also be enforced through the individual petition procedures under the American Convention.[201]

---

[200] The Annual and Special Reports of the Inter-American Commission on Human Rights are replete with observations concerning the exercise of the right to strike in the Americas. For recent examples, see, eg, IACHR, Protest and Human Rights Standards on the rights involved in social protest and the obligations to guide the response of the State, OEA/SER.L/V/II CIDH/RELE/INF.22/19 (September 2019) 13. ('The right to freedom of association has particular dimensions when it comes to specific groups and collectives or specific forms of protest. One example of this is trade unions and strikes, respectively. In this field, the right of association is especially protected by Article 8 of the Additional Protocol to the American Convention in the Area of Economic, Social, and Cultural Rights – "Protocol of San Salvador." The right to freedom of trade union association consists of "freedom of association consists basically of the ability to constitute labor union organizations, and to set into motion their internal structure, activities and action program, without any intervention by the public authorities that could limit or impair the exercise of the respective right." The right to strike is one of the expressions of this right, and has been considered one of the most common forms of exercising the right to protest.') IACHR, 'Criminalization of the Work of Human Rights Defenders', OEA/Ser.L/V/II Doc. 49/15 (31 December 2015) 32–33 (concerning the exercise of the right to strike in Venezuela); and 55 (finding that '[S]trikes, road blockages, the occupation of public space, and even the disturbances that might occur during social protests may naturally cause annoyances or even damages that are necessary to prevent and repair. Nevertheless, disproportionate restrictions to protest, in particular in cases of groups that have no other way to express themselves publicly, seriously jeopardize the right to freedom of expression. The Commission has expressed its concern about the existence of provisions that make criminal offenses out of the mere participation in a protest, road blockages (at any time and any kind), or acts of disorder that in reality, in and of themselves, do not adversely affect legally protected rights such as those to life, security, or the liberty of individuals'); 'Annual Report of the Inter-American Commission on Human Rights 2014'; Volume II 'Annual Report of the Office of the Special Rapporteur for Freedom of Expression', OEA/Ser.L/V/II Doc. 13 (9 March 2015) 93 ('The Office of the Special Rapporteur expresses its concern over the new law enacted by the Government of Alberta (Bill 45), which makes it unlawful to advocate for government employees to go on strike and assesses financial penalties against those who advise taking such action'); IACHR, 'Second Report on the Situation of Human Rights Defenders in the Americas', OEA/Ser.L/V/II Doc. 66 (31 December 2011) 50–51 and 109 (expressing concern over violence against striking banana workers in Panama)' 56 (calling on Member States not to use the armed forces to put down social protest or labour strikes); 100 (noting that the Commission has 'received information to the effect that in some States the right to strike is not recognized in law'); and 108 (observing in Venezuela 'that a crime called "obstruction of work" has frequently been invoked to charge persons who call for and lead labor strikes').

[201] The draft of the Protocol of San Salvador included the right to strike, then in Article 9, in the list of those rights which could be subject to individual petitions. See OAS, 'Annual Report 1985/86', Chapter 5, Section II, available at: www.cidh.org/annualrep/85.86eng/chap.5.htm. 'Without prejudice to the foregoing, the Commission considers that three rights defined in the protocol – trade union rights, the right to strike and freedom of education – should enjoy the same system of protection that

B. Inter-American Human Rights Jurisprudence

The Inter-American Court of Human Rights has considered the scope of trade union rights in only a few cases. The first and most often cited case on the right to freedom of association is *Ricardo Baena et al v Panama*, in which the Court concluded that the government of Panama had violated the right to freedom of association enshrined in Article 16 of the American Convention when it dismissed 270 union workers. In that case, the State Enterprise Workers Union had submitted a 13-point petition on a number of labour-related issues, including reforms to the labour code, to the government. Following the rejection of that petition, the union called for a march on 4 December 1990, and a 24-hour work stoppage the following day. The march took place peacefully; however, it coincided with the escape from prison by an army colonel and the takeover of the central police station by him and a group of military troops. The work stoppage planned for 5 December took place but was eventually suspended to prevent it being associated with the colonel's actions.

Although the government had not decreed a state of emergency or the suspension of guarantees, the Minster of the Interior forwarded a draft bill to the Legislative Assembly on 6 December proposing the dismissal of all public servants who had participated in the 5 December work stoppage on the grounds that it was intended to subvert the democratic constitutional order. Before this law was enacted, the State dismissed hundreds of workers by written notice. Under the then prevailing law, the employer had to notify the worker in advance and in writing about the date and cause of dismissal and with the right to appeal such a decision. Labour leaders could not be dismissed without authorisation from the labour courts. On 14 December, the Legislative Assembly passed Law 25, which was made retroactively effective from 4 December. On 23 January 1991, the Cabinet Council established that the work stoppages in the public sector were attempts against democracy and the constitutional order, and that any public servant who, as of 4 December 1990, had

> promoted, convoked, organized or participated in, or who would in the future promote, convoke, organize, or participate in work stoppages without complying with the established procedures and restrictions established in the Law, or in abrupt collective interruptions of the work in the public sector, would be subject to dismissal for cause.

As a preliminary matter, the Court addressed the applicability of the Protocol, which Panama had signed in 1988 but had not ratified until 1992, which was after the events which gave rise to the case. The Commission argued before the Court that Law 25 'affected the exercise of the right to organise and join trade unions freely (one of whose expressions is the right to strike, which is guaranteed by Article 8

---

was established for civil and political rights. Thus, paragraph 5 of Article 21 of the draft makes applicable the system of individual petitions of the Convention – with the participation of the Commission or where appropriate of the Court – when one of these rights is violated by an order directly attributable to a State Party'. It was removed from that list in the final draft of Article 19.

of the Protocol)'.[202] By signing the Protocol, they argued, Panama had committed to refrain from acts 'that would oppose the objective and purpose of the treaty' and that Panama is liable for the violations committed by State actors after signing the Protocol, namely dismissing the union workers, as the objective and purpose is to protect trade union rights.[203] The Court found that while Panama could not be found to have violated the Protocol itself, it nevertheless had 'a duty to abstain from committing any act in opposition of the objective and purpose'.[204]

With regard to the scope of the right to freedom of association, the Court held that:

> In labor union matters, freedom of association consists basically of the ability to consti-tute labor union organizations, and to set into motion their internal structure, activities and action program, without any intervention by the public authorities that could limit or impair the exercise of the respective right.[205]

The Court further explained that 'freedom of association is of the utmost impor-tance for the defence of the legitimate interests of the workers and falls under the *corpus juris* of human rights'.[206]

With regard to the specific facts of the case, the Inter-American Court concluded that:

> [T]he entirety of the evidence in the instant case shows that, in dismissing the State workers, labor union leaders who were working on a number of claims were dismissed. In addition, the members of workers organizations were dismissed for acts that were not causes for dismissal according to the legislation in force at the time of the events. This proves that the intention in making Law 25 retroactive in compliance with orders from the Executive Branch, was to provide a basis for the massive dismissal of public sector trade union leaders and workers, such actions doubtlessly limiting the possibili-ties for action of the trade union organisations in the cited sector.[207]

The Court's conclusions were bolstered by the decision of the ILO Commit-tee on Freedom of Association, which had earlier found that the mass dismissal of trade union leaders and workers in the public sector on account of the strike of 5 December 1990 was a measure which could seriously compromise the ability of public sector trade union organisations to take action in the institutions in which they operate and was a serious violation of ILO Convention 98.[208]

In two subsequent cases, which concern the assassination of union leaders, the Court further clarified that the right to freedom of association includes not merely the recognition of trade unions but the ability to exercise that freedom.[209]

---

[202] *Case of Baena-Ricardo et al v Panama*, Inter-American Court of Human Rights, Merits, Repara-tions and Costs, Judgment of 2 February 2001, Series C No 72, para 95.

[203] ibid.

[204] ibid, para 98.

[205] ibid, para 156.

[206] ibid, para 158.

[207] ibid, para 160.

[208] ILO CFA, Report No 281, Case No 1569 (1992).

[209] Not discussed here, the Inter-American Commission on Human Rights has also determined that violence against trade union leaders violates Article 16 of the American Convention. See, eg, *Carlos*

The case of *Pedro Huilca Tecse v Peru*[210] concerned the murder of the General Secretary of the Confederación General de Trabajadores de Perú on 18 December 1992. The Court determined that the killing was motivated by the fact he was a trade union leader who opposed and criticised the policies of the government. The Court explained that Article 16 conferred not only the individual right and freedom 'to associate freely with other persons, without the interference of the public authorities limiting or obstructing the exercise of the respective right', but also the collective right 'to seek the common achievement of a licit goal, without pressure or interference that could alter or change their purpose'.[211] The Court further explained that,

> labor-related freedom of association is not exhausted by the theoretical recognition of the right to form trade unions, but also corresponds, inseparably, to the right to use any appropriate means to exercise this freedom. When the Convention proclaims that freedom of association includes the right to freely associate 'for [... any] other purposes', it is emphasizing that the freedom to associate and to pursue certain collective goals are indivisible, so that a limitation of the possibilities of association represents directly, and to the same extent, a limitation of the right of the collectivity to achieve its proposed purposes. Hence the importance of adapting to the Convention the legal regime applicable to trade unions and the State's actions, or those that occur with its tolerance, that could render this right inoperative in the practice.[212]

The Court clearly articulated what we have argued: that the right to freedom of association must also encompass 'the appropriate means to exercise this freedom'. While not explicitly stated, this should encompass the right to strike.

Two years later, the Inter-American Court reaffirmed its views articulated in *Huilca-Tecse* on the nature of the right to freedom of association in another case against Peru concerning the murder of trade unionists, namely *Cantoral Huamaní and García Santa Cruz v Peru*.[213] The Court found that the murder of the two leaders not only affected their individual right to freedom of association but also had a chilling effect on the miners' right to exercise collectively their right to associate. Of note, Garcia Cruz was murdered for his support for the miners' strikes.[214]

In *Case of Acevedo-Jaramillo et al v Peru*,[215] the petitioners, workers who had, in several different cases, obtained judgments in their favour but which were not

---

Gomez Lopez, Report No 29/96; Case No 11.303 *Guatemala* (16 October 1996); *Finca 'La Exacta'*, Report No 57/02; Case No 11.382 *Guatemala* (21 October 2002).

[210] *Case of Huilca-Tecse v Peru*, Inter-American Court of Human Rights, Merits, Reparations and Costs, Judgment of 3 March 2005.

[211] ibid, para 69.

[212] ibid, para 70.

[213] See, *Case of Cantoral Huamaní and García Santa Cruz v Peru*, Preliminary Objections, Merits, Reparations and Costs, Judgment of July 10, 2007, Series C No 167, paras 141–49. In 2017, the Inter-American Commission on Human Rights restated the views on the right to freedom of association in *Huilca-Tecse* in a case concerning the murder of a trade union leader in Guatemala in 1995. See CIDH, Informe No 33/17, Caso 11.639 *Admisibilidad y Fondo, Alejandro Yovany Gómez Virula y familia, Guatemala* (21 de marzo de 2017) para 91.

[214] ibid, 147–48.

[215] *Case of Acevedo-Jaramillo et al v Peru*, Inter-American Court of Human Rights, Preliminary Objections, Merits, Reparations and Costs, Judgment of 7 February 2006, Series C, No 144.

enforced, brought a claim arguing violations of the right to judicial protection under Article 25 of the American Convention. One set of petitioners included workers unionised by SITRAMUN-LIMA and who had been dismissed for having taken strike action. They had obtained numerous judgments ordering their reinstatement and other relief.[216] As such, the Court did not have case to explore the nature of the right to strike or its relation to the right to freedom of association (which was not pleaded by the petitioners in any case).[217]

A possible explanation for the paucity of jurisprudence by the Inter-American Court on the right to strike *per se* is that while the right to strike is explicitly protected in various instruments, there has been a long-standing debate as to whether economic, social and cultural rights, such as the right to strike, are supervised through reporting obligations or may also be the subject of individual petitions under Article 26 of the American Convention.[218] That article requires the progressive realisation of the economic, social and cultural rights that were introduced during the 1967 amendments to the OAS Charter.[219]

The case of *Lagos del Campo v Peru*,[220] decided in 2017, appears to have put to rest the debate on the justiciability of economic, social and cultural rights and

---

[216] ibid, 61–65.

[217] The Court took note that neither the Commission nor the common intervener alleged a violation of Article 16 of the Convention. Without analysis, the Court found that 'the facts at issue in this case do not fall within the scope of Article 16 of the Convention, and therefore, the Court shall not deliver opinion on the alleged violation of said Article'. ibid, 104.

[218] The Inter-American Commission on Human Rights has on one occasion considered a contentious case concerning the right to strike. See, *Milton García Fajardo et al v Nicaragua*, Case 11.381, 11 October 2000. The case concerned the dismissal of customs service workers who went on strike. The strike was deemed illegal by the Ministry of Labor, as public sector workers were not afforded the right to strike under the labor code. That union filed for an amparo, citing the constitution, and the Court of Appeals issued an injunction suspending the dismissal of the customs workers. One year later, the Supreme Court upheld the Ministry's decision, though the union alleged that the Court had based its decision on the facts of another case. While the petitioners prevailed before the Commission on the grounds of the right to a fair trial and judicial protection, the Commission held that the petitioners had not proven a violation of the right to freedom of association. It held that 'the right to unionize is a substantive labor right' and regardless of an 'intrinsic link that the right to freedom of association … [and] the right to strike' (para 106) the petitioners allegations were unclear and that they had failed to provide evidence to establish a violation of the right of association. Notably, the ILO Committee on Freedom of Association also concluded that it was not a violation of the right to freedom of association to prohibit customs officials from going on strike. See, ILO Committee on Freedom of Association, Case No 1719, Report 304, June 1996, para 413. Though not stated in the decision, it might explain why the Commission held that the union was able to exercise its right to associate by challenging the matter in court. The Commission did find however that the Nicaraguan State violated Article 26, in that 'instead of adopting measures with the purpose of achieving the progressive development of the customs workers, sought to curtail their rights, thereby causing grave injury to their economic and social rights' (para 101).

[219] Article 26 states: 'The States Parties undertake to adopt measures, both internally and through international cooperation, especially those of an economic and technical nature, with a view to achieving progressively, by legislation or other appropriate means, the full realization of the rights implicit in the economic, social, educational, scientific, and cultural standards set forth in the Charter of the Organization of American States as amended by the Protocol of Buenos Aires'.

[220] *Caso Lagos del Campo v Peru*, Excepciones Preliminares, Fondo, Reparaciones y Costas, Sentencia de 31 de Agosto 2017, Serie C No 340. The case has been the subject of recent commentary, including F Ebert and C Fabricius, 'Strengthening Labor Rights in the Inter-American Human Rights System

the relationship between Article 26 of the Convention and the Protocol. In that case, Mr Lagos del Campo had observed employer interference in the election of an 'industrial committee' in 1989. He reported the interference to the authorities and described them in an interview with a national newspaper. As a result of his statements to the media, he was fired. He won his case at the court of first instance, but the decision was reversed on appeal. The case was taken up by the Inter-American Court in 2015. In finding that his right to freedom of association was violated, the Court relied not only on Article 16 but on Article 26.

Importantly, the Court reiterated that it had jurisdiction to hear a claim arising under any article of the American Convention, including Article 26. It noted also that the location of Article 26 in Part I of the Convention concerning 'State Obligations', along with civil and political rights, creates the same obligations.[221] As such, Article 26 was deemed to allow the Court to protect ESC rights directly in individual cases. As to the content of Article 26, the Court applied the plain language and looked to the articles of the OAS Charter pertaining to labour, including Articles 34.g, 45.b and c, and 46.[222] It also looked to international and regional human rights instruments.[223] The Court thus found that the right to work included a right not to be unfairly deprived of employment and found that a worker dismissed from their work without justification had a cause of action.[224]

As Franz Ebert and Charlotte Fabricius explain, while the decision provides important protection to workers from unjust dismissal, it likely has much broader implications for the world of work including protection for other labour rights under Article 26.[225] Indeed, it would appear beyond a doubt after *Lagos del Campo*, whose approach has been confirmed by the Court in two cases,[226] that Article 26 of the American Convention protects the right to strike and could serve as the basis for future petitions.[227]

(2018) 4 *International Labor Rights Case Law* 179; and M Canessa, 'La Proteccion Interamericana de la Libertad Sindical y de la Establidad Laboral: El caso de Lagos del Campo v Peru' (2017) 8 *Revista Chilena de Derecho de Trabajo y de la Seguridad Social* 143.

[221] *Caso Lagos del Campo* (n 219 above) para 142.

[222] ibid, 143.

[223] ibid. 145.

[224] ibid 147.

[225] Ebert and Fabricius (n 219 above) 184.

[226] See, *Trabajadores Cesados de Petroperú y otros vs. Perú*, Excepciones Preliminares, Fondo, Reparaciones y Costas, 23 November 2017, Serie C, No 344, paras 192–193; IACtHR, *Poblete Vilches y otros vs Chile*, Fondo, Reparaciones y Costas, 8 March 2018, Series C, No 349, paras 100–43.

[227] Indeed, 10 years before *Lagos del Campo*, Victor Abramovich, a commissioner of the Inter-American Commission, argued that Article 26 created justiciable rights and that the right to strike is included in the scope of Article 26 and thus amenable to individual petitions without regard to the limitations of Article 19(6) of the Protocol. Given that the right to strike is explicitly protected by Article 45 of the Charter and that the right to strike is intimately related to the right to freedom of association protected under Article 8(1) of the Protocol, there is little concern that the American Convention protects a right through individual petitions which are not explicitly listed in Article 19(6) of the Protocol. J Rossi and V Abramovich, 'La Tutela de los Derechos Economics, Sociales y Culturales en Articulo 26 de la Convencion Americana Sobre Derechos Humanos' (2007) 9 *Revista Estudios Socio-Juridicos* 34. See also T Melish, 'Rethinking The "Less As More" Thesis: Supranational Litigation of Economic, Social, and Cultural Rights in The Americas' (2006) 39 *New York University Journal of International Law and Politics* 1.

V. African Charter on Human and Peoples' Rights

Though far less developed, the African Charter on Human and Peoples' Rights also protects the right to freedom of association, including the right to strike.

Article 10 – Freedom of Association

1. Every individual shall have the right to free association provided that he abides by the law.
2. Subject to the obligation of solidarity provided for in Article 29, no one may be compelled to join an association.[228]

Unlike other international instruments with similar provisions,[229] Article 10 does not explicitly recognise the right to form trade unions as a corollary of the right to free association.[230] Of course, when this provision is read in conjunction with other international instruments that African Member States have adopted, including ILO Convention 87, the right to freedom of association guaranteed by Article 10 must necessarily include the right to form a trade union.[231] A trade union is, by definition, an association and therefore the right to form a trade union is necessarily guaranteed by a State's obligation to uphold the rights enshrined in Article 10.[232]

Despite the protection of freedom of association under Article 10, trade union rights have been deemed protected under Article 15 of the Charter, concerning Conditions of Work.

Article 15 – Conditions of Work

Every individual shall have the right to work under equitable and satisfactory conditions, and shall receive equal pay for equal work.[233]

Notwithstanding its express language,[234] Article 15 appears to have been intended as a vehicle for trade union rights as well. Article 59 of the African Commission's *Principles and Guidelines on the Implementation of Economic, Social and Cultural Rights in the African Charter on Human and Peoples' Rights*[235] explains that the right to work includes State obligations to:

Ensure the right to freedom of association, including the rights to collective bargaining, to strike and other related organisational and trade union rights. These rights include

---

[228] Text available at: www.achpr.org/files/instruments/achpr/banjul_charter.pdf.

[229] See, eg, Second Optional Protocol to the International Covenant on Civil and Political Rights, Article 22(1).

[230] F Ouguergouz, *The African Charter on Human and Peoples' Rights: A Comprehensive Agenda for Human Dignity and Sustainable Democracy in Africa* (Alphen aan den Rijn, Kluwer Law, 2003) 170.

[231] ibid.

[232] ibid.

[233] African Charter, Article 15.

[234] Ouguergouz (n 229 above) 183.

[235] African Commission on Human and Peoples' Rights, *Principles and Guidelines on the Implementation of Economic, Social and Cultural Rights in the African Charter on Human and Peoples' Rights*, available at: www.achpr.org/files/instruments/economic-social-cultural/achpr_instr_guide_draft_esc_rights_ eng.pdf.

the right to form and join a trade union of choice (including the right not to), the right of trade unions to join national and international federations and confederations, and the right of trade unions to function freely without undue interference.

Under Article 62 of the Charter, States must submit periodic reports to the African Commission on Human and Peoples' Rights detailing how the State implements and safeguards the fundamental rights guaranteed by the Charter.[236] In October 2011, the African Commission published the *State Party Reporting Guidelines for Economic, Social and Cultural Rights in the African Charter on Human and Peoples' Rights* (Tunis Reporting Guidelines).[237] Under section 7(B)(ii), nations submitting a periodic report to the Commission must 'Indicate the legislative and administrative measures taken to ensure the rights to unionise, to collective bargaining, and to strike'.[238]

It appears that neither the African Commission nor the African Court have yet explored the contours of the right to strike under Article 10 or Article 15 of the African Charter.

VI. The Right to Strike and Trade Arrangements

The inclusion of the right to strike, explicitly or implicitly, in the labour provisions of free trade agreements (FTAs) and in trade preference programmes is further evidence that economically important States recognise that the right to strike is a fundamental labour right and is protected by the broader right to freedom of association. It also demonstrates that these countries view the right as having specific contours under international law, and not merely an abstract right which is given articulation only through regulation at the national level.

A. United States Agreements

The first modern trade agreement to incorporate labour obligations was the North American Free Trade Agreement (NAFTA). In 1993, the North American Agreement on Labor Cooperation (NAALC) was annexed as a side agreement in an (unsuccessful) attempt to assuage the concerns of organised labour over the employment impacts of NAFTA.[239] The idea was that by improving labour standards in

---

[236] African Charter, Article 62. For a discussion of the importance of these period reports, see the section below on the African Commission.

[237] African Commission on Human and Peoples' Rights, *State Party Reporting Guidelines for Economic, Social and Cultural Rights in the African Charter on Human and Peoples' Rights* (Tunis Reporting Guidelines) 24 October 2011, available at: www.achpr.org/files/instruments/economic-social-cultural-guidelines/achpr_instr_tunis_reporting_guidelines_esc_rights_2012_eng.pdf.

[238] ibid.

[239] See, North American Agreement on Labor Cooperation, available at: www.dol.gov/ilab/reports/pdf/ naalc.htm.

Mexico, this would reduce the unfair competitive advantage of artificially low wages obtained by Mexican employers through worker repression.[240] Article 2 of NAALC provides that 'each Party shall ensure that its labor laws and regulations provide for high labour standards, consistent with high quality and productivity workplaces, and shall continue to strive to improve those standards in that light.'[241] Article 49 defined the term 'labor law' to include the 'right to strike.'[242] The right to strike is further described in Annex I, Statement of Principles, as 'the protection of the right of workers to strike in order to defend their collective interests.'[243]

Over the years, three petitions were filed against Mexico specifically alleging the failure to protect the right to strike in law and in practice. These are (1) Submission 1998-01,[244] concerning measures taken by the government to force back to work striking flight attendants at Aeroméxico; (2) Submission 2005-01,[245] concerning then proposed reforms to the federal labour law that would have made the right to strike exceedingly difficult to exercise; and (3) Submission 2005-03,[246] concerning a labour conflict at Rubies' Apparel. In the first case, the United States acknowledged that the right to strike was within the scope of the agreement but declined to accept the case claiming that it would 'not further the objectives of the agreement' but with no further explanation. The US Department of Labor promised however to undertake a trinational study on the right to strike though it does not appear that any such study was undertaken.[247] In the second case, the US Department of Labor declined to review whether the proposed legislation violated the NAALC, apparently in deference to the legislative process, again arguing it would not further the objectives of the agreement.[248] The third case was accepted for review

---

[240] See MA Cameron and BW Tomlin, *The Making of NAFTA: How the Deal Was Done* (Ithaca NY, Cornell University Press, 2000). Indeed, the same argument has resurfaced in 2017 as the Trump Administration has sought to renegotiate NAFTA and has insisted that Mexico raises wage rates (though by fiat rather than insisting instead that Mexico protect the right to freedom of association – in particular outside the corporatist trade union structures).

[241] NAALC, Article 2, available at: www.dol.gov/ilab/reports/pdf/naalc.htm.

[242] ibid, Article 49.

[243] ibid, Annex I.

[244] See, Association of Flight Attendants, 'Public Communication on Labor Law Matters Arising in Mexico: Strike by ASSA-Mexico Vs Aerovias De Mexico, SA De C V', filed 17 August 1998, available at: www.dol.gov/ilab/ submissions/pdf/US_9801_flight_attendants_submission.pdf.

[245] See, Washington Office on Latin America, 'Public Communication to the US National Administrative Office under the North American Agreement on Labor Cooperation (NAALC) Concerning the Introduction of Reforms to the Federal Labor Code of Mexico', 17 February 2005, available at: www.dol.gov/ilab/submissions/pdf/US_2005-01_labor-law-reform_submission.pdf.

[246] Progressive Union of Workers of the Textile Industry, 'Public Communication to the US National Administrative Office (NAO) under the North American Agreement on Labor Cooperation (NAALC) concerning labor rights violations at RUBIE'S DE MEXICO, S de RL de C V', 14 October 2005, available at: www.dol.gov/ilab/submissions/pdf/US_2005-3_Hidalgo_submission.pdf.

[247] Letter from Irasema Garza, Secretary, National Administrative Office, to Patricia Friend, President, Association of Flight Attendant, 19 October 1998, available at: www.dol.gov/ilab/reports/pdf/US_9801_flight_attendants_decision.pdf.

[248] See US Department of Labor, 'Submissions under the North American Agreement on Labor Cooperation (NAALC)', available at: www.dol.gov/ilab/trade/agreements/naalc.htm.

and resulted in a report and recommendation for further consultation between the governments, although it did not treat specifically the right to strike.[249]

The explicit reference to the right to strike was dropped in subsequent US trade agreements. This is likely explained by the subsequent adoption of the ILO Declaration on Fundamental Principles and Rights at Work in 1998.[250] The ILO Declaration set forth four labour principles, deemed fundamental, which all States have a duty to 'respect, promote and realize' regardless as to whether the corresponding conventions have been ratified. Among the principles protected in the ILO Declaration are the right to 'freedom of association and the effective recognition of the right to collective bargaining'.[251] In 1993, the drafters of NAALC had no such reference point and thus enumerated its own list of labour principles (which turned out to overlap substantially with the ILO Declaration). The explicit mention of a right to strike was most likely meant for clarity rather than to imply that it was not protected by the right to freedom of association.

This contention is supported by subsequent practice in the negotiation and application of all post-NAFTA US trade agreements.[252] The United States has repeatedly invoked the ILO Declaration's reference to freedom of association to raise concerns with regard to the right to strike, as evidenced by: (1) the review by the US Department of Labor of a complaint filed by the AFL–CIO against the Kingdom of Bahrain concerning violations of the right to strike as interpreted by the ILO; and (2) the requirement that trade partners amend their labour laws, including laws relating to the right to strike, prior to certifying them as compliant with the terms of the trade agreement.[253]

i. AFL–CIO Complaint against Bahrain

In February 2011, as the Arab Spring protests swept the region, workers and trade unionists engaged in demonstrations and strikes to oppose political repression – in particular the crackdown on protestors at the Pearl Roundabout by government

[249] See US Department of Labor, 'Public Report of Review of Office of Trade and Labor Affairs Submission 2005-03, Aug 31, 2007', available at: www.dol.gov/ilab/reports/pdf/publicrep2005-3.pdf.

[250] ILO Declaration on Fundamental Principles and Rights at Work and its Follow-Up, 18 June 1998, available at: www.ilo.org/wcmsp5/groups/public/---ed_norm/---declaration/documents/publication/wcms_467653.pdf.

[251] ibid, Article 2(a).

[252] See J Vogt, 'The Evolution of Labor Rights and Trade: A Transatlantic Comparison and Lessons for the Transatlantic Trade and Investment Partnership' (2015) 18 *Journal of International Economic Law* 827.

[253] In its trade agreements ratified after May 2007, the United States required its partners to harmonise their laws and regulations with the principles of the ILO Declaration. This gave the United States a legal basis to require amendments be made in labour legislation prior to the agreement entering into force. See, J Vogt, 'Trade and Investment Arrangements and Labor Rights' in L Blecher, N Kaymar Stafford and G Bellamy (eds), *Corporate Responsibility for Human Rights Impacts: New Expectations and Paradigms* (Chicago, IL, American Bar Association, 2015). The United States made similar demands prior to 2007 explaining to trade partners that Congress would be unlikely to support the agreement without requested reforms.

forces and, later, the declaration of a state of emergency and the incursion of the Saudi and UAE military to quell further protests.[254] The AFL–CIO filed a petition with the US Department of Labor arguing that the crackdown on workers and unions, including mass dismissals for participating in strikes, violated the labour chapter of the US–Bahrain Free Trade Agreement (US–Bahrain FTA) and urged immediate intervention to stop the repression. The US Department of Labor accepted the petition for review and, in December 2012, issued its report on the petition.[255] In its findings, US Department of Labor explained that it had reviewed the complaint in light of Article 15.1.1 of the US–Bahrain FTA, which provides that:

> The Parties reaffirm their obligations as members of the ILO and their commitments under the ILO Declaration on Fundamental Principles and Rights at Work and its Follow-up (1998). Furthermore, each Party 'shall strive to ensure that such labour principles', including *freedom of association* and the effective recognition of the right to collective bargaining, the elimination of discrimination in employment and occupation, and 'the internationally recognized labour rights set forth in Article 15.7, are recognized and protected by its law' (emphasis added).

The US Department of Labor report explained that Bahrain repeatedly violated this provision, as it relates to the right to strike, by: (1) the existence and application of a ban on strikes in broadly defined 'strategic undertakings'; (2) the existence and application of criminal sanctions for engaging in or encouraging strikes in the public sector or in undertakings related to public services or public service requirements; and (3) retaliation, including criminal cases, against trade unionists and union leaders who organised and participated in the March 2011 general strike.[256]

ii. Law Reforms

Additionally, the United States has a long history of insisting that countries amend their laws as a condition prior to allowing the trade agreement to enter into force. The most recent examples include the labour consistency plans with Brunei Darussalam, Malaysia and Vietnam developed pursuant to the labour chapter of the Trans-Pacific Partnership.[257] Each of these plans require the corresponding country to enact reforms relating to the right to strike. None of these

---

[254] See AFL–CIO, 'Public Submission Concerning the Failure of the Government of Bahrain to Comply With Its Commitments Under Article 15.1 of the US–Bahrain Free Trade Agreement', available at: www.dol.gov/ilab/reports/pdf/BahrainSubmission2011.pdf.

[255] US Department of Labor, 'Public Report of Review of US Submission 2011-01 (Bahrain)', available at: www.dol.gov/ilab/reports/pdf/20121220Bahrain.pdf.

[256] See ibid, 'Findings and Recommendations' ii–v.

[257] Once negotiated, the Trump Administration decided to withdraw from the agreement. Peter Baker, 'Trump Abandons Trans-Pacific Partnership, Obama's Signature Trade Deal' *New York Times* (23 January 2017).

countries have ratified Convention 87 and thus there are no observations of the ILO Committee of Experts; however, the plans clearly draw their recommendations from ILO jurisprudence drawn from the Committee of Experts and the ILO Committee on Freedom of Association. For example, under the Brunei plan, the country 'shall amend relevant sections of the Trade Disputes Act (TDA), Section 9, to ensure workers' right to strike, except in the limited circumstances noted under Section 7 and Section 8'.[258] Under the Malaysia plan, the country 'shall amend relevant sections of Act 177 to remove penal sanctions for peaceful strikes, regardless of whether such strikes are inconsistent with IRA provisions (relevant sections of current law include Section 46, Section 47 and Section 48)'.[259]

The amendments demanded of Vietnam on the right to strike are extensive (and explicitly refer to the ILO):

1. Viet Nam shall ensure that its law allows for rights-based strikes, consistent with ILO guidance. Relevant articles in current law include LC Article 215(1).
2. Viet Nam shall ensure that its law provides for 50 per cent plus one of the Executive Committee to be required to approve a strike. Relevant articles in current law include LC Article 212 and Article 213(1).
3. Acknowledging that collective bargaining at the sectoral level and for more than one enterprise is recognised under the LC, Viet Nam shall ensure that strikes are permitted when organized for workers of different enterprises at the same levels at which collective bargaining is permitted under law, subject to compliance with domestic procedures that are not inconsistent with the labour rights as stated in the ILO Declaration. Relevant articles in current law include LC Article 215(2).
4. Viet Nam shall amend Decree 41/2013/ND-CP to delete Article 2.1.b of the Decree and the resultant list of affected entities to ensure that strikes are permitted in the exploration and exploitation of oil and gas and supply and production of gas.
5. Viet Nam shall amend Decree 46/2013/ND-CP to delete Article 8.1.[260]

In an unanticipated development, Chapter 23 of the recently negotiated US–Mexico–Canada (USMCA) Trade Agreement contains not only an explicit reference to the right to strike but affirms its linkage to the right to freedom of association. Footnote 5 of that chapter states, 'For greater certainty, the right to strike is linked to the right to freedom of association, which cannot be realized without protecting the right to strike'.[261] The US position thus could not be clearer. The 'greater certainty' clause also suggests that it has always been the view of the parties that any reference to freedom of association in trade agreements implicitly included the right to strike.

---

[258] USTR, US–Brunei Darussalam Consistency Plan, 4 February 2016, available at: www.ustr.gov/sites/default/files/TPP-Final-Text-Labour-US-BN-Labour-Consistency-Plan.pdf.

[259] USTR, US–Malaysia Consistency Plan, 4 February 2016, available at: www.ustr.gov/sites/default/files/TPP-Final-Text-Labour-US-MY-Labour-Consistency-Plan.pdf.

[260] USTR, US–Vietnam Consistency Plan, 4 February 2016, available at: www.ustr.gov/sites/default/files/TPP-Final-Text-Labour-US-VN-Plan-for-Enhancement-of-Trade-and-Labour-Relations.pdf.

[261] USMCA, Chapter 23 (Labor), available at: ustr.gov/sites/default/files/files/agreements/FTA/USMCA/ Text/23_Labor.pdf.

B. Canadian Agreements

Canada's practice with regard to trade and labour standards largely follows the US practice, though Canada has received relatively few post-NAALC petitions and does not, as a rule, demand labour law amendments of their partners prior to the agreement entering into force. This is likely owing to the relatively small market power compared with the United States, and thus the limited leverage to make such demands. However, the progression of the text of the labour provisions of Canadian FTAs post-NAALC is instructive.

For example, its labour cooperation agreement with Costa Rica in 2002, paraphrases the labour principles under the ILO Declaration, though it continues to specifically mention the right to strike in its list of labour principles.[262] In its trade agreement with Peru, in 2009, the right to strike is again specifically mentioned but this time is expressed as a right encompassed by the right to freedom of association.[263] It remains this way until 2013 when the right to strike is no longer specifically mentioned, as in the cooperation agreement with Panama.[264] In 2015, the labour provisions migrate from cooperation agreements to labour chapters within the FTAs, as with the Canada–Korea FTA. The right to strike is, as with Panama, implicit as a right protected by freedom of association and continues to be so. Despite the evolution in the expression of the right to strike in FTAs, the government has consistently held that the right to strike is protected by the agreements. The USMCA, to which Canada is a party, does, as mentioned above, bring back the right to strike as an explicit commitment.

Canada has received only one labour complaint not arising under NAALC. It concerns violations of the right to freedom of association, to bargain collectively and to strike in Colombia. The Canadian government found that the right to strike had been violated through the illegitimate use of labour intermediation/short-term contracting and by the use of violence.[265]

---

[262] See, Canada–Costa Rica Agreement on Labour Cooperation, April 2001, available at: www.canada.ca/en/employment-social-development/services/labour-relations/international/agreements/costa-rica.html.

[263] See, Article 1(a), Canada–Peru Agreement on Labour Cooperation, 29 May 2008 ('freedom of association and the right to collective bargaining (including protection of the right to organize and the right to strike'), available at: www.canada.ca/en/employment-social-development/services/labour-relations/international/agreements/peru.htm l.

[264] See, Article 1, Canada–Panama Agreement on Labour Cooperation, 14 May 2010, available at: www.canada.ca/en/employment-social-development/services/labour-relations/international/agreements/panama.html.

[265] See, Review of public communication CAN 2016-1, available at: www.canada.ca/en/employment-social-development/services/labour-relations/international/ agreements/2016-1-review.html ('While the right to strike is protected under Colombian law, the Canadian NAO observes that the systemic use of short-term contracts puts workers in precarious employment relationships and makes it difficult for them to effectively exercise their right to strike. The Canadian NAO notes that this precarious labour situation may give an unjustified reason to the government to deny workers the ability to take legitimate labour actions'.)

C. European Union Agreements

Like the United States and Canada, the European Union has included labour standards in its recent trade agreements. For example, Article 269(3) of the EU–Colombia–Peru Trade Agreement provides that the parties commit to 'the promotion and effective implementation in its laws and practice and in its whole territory of internationally recognised core labour standards as contained in the fundamental Conventions of the International Labour Organisation'. The Article of course refers to 'freedom of association and the effective recognition of the right to collective bargaining'.

The EU–Korea FTA, which has a more substantial Trade and Sustainable Development chapter, provides, inter alia, at Article 13.4(3) that

> the parties, in accordance with the obligations deriving from membership of the ILO and the ILO Declaration on Fundamental Principles and Rights at Work and its Follow-up, adopted by the International Labour Conference at its 86th Session in 1998, commit to respecting, promoting and realising, in their laws and practices, the principles concerning the fundamental rights, namely: (a) freedom of association and the effective recognition of the right to collective bargaining.

Subsequent supervision of Chapter 13 of the EU–Korea FTA indicates that the parties understand that the right to strike as elaborated by the ILO is protected under the FTA's labour provisions. On 29 May 2013, the EU Domestic Advisory Group (DAG) constituted under the FTA, issued an opinion, with bipartite (labour/NGO and business) support, which catalogued the DAG's various concerns as it related to Korean labour law and practice. Concerns related to the right to strike, drawn from the ILO Committee on Freedom of Association, were adopted without controversy.[266] On January 13, 2014, the EU DAG urged the EU to initiate consultations under Chapter 13 for serious violations of the right to freedom of association, including violations of the right to strike of railway workers.[267] While the EU had rejected the request to initiate formal consultations, these issues were raised through informal channels. At no time did the EU, or EU employers, suggest that the right to strike claims were outside the scope of the FTA. In fact, on 17 December 2018, the EU did finally request consultations on the FTA over the

---

[266] Domestic Advisory Group under the EU–Korea Free Trade Agreement, 29 May 2013, OPINION on the Fundamental rights at work in the Republic of Korea, available at: www.eesc.europa.eu/sites/default/files/resources/docs/eu-dag-opinion-on-labour-standards_en.pdf.

[267] A copy of the letter of the EU Domestic Advisory Group is available at: www.finunions.org/files/225/ Letter_to_Mr_Karel _De_Gucht_Art_13-_Korea_-FTA.pdf. Of note, the EU Domestic Advisory Group reiterated their demand for consultations in a December 2016 letter to Trade Commissioner Malmstrom, citing Korea's failure to comply with Chapter 13 of the FTA, available at: www.ec.europa.eu/carol/?fuseaction=download&documentId=090166e5af1bf802&title=EU_DAG%20letter%20to%20Commissioner%20Malmstrom_signed%20by%20the%20Chair%20and%20Vice-Chairs.pdf. The Annexes to that letter refer frequently to violations of the right to strike. See Annexes at www.epsu.org/sites/default/files/article/files/Annexes%20to%20EU%20DAG%20letter.pdf

Korean government's failure to comply with its labour obligations.[268] In its request for consultations, the EU listed among the matters to be addressed, 'Section 314 of the Korean Criminal Code (obstruction of business) and its application by the Korean police and public prosecutor's office to certain peaceful strike actions'.[269] On 4 July 2019, the EU requested the establishment of a Panel of Experts following the failure of consultations to bring about the desired reforms by the Korean government.[270]

Of particular interest, the EU undertook an impact assessment of the draft Trans-Atlantic Trade and Investment Partnership (TTIP), a draft agreement between the EU and the United States. In an assessment based on the EU proposal for the labour chapter, the EU raised concerns with US labour law and its inconsistency with the right to freedom of association. It noted specifically, 'Another significant difference regarding Convention 87 and US legislation concerns the right to strike, including the many limitations and restrictions placed on the right to strike'.[271]

In addition to its trade agreements, like the United States the EU conditions its trade preferences on continued compliance with labour rights. The EU also maintains a special incentive programme known as GSP+ which requires applicant States to have already ratified 27 core international conventions, including the eight ILO core conventions – including Convention 87 on the right to freedom of association. In 2016, the EU published a Working Document entitled, 'The EU Special Incentive Arrangement for Sustainable Development and Good Governance ('GSP+') covering the period 2014–2015'. The report identified the areas in which the GSP+ beneficiary countries had failed to comply with the requirements of the 27 ratified conventions as indicated by the relevant monitoring bodies.[272] The report detailed the shortcomings with regard to the right to strike in each country, as described by the ILO Committee of Experts, under Convention 87. In 2018, the EU issued a follow-up report covering the period from 2016 to 2017,[273] together with separate reports for each GSP+ beneficiary identifying where they

---

[268] European Commission, Press Release, 'EU steps up engagement with Republic of Korea over labour commitments under the trade agreement', 17 December 2018, available at: www.trade.ec.europa.eu/doclib/press/index.cfm?id=1961.

[269] EU, Request for Consultations by the European Union, 17 December 2018, available at: www.trade.ec.europa.eu/doclib/docs/2018/december/tradoc_157586.pdf.

[270] EU, Request for the establishment of a Panel of Experts by the European Union, 4 July 2019, available at: trade.ec.europa.eu/doclib/docs/2019/july/tradoc_157992.pdf.

[271] European Commission, 'Sustainability Impact Assessment in support of the negotiations on a Transatlantic Trade and Investment Partnership (TTIP), Final Report', March 2017, available at: www.trade.ec.europa.eu/doclib/docs/2017/april/tradoc_155464.pdf, 146.

[272] European Commission, Joint Staff Working Document, 'The EU Special Incentive Arrangement for Sustainable Development and Good Governance ('GSP+') covering the period 2014–2015', 28 January 2016, available at: www.eeas.europa.eu/sites/eeas/files/european_commission_2016_report_on_the_generalised_scheme_of_preferences_during_the_period_2014-2015.pdf.

[273] European Commission, 'Report from the Commission to the European Parliament and the Council Report on the Generalised Scheme of Preferences covering the period 2016–2017', 19 January 2018, available at: www.trade.ec.europa.eu/doclib/docs/2018/january/tradoc_156536.pdf.

continue to fail on compliance with labour standards – including the right to strike.[274] It is clear therefore that the EU has expectations of its trading partners concerning the right to strike, as identified by the Committee of Experts, protected by Convention 87.

VII. High Court Cases Since 2012 Affirm the Right to Strike

A. *Saskatchewan Federation of Labour v Saskatchewan*

In 2015, the Supreme Court of Canada, in *Saskatchewan Federation of Labour v Saskatchewan*, rendered a significant decision that expanded the reach of the Constitution (Charter of Rights) to encompass the right to strike. The case turned on a statutory prohibition of certain public sector workers who perform 'essential' services to strike.[275] The Court found that the absence of the right to strike would render meaningless the right to bargain collectively:

> A meaningful process of collective bargaining requires the ability of employees to participate in the collective withdrawal of services for the purpose of pursuing the terms and conditions of their employment through a collective agreement. Where good faith negotiations break down, the ability to engage in the collective withdrawal of services is a necessary component of the process through which workers can continue to participate meaningfully in the pursuit of their collective workplace goals. The suppression of the right to strike amounts to a substantial interference with the right to a meaningful process of collective bargaining.[276]

In reaching its decision, the Supreme Court recognised that ILO Convention 87 protected the right to strike and explained that the Committee of Experts should be treated as persuasive authority on the scope of that right:

> Although Convention No 87 does not explicitly refer to the right to strike, the ILO supervisory bodies, including the Committee on Freedom of Association and the Committee of Experts on the Application of Conventions and Recommendations, have recognized the right to strike as an indissociable corollary of the right of trade union association that is protected in that convention.[277]

> ...

---

[274] see, eg, European Commission, Joint Staff Working Document, 'The EU Special Incentive Arrangement for Sustainable Development and Good Governance ('GSP+') assessment of Pakistan covering the period 2016–2017', 19 January 2018 (identifying several areas in which national law on the right to strike does not comply with ILO obligations), available at: www.trade.ec.europa.eu/doclib/docs/2018/january/tradoc_156544.pdf, 14–15. All country assessment are online at: www.ec.europa.eu/trade/policy/countries-and-regions/development/generalised-scheme-of-preferences/.

[275] See Fudge (n 161 above).

[276] *Saskatchewan Federation of Labour v Saskatchewan* 2015 SCC 4, [2015] 1 SCR 245, para 75.

[277] ibid, para 67.

Though not strictly binding, the decisions of the Committee on Freedom of Association have considerable persuasive weight and have been favourably cited and widely adopted by courts, tribunals and other adjudicative boards around the world, including our Court. The relevant and persuasive nature of the Committee on Freedom of Association jurisprudence has developed over time through custom and practice and, within the ILO, it has been the leading interpreter of the contours of the right to strike.[278]

B. *Francisco Daniel Orellano v el Correo Oficial de la República Argentina SA*

In June 2016, the Supreme Court of Argentina explored the nature of the right to strike under its Constitution.[279] In that case, the Post Office had dismissed Orellano for having participated in multiple meetings with other workers to discuss a wage increase. The Post Office claimed that these meeting were highly disruptive forms of industrial action and created serious delays in the delivery of mail. It also argued that since the union representing the postal workers didn't authorise these meetings, Orellano had no protection from dismissal as the right to strike is vested in the union, not its members. The National Chamber of Labour Appeals had ordered the reinstatement of Orellano, finding that he was dismissed for no other reason that his participation in these meetings, supported by a number of workers, concerning wages and condition of work. In the Court's view, this was protected collective activity.

The Postal Service appealed, causing the Supreme Court to undertake a lengthy examination on the nature of the right to strike as an individual and/or collective right in domestic, regional and international jurisprudence and concluded that under the Constitution of Argentina, the right to call a strike (or to end one) is reserved to trade unions alone. Though not central to the Court's finding, the Court nevertheless reaffirmed that Convention 87 does protect the right to strike:

> In this regard, it should be noted that Convention 87 – on freedom of association and protection of the right to organize – although it does not expressly mention the right to strike, does consecrate the right of 'workers' organizations' and employers 'to organize their administration and its activities and to formulate its program of action' (Article 3) and establishes as object of said organizations 'to promote and defend the interests of workers or employers' (Article 10). In support of these provisions, two bodies established to monitor the application of ILO standards, the Committee on Freedom of Association and the Committee of Experts on the Application of Conventions and Recommendations have given wide recognition to this right, considering it as an indissociable corollary from freedom of association.[280]

---

[278] ibid, para 69.
[279] *Orellano v el Correo Oficial de la República Argentina SA*, CSJ 93/2013 (49-0)/CS1.
[280] Para 11 (authors' translation from the Spanish text).

The Court noted that the Committee on Freedom of Association, in interpreting Convention 87, had found that systems which reserve the right to strike to union organisations exclusively did not violate Convention 87.

In an interesting counterpoint to the *Orellano* case, the Court of Appeals of Santiago, in an appeal brought by Actionline Chile SA, took the opposite approach on the question as to who bears the right to strike. There, the employer, Actionline Chile, argued that a sit-in strike organised outside the collective bargaining process should be declared illegal.[281] In October 2015, the Court rejected this position as a matter of national law (and without reference to the ILO supervisory system), recognising that 'the right to strike is a fundamental right of the person'. In March 2016, the Supreme Court of Chile rejected Actionline Chile's appeal.[282]

While the Committee on Freedom of Association has held that, 'It does not appear that making the right to call a strike the sole preserve of trade union organizations is incompatible with the standards of C87',[283] it of course does *not follow* that a national law making the right to strike also the preserve of individual workers is incompatible. Indeed, the Committee on Freedom of Association has referred to the right as 'a fundamental right of workers and their organizations'.[284] It would appear that Convention 87 is expansive enough to support national laws on the right to strike that point in both directions.

C. *Syndicat indépendent pour cheminots (SIC) v le Conseil des Ministres*

On 26 July 2017, the Belgian Constitutional Court struck down legislation which had the effect of outlawing strikes on the Belgian Railways. The Court there took note that strike procedures for labour disputes on the Belgian Railways were reserved only for representative and recognised trade union organisations, and thus deprived other unions the ability to exercise the 'very essence of freedom of association'. The Court found:

> B.23.9. The fact that the procedure of notice and consultation in the context of social conflicts within the Belgian Railways is reserved exclusively for representative and recognised trade unions is therefore a restriction which is not compatible with the freedom of association and the right to collective bargaining, including the right to take collective action, as guaranteed by the provisions mentioned in B.13, in particular Article 6 § 4 of the revised European Social Charter. While the legislator may grant certain prerogatives, in particular as regards representation, to the most representative trade union organisations, this distinction may not, however, have the effect of

---

[281] See: www.pjud.cl/documents/396729/0/DESAFUERO+SINDICAL+BRAZOS+CAIDOS+CORTE.pdf/.
[282] See: www.pjud.cl/documents/396729/0/DESAFUERO+SINDICAL+BRAZOS+CAIDOS+SUPREMA.pdf/.
[283] Para 756.
[284] ibid, 751–53.

excluding authorised trade union organisations from a prerogative which goes to the very essence of freedom of association by depriving them of a means indispensable to ensure the effective exercise of the right to conduct collective bargaining and to be able to defend effectively the interests of their members.

By depriving the trade union organisations authorised within the Belgian Railways of an essential prerogative of freedom of association and the right to collective bargaining, the contested measure constitutes, in the light of the objective of a fair balance between the rights in question, a disproportionate infringement of the rights of those trade unions.[285]

The instruments cited in B.13, referred to above, included Articles 3 and 10 of ILO Convention 87. It also relied on Article 11 of the ECHR and many of the ECtHR cases cited herein.

---

[285] Arrêt No 101/2017, 26 July 2017, available at: www.const-court.be/public/f/2017/2017-101f.pdf.

9

Other Methods under Article 31 of the Vienna Convention on the Law of Treaties (VCLT) Support the Existence of the Right to Strike

The methods of interpretation available under Article 31 examined above should remove any doubt as to the fact that the right to strike is protected in international law, and in particular by the ILO Constitution and conventions. For thoroughness, we briskly examine other elements of Article 31 of the VCLT here.

I. 'Any Relevant Rules of International Law Applicable in the Relations between the Parties' (Article 31(3)(c) VCLT)

This provision requires one to take account of other relevant rules of international law. This element of interpretation is not limited to the time of the adoption of the instrument concerned. The European Court of Human Rights (ECtHR) has applied this element of interpretation in a wider sense. In its *Demir and Baykara* judgment, it referred in a general way to Article 31(3)(c) of the VCLT[1] and applied it in the following words: 'The Court observes that these considerations find support in the majority of the relevant international instruments'.[2] This is followed by explicit references to many relevant international instruments (concerning the right to organise) such as the UN Covenants (Article 8 International Covenant on Economic, Social and Cultural Rights (ICESCR); Article 22 International Covenant on Civil and Political Rights (ICCPR)), ILO Convention 87 (Article 2),

---

[1] ECtHR (Grand Chamber), *Demir and Baykara v Turkey* App No 34503/97 Judgment (12 November 2008) 28 EHRR 54: 'In addition, the Court has never considered the provisions of the Convention as the sole framework of reference for the interpretation of the rights and freedoms enshrined therein. On the contrary, it must also take into account any relevant rules and principles of international law applicable in relations between the Contracting Parties (citations omitted); see also Article 31(3)(c) of the Vienna Convention'.

[2] ibid, para. 98.

and the European Social Charter (Article 5). In referring also to the instruments mentioned in the *Demir and Baykara* judgment, the ECtHR recognised the right to strike in its judgment *Enerji Yapi-Yol Sen*.[3]

As has been noted above, in *RMT v UK*[4] the ECtHR applied Article 31(3)(c) of the Vienna Convention after an extensive review of the ILO Committee of Experts' and Committee on Freedom of Association (CFA) materials relevant to the right to strike[5] had led it to conclude that secondary industrial action 'is recognised and protected as part of trade union freedom under ILO Convention No 87 and the European Social Charter'[6] so that it

> would be inconsistent with this method [ie that prescribed by Article 31(3)(c) of the Vienna Convention] for the Court to adopt in relation to Article 11 an interpretation of the scope of freedom of association of trade unions that is much narrower than that which prevails in international law.[7]

II. 'A Special Meaning Shall be Given to a Term if it is Established that the Parties So Intended' (Article 31(4) VCLT)

The parties to Convention 87 did not intend at the time of drafting that the right to strike was to be excluded from the rights conferred by that Convention. Of course, the Workers' Group had no intention of excluding the right from Convention 87. But the same absence of intention appears also true of the other parties since, had their intention been to do so, it would have been simple to draft words to limit the broad rights conferred by the Convention so as to specifically exclude the right to strike. There was apparently no attempt to do so by *any* party.

The main argument advanced by the Employers' Group is the rejection, during the drafting process of what became Convention 87, of two amendments asking for the inclusion of the right to strike in the Convention.[8] However, this is not sufficient to 'establish that the parties … intended' (ie, *all* the parties intended) to exclude the right to strike. Given that the plain meaning of Convention 87 comprehended

---

[3] ECtHR (Third Section), 2009 *Enerji Yapi-Yol Sen v Turkey* App No 68959/01 Judgment (21 April 2009) para 16 referring to the description of international law in *Demir and Baykara* (paras 31, 34–52); see the further reference to *Demir and Baykara* in para 31.

[4] *RMT v UK* App No 31045/10 (8 April 2014).

[5] See *RMT*, ibid, paras. 27–33; likewise the review of the European Committee on Social Rights case law, paras 34–37.

[6] *RMT*, ibid, para 76.

[7] ibid.

[8] In any event, the argument of the Employers' Group comes close to proposing that the supplementary means of interpretation (Article 32 VCLT) would displace the primary means (Article 31 VCLT).

the right to strike, a specific inclusion of it was unnecessary and impractical.[9] The reality is that there is not sufficient evidence to *establish* an intention on the part of the parties to exclude the right to strike from the broad and ordinary words which, as submitted above, plainly includes that right among others.

III. Further Interpretation Principles

Obviously, rules or principles of interpretation not mentioned in Articles 31–33 VCLT may also be considered in the interpretative process. In the *Georgia v Russian Federation (CERD)* case, the Court referred to the jurisprudence of the Permanent Court of International Justice (ie, before the VCLT) in order to introduce an interpretation element not (directly) mentioned in the VCLT's interpretation rules:

> In the *Free Zones of Upper Savoy and the District of Gex* case, the Permanent Court of International Justice had occasion to apply the well-established principle in treaty interpretation that words ought to be given appropriate effect.[10]

Taking into account the element of effectiveness, an interpretation of the word 'activities' in Article 3(1) Convention 87 as excluding the right to strike would not give it the appropriate effect. This additional principle even strengthens the result of the interpretation process on the basis of Article 31 of the VCLT.

The 'living instrument' concept is also a common means of interpretation, particularly in the interpretation of human rights instruments. In *Demir and Baykara v Turkey*, the ECtHR referred to 'the "living" nature of the Convention, which must be interpreted in the light of present-day conditions, [and take] account of evolving norms of national and international law in its interpretation of Convention provisions'.[11] The Inter-American Court on Human Rights has held similarly, finding for example in the *Case of the Mapiripán Massacre v Colombia* that the interpretation of human rights treaties 'must go hand in hand with evolving times and current living conditions'.[12] Given the universality of the right to strike in international law, even if Convention 87 did not include the right to strike in 1949, which we do not argue, it must do so now.

---

[9] Indeed, had it been included specifically it would have had to have been enveloped with clumsy protective words to prevent Article 3 being confined only to the right to strike or to rights construed *eiusdem generis* with the right to strike. So phraseology such as 'including, for the avoidance of doubt and without prejudice to the generality of the foregoing, the right to strike or organise, support or take other forms of industrial action' would have been required. No doubt even such language would have given rise to subsequent questions as to whether the unexpressed right to collective bargaining (on the part of employers' associations and trade unions), political lobbying, organising marches and demonstrations and other activities were included.

[10] ICJ Judgment, *Georgia v Russian Federation (CERD)* (1 April 2011) para 133.

[11] *Demir and Baykara v Turkey* (n 1 above) para 68.

[12] *Case of the Mapiripán Massacre v Colombia*, Inter-American Court of Human Rights, Judgment of 15 September 2005, Series C No 122, para 106.

IV. Inadmissible 'Creative Interpretation'?

A further criticism by the Employers' Group is that the Committee of Experts (and presumably, the CFA) has created a right to strike by 'interpreting' Convention 87. In one sense this is correct – the ascertainment of the meaning of words is a process of interpretation. But the Employers' Group implies that the use of interpretation as a creative tool has gone beyond the literal meaning of the words. But, as above, the suggestion that the ILO bodies have been creative in their interpretation of Convention 87 as containing the right to strike is simply factually wrong. The right to strike is found, as shown above, in the very words of Convention 87; no process of creative interpretation is required to find it.

It is true, however, that the ILO committees have used a process of creative interpretation in relation to one feature of the right to strike in Convention 87. The ILO bodies have created *limitations* on the right to strike. Convention 87 contains no limiting words or context.[13] For example, there is no parallel to the wording of Article 11(2) of the European Convention on Human Rights which permits restrictions on freedom of association:

> No restrictions shall be placed on the exercise of these rights other than such as are prescribed by law and are necessary in a democratic society in the interests of national security or public safety, for the prevention of disorder or crime, for the protection of health or morals or for the protection of the rights and freedoms of others. This Article shall not prevent the imposition of lawful restrictions on the exercise of these rights by members of the armed forces, of the police or of the administration of the State.

Many other international human rights provisions have analogous wording. The ILO committees therefore have, by construing Convention 87, constructed limitations on what would otherwise be an unfettered right to strike. The Committee of Experts (and the CFA) has accepted a wide variety of limitations on the right to strike. For example, as the CFA has ruled as follows:

> The Committee has considered that the occupation of plantations by workers and by other persons, particularly when acts of violence are committed, is contrary to Article 8 of Convention No 87. It therefore requested the Government, in future, to enforce the evacuation orders pronounced by the judicial authorities whenever criminal acts are committed on plantations or at places of work in connection with industrial disputes.[14]

In so interpreting Convention 87, these two supervisory bodies have not *created a right to strike*; on the contrary, they have done the very opposite. They have *created permissible restrictions* on what would otherwise be an unfettered right to strike created, not by them, but by the very words of Convention 87.

---

[13] Save perhaps for Article 8, the requirement of conformity to national law balanced by the requirement that national laws must not impair Convention 87 rights, and Article 9 which permits restrictions in relation to armed forces and police.

[14] CFA *Digest of Decisions*, 5th edn (Geneva, ILO, 2006) para 546.

In sum, the Employers' Group does not and cannot point to any other rule of construction which would defeat the long-standing rules now contained in Article 31 of the VCLT which could lead to the conclusion that Article 3(1) of ILO Convention 87 is to be interpreted as excluding the right to strike. In both the academic field[15] and in judicial practice,[16] it is recognised that ILO case law is to be taken into consideration in cases to which it is relevant. Any systematic approach to the international context would be incomplete if the practice of the competent bodies tasked with applying the relevant international standards were left aside. Insofar as these bodies have their own case law demonstrating consistency and continuity in interpretation, reference to that case law reflects state-of-the-art practice by national and regional courts across the globe.

[15] See, eg N Ando, 'The Development of the Human Rights Committee's Activities under the ICCPR and its Optional Protocol through my Twenty-Year Experience as a Committee Member' in G Venturini and S Bariatti (eds), *Liber Fausto, Pocar* (Milan, Giuffrè Editore, 2009) 15 (No 6.2) referring to the case of the application of the term 'territory' in respect of the US report on Guantanamo (outside US 'territory'); to a certain extent also R Gardiner, *Treaty Interpretation* (Oxford, Oxford University Press, 2008) 246.

[16] See, eg, Constitutional Court of South Africa, Judgment 13 December 2002, CCT 14/02, *National Union of Metalworkers of South Africa*, para 32: 'Although none of the ILO Conventions specifically referred to mentions the right to strike, both committees engaged with their supervision have asserted that the right to strike is essential to collective bargaining'; para 33: 'These principles culled from the jurisprudence of the two ILO committees are directly relevant to the interpretation both of the relevant provisions of the Act and of the Constitution'. See also: Supreme Court of Canada, Judgment, *Health Services and Support – Facilities Subsector Bargaining Association v British Columbia* 2007 SCC 27, [2007] 2 SCR 391, para 76: 'Convention No 87 has been the subject of numerous interpretations by the ILO's Committee on Freedom of Association, Committee of Experts and Commissions of Inquiry. These interpretations have been described as the 'cornerstone of the international law on trade union freedom and collective bargaining'; para 79: 'In summary, international conventions to which Canada is a party recognize the right of the members of unions to engage in collective bargaining, as part of the protection for freedom of association'.

10

Though Unwarranted, Article 32 of the Vienna Convention on the Law of Treaties (VCLT) also Supports the Existence of the Right to Strike

I. Resort to the Preparatory Work of Convention 87 is Unwarranted

Article 32 of the VCLT allows recourse to the preparatory works of a treaty only if at least one of the conditions of Article 32(a) or (b) are fulfilled. To do so, the meaning derived by recourse to Article 31 of the VCLT (a) must leave the meaning ambiguous or obscure or (b) lead to a result which is manifestly absurd or unreasonable. If the primary meaning is neither, then the justification for the use of the supplementary means of interpretation under Article 32 of the VCLT is unjustifiable. As explained in the previous chapter on the application of Article 31, it is clear that the meaning of Article 3 of ILO Convention 87 is that trade unions have the right to draft rules and make constitutional provision for the organisation of or support for industrial action, the right to organise activities including the organisation of or support for industrial action and the right to formulate programmes which include plans to organise or support the taking of industrial action. The question is whether that meaning is ambiguous or obscure or leads to results which are manifestly unreasonable or absurd. They are not.

As to ambiguity or obscurity, the existence of a right to strike protected by Convention 87 is neither. Only permissible restrictions on it require any further elaboration but that task cannot render the existence of the right itself ambiguous or unclear. As to manifest absurdity or unreasonableness, the practice of the ILO and its supervisory system to trade unions of the right to strike is the antithesis of absurdity. That this is so is demonstrated by multiple other international instruments protecting the right to strike. Indeed, the idea that unions would have the right to associate and to bargain collectively but have no right to carry out activities in furtherance of those rights, including exercising leverage at the bargaining table through the strike, is manifestly absurd. This is plain to anyone familiar with the practice of industrial relations the world over.

As the Committee of Experts has noted:

> Although the exercise of the right to strike is in most countries fairly commonly subject to certain conditions or restrictions, the principle of this right as a means of action of workers' organizations is almost universally accepted.[1]

So, while there may be arguments as to the extent and scope of the freedom which trade unions have to engage in industrial action, it cannot be argued (save by the most repressive dictatorships) that granting trade unions the rights to do such things is unreasonable or absurd. The fact that so many countries in the world have a legal right to strike is all but conclusive on the point.[2] Therefore, the conditions necessary before resort may be made under Article 32 of the VCLT to supplementary means of interpretation such as the *travaux préparatoires* of Convention 87 to determine the meaning of Article 3(1) of that Convention, are non-existent.

II. Application of Article 32 VCLT would Not Affect the Outcome were it Applied

The practice of the ILO supervisory bodies recognising the right to strike as being included in Article 3(1) of ILO Convention 87 is not only in conformity with the interpretation rules contained in Article 31 VCLT but is required by application of those principles. Even assuming that Article 32 VCLT would apply, however, the outcome would remain unchanged. First, the preparatory work for the ILO Constitution makes clear that from the beginning the right to strike was protected by the right to freedom of association. Secondly, it would have been peculiar for the drafters of Convention 87 to posit that the right to freedom of association was something other, or lesser, than the right as set forth in the Organization's Constitution. And, indeed, there is nothing in the *travaux préparatoires* of Convention 87 which would support such a claim.

A. The Preparatory Work of the Treaty of Versailles and the Circumstances of its Conclusion Confirm the Existence of a Right to Strike

i. Freedom of Association and the Paris Conference

The term 'freedom of association' appears twice in Part XIII of the Treaty of Versailles which established the ILO. However, most contemporary academic

---

[1] ILO, Report of the Committee of Experts on the Application of Conventions and Recommendations, *General Survey on the Fundamental Conventions concerning rights at work in light of the ILO Declaration on Social Justice for a Fair Globalisation 2008*, Report III (Part 1B); ILC, 101st Session, 2012 (*General Survey* 2012), available at: www.ilo.org/wcmsp5/groups/public/---ed_norm/---relconf/ documents/ meetingdocument/wcms_174846.pdf, 50, para 123.

[2] See ch 11 and Annex III.

writing does not examine why it was included in the Treaty and what it meant to those who drafted the relevant sections.[3] The term 'freedom of association' was not a common term in the first part of the twentieth century. Yet, when this term made its appearance during the discussions of the Labour Commission at the Paris Peace Conference, the Committee which was dealing with the labour and social policy items to be included in the Treaty of Versailles raised no controversy among the Commission members. Further, both the context and statements by those who participated in the Conference make clear that the right to strike was considered a bedrock activity of trade unions and a normal part of the collective bargaining process. It would be difficult to imagine that those drafting Part XIII would have considered the right to strike as excluded from the right to freedom of association.

a. The British Legal Situation

In nearly all European countries, legal concepts from the seventeenth and eighteenth centuries recognised property rights, and these were 'allied in some countries to relics of paternalism or feudal status for certain workers'.[4] At the beginning of the nineteenth century, the law in Britain and most European countries recognised almost no worker rights. Thus, when combinations of workers acted to increase their bargaining power, those actions had the effect of harming the employer economically, that is, harming his property interests, and for much of the nineteenth century courts in nearly all countries viewed the workers' actions as unlawful. Looking back at almost two centuries of labour cases, Lord Wedderburn saw two stages of labour law development. In the first, 'the most repressive, penal restrictions upon organisations of workers were removed' as a country industrialised with the new working class 'troublesome to those in control of social and economic power but necessary for their new economy' but while these created narrow areas where associations could exist, 'other types of illegality remained and were sometimes extended ... especially in respect of strikes and industrial struggle'.[5] The second stage of development gave rise to positive rights, such as the right of association, to organise, to bargain and to strike.

Britain, having experienced the world's first industrial revolution, was also the first country to confront labour conflict. Moreover, Britain (unlike countries on the Continent) was a common law country, and as Phelps Brown has stated succinctly: '[a]ny combination conflicts by its very nature with the endeavour of

---

[3] Most authors pinpoint the 1919 Treaty of Versailles as the first international recognition of freedom of association and move forward in time to examine the meaning of the right. See, eg, T Novitz, *International and European Protection of the Right to Strike* (Oxford, Oxford University Press, 2003) 88–99.

[4] KW Wedderburn, 'Industrial Relations and the Courts' (1980) 9 *Industrial Law Journal* 65.

[5] ibid, 65–66.

the common law to preserve the freedom of the individual'.[6] The initial reaction was to ban unions. In 1799 and 1800, the British Parliament passed the wide-ranging Combination Acts. Prior to this, it had prohibited workers from combining and seeking higher wages as this would disturb the arrangement of prices and wages that Parliament was enforcing in that industry. But in 1799, Parliament banned all wage earners in all industries from combining. The word 'combination' had been used in prior laws, and it was used to denote the problem the legislature saw: namely, that workers would join together, or combine, seeking to secure an increase in wages or a decrease in hours. The actions the workers took in furtherance of their goal was the key to the law's hostility. The illegality arose not from the mere fact that workers joined together, but from the reason they joined together.[7]

Although the Combination Acts were repealed in 1824, the lack of an affirmative right to combine meant that throughout the nineteenth century British employers continued to battle unions in the courts by using common law theories, based on contract and tort law. Any strike or work stoppage meant that workers had breached their contract of employment (which of course required that they work if the employer so wished), and anyone organising a work stoppage was inducing a breach of contract which itself was a tort. The usual remedy for a breach of contract or a tort is damages, which in the case of poor nineteenth-century workers was often not a realistic remedy. In any case, what employers wanted was for the work stoppage to cease immediately if not to be prevented altogether. This led employers to bring cases charging workers acting together with conspiracy.

Following the 1872 conviction of gas workers who went on strike in support of a co-worker who had been dismissed for union activity,[8] Parliament passed the 1875 Conspiracy and Protection of Property Act which stated that a court could not convict the defendants, who were acting in furtherance or contemplation of a trade dispute, unless the act they aimed to do was in itself was a crime.[9] Thus, the mere act of combination was not unlawful. But it soon became clear that the 1875 statute only partially responded to the problem of legal liability for engaging in industrial action. Although they were no longer subject to criminal prosecution, workers were still exposed to civil liability as trade union industrial action was nearly always intended to inflict some amount of economic pain on the employer in order to persuade the employer to accede to the union's demands, and withdrawing labour was the main way of applying economic pressure. This was (and is) an integral aspect of the bargaining process. As one scholar, appealing to everyday

---

[6] H Phelps Brown, *The Origins of Trade Union Power* (Oxford, Oxford University Press, 1983) 28.

[7] For an explanation in common language, see Phelps Brown, ibid, ch II, 'The Trade Union as a Combination and the Principles of the Common Law'.

[8] *R v Bunn* [1872] 12 Cox CC. 316. The Court held that the men had broken their contracts of employment by going on strike, and that they had agreed to do a lawful act by use of unlawful means and that this was sufficient to prove criminal conspiracy.

[9] Section 3 states: 'An agreement or combination by two or more persons to do or procure to be done any act in contemplation or furtherance of a trade dispute ... shall not be indictable as a conspiracy if such act committed by one person would not be punishable as a crime'.

experience, has observed: 'The very point of joining a trade union is to have more impact in bargaining, with its clearly detrimental effect on the interests of the employer'.[10]

Following landmark decisions in *Quinn v Leathem*[11] and *Taff Vale*,[12] which allowed individuals (Quinn) and the union (Taff Vale) to be sued for damages in tort for having engaged in industrial action, the legislature overturned them via the Trade Disputes Act 1906 which stated:

> An act done in pursuance of an agreement or combination by two or more persons shall, if done in contemplation or furtherance of a trade dispute, not be actionable unless the act, if done without any such agreement or combination, would be actionable.

Termed 'the golden rule' of British labour law,[13] this linked workers, combination and industrial action and gave workers legal protection. This 1906 legislation meant that for the British at the 1919 Peace Conference, the term 'freedom of association' for workers was understood as more than simply the ability to join together lawfully; rather it was seen as being inextricably linked to the right of workers through their union to formulate collective bargaining demands and to take industrial action, and for the union not be put out of existence by having to pay damages resulting from industrial action.

The British government and employers had also by 1919 adopted the conclusions of the 'Whitley' Committee on Relations between Employers and Employed of 1917[14] recommending that 'the government should propose, without delay, to the various associations of employers and employed, the formation of Joint Standing Industrial Councils in each industry'[15] consisting of representatives of employers' associations on the one side and trade unions on the other for the purpose of industry-wide collective bargaining in order to avoid the widespread

---

[10] Novitz (n 3 above) 126.

[11] *Quinn v Leathem* [1901] AC 495, 510.

[12] *Taff Vale Railway Co v Amalgamated Society of Railway Servants* [1901] AC 426. The union went on strike to protest against the company's treatment of a worker who had demanded higher pay. When the Taff Vale Railway Company hired strike replacements, the strikers engaged in various acts designed to stop the trains from running. At this point, the company decided to bargain collectively with the union and the strikers were returned to their jobs. The company, however, decided to sue the union in tort for damages and won. The House of Lords upheld the decision. Previously it had been thought that under the law of trusts a trade union (versus an individual) could not be sued, because it was an unincorporated entity.

[13] KW Wedderburn, *Cases and Materials on Labour Law* (Cambridge, Cambridge University Press, 1967). Professor Wedderburn referred to the statutory language used which delineated who, acting in what circumstances, would receive immunity as the 'golden formula': 388–421.

[14] Originally set up by the Ministry of Reconstruction as part of the planning for reconstruction after the First World War, its task was to 'make and consider suggestions for securing a permanent improvement in the relations between employers and workmen', Whitley Committee, *Final Report* (Cd 9153, 1 July 1918) para 1.

[15] Whitley Committee, *Interim Report on Joint Standing Industrial Councils* (Cd 8606, 8 March 1917) para 6. These were subsequently known as 'Joint Industrial Councils' (JICs).

and damaging strikes that had marked the previous 50 years.[16] The objective, adopted by government, was to 'constitute a scheme designed to cover all the chief industries of the country and to equip each of them with a representative joint body capable of dealing with matters affecting the welfare of the industry in which employers and employed are concerned'.[17] In this way, it was hoped that reliance on industrial action would be diminished.

b. The US Legal Situation

The US representatives at the 1919 Peace Conference faced a more complex legal situation as labour cases at the time were typically litigated on a torts or contracts theory, which is a matter for state, not federal (national) law. As such, 48 state courts could apply common law concepts to a labour situation and their views as to the legality of specific manifestations of industrial action varied. Similar to Britain,[18] the view of most state courts had evolved during the course of the nineteenth century, with combinations of workers taking some concerted action no longer seen as a criminal conspiracy but with various forms of civil liability still applicable. US unions faced an even more hostile climate than the British. By 1919, there had been no statute recognising a right of association or granting immunity from civil suits in tort or contract. Moreover, the 1890 Sherman Antitrust Act, a federal statute enacted to curb anti-competitive business practices, had an unintended effect due to the broad wording of section 1 which stated: 'Every contract, combination ... or conspiracy, in restraint of trade or commerce among the several States is declared to be illegal'. Latching onto this section, courts found that workers combining together could be deemed in restraint of trade, and if so, they were subject to the treble damages provisions of the statute.[19]

An 1892 general strike in New Orleans gave rise to the first US case which considered the applicability of the Sherman Act to workers' industrial action. The trial court expressed a viewpoint that essentially made most strikes unlawful. The court said: 'The evil, as well as the unlawfulness, of the act of the defendants, consists in this: that, until certain demands of theirs were complied with, they endeavored to prevent, and did prevent, everybody from moving the commerce of the country'.[20] In the famous *Danbury Hatters'* case which involved a nationwide

---

[16] Where such Joint Committees did not already exist, the second report recommended 'an adaptation and expansion of the system of trade boards' working under an amended Trade Boards Act 1909 to conduct bi-partite collective bargaining with the presence of government appointees to facilitate negotiations, Whitley Committee, *Final Report* (n 14 above).

[17] Whitley Committee, *Final Report* (n 14 above).

[18] Prior to 1935 when the first federal (national) labour relations statute was enacted, American labour law case books typically referred not only to leading state cases but also to British decisions to explain how the common law regulated conduct. See, eg, JM Landis, *Cases on Labor Law* (Chicago, IL, The Foundation Press Inc, 1934).

[19] For a discussion of early Sherman Act cases, see A Cox, 'Labor and the Antitrust Laws – A Preliminary Analysis' (1955–56) 104 *University of Pennsylvania Law Review* 252, 256–62.

[20] *US v Workingmen's Amalgamated Council of New Orleans* 54 Fed 994, 1000 (ED Louisiana, 1893).

boycott of a hat manufacturer, the US Supreme Court expressed the same view: '[The statute] prohibits any combination whatever to secure action which essentially obstructs the free flow of commerce between the States, or restricts, in that regard, the liberty of a trader to engage in business'.[21]

Compared with Britain in the first years of the twentieth century, American courts appeared not only hostile to nearly all industrial action, but even more restrictive than they had been before the 1890 Sherman Act. There had been no legislative action to grant immunity in certain situations, let alone to grant positive rights, with the exception of a carve-out in the Clayton Act of 1914, but one which would prove not to insulate industrial action from legal action. Boycotts appear to have been utilised more in the United States than in Britain, perhaps because of the illegality of typical industrial action, such as strikes. But this too was fraught with peril. Even the president of America's central labour federation, Samuel Gompers, had faced being jailed for contempt when he refused to cease publishing a list of unfair employers for consumers to boycott.[22]

ii. Freedom of Association and the Treaty of Versailles

There were several occasions at the end of the nineteenth and beginning of the twentieth century when government representatives from several countries met and proposed action on a labour matter, often lobbied to do so by the International Association for Labour Legislation.[23] The Swiss government took the lead in proposing an international labour organisation that would deal with these matters, with the Berne Conference of 1906 particularly notable in reaching a multilateral agreement on a convention dealing with the use of white phosphorus in the manufacture of matches.[24] By 1914, there were 20 bilateral treaties on labour issues.[25] However, by 1914 only two multilateral treaties relating to labour

---

[21] *Loewe v Lawlor* 208 US 274, 275 (1908).

[22] In 1906 workers at a company in St Louis, Missouri went on strike in support of their demand for a 9-hour day. The American Federation of Labor (AFL) put the company on its 'unfair list' which was circulated to union members asking them to boycott companies on the list. The company went to court and was granted an injunction forbidding the publication of this list. Gompers and several other AFL leaders refused to comply and were sentenced to prison for contempt. The sentence was overturned by the US Supreme Court on technical grounds: *Gompers v Buck's Stove and Range Company* 221 US 418 (1911). The defendants were tried again a year later, and once again were found guilty of contempt and sentenced to prison. The Supreme Court overturned these convictions on grounds relating to the statute of limitations: *Gompers v US* 233 US 604 (1914).

[23] Sir Malcolm Delevingne, 'The Pre-War History of International Labor Legislation' in J Shotwell (ed), *The Origins of the International Labor Organization* (New York, Columbia University Press, 1934). Delevingne chronicles various meetings beginning in 1881 where several European nations came together, often at the invitation of Kaiser Wilhelm of Germany or the government of Switzerland.

[24] This later became Recommendation 006 of the new ILO. Recommendation concerning the Application of the Berne Convention of 1906, on the Prohibition of the Use of White Phosphorus in the Manufacture of Matches (1919), available at: www.ilo.org/dyn/normlex/en/f?p=NORMLEXPUB:12100:0::NO::P12100_ILO_CODE:R006.

[25] J Solano and GN Barnes (eds), *Labour as an International Problem* (London, Macmillan, 1920) 161–94. Here, Arthur Fontaine reviews the efforts before 1919 to achieve the agreement of countries on specific labour standards.

conditions had been concluded.[26] In the same period, several union and socialist groups came together to propose international labour legislation. Union leaders were also active in the most famous pre-war association, the Second International, which was formed at a meeting in Paris in 1889 organised by socialist, social democratic and labour parties and attended by delegates from 20 countries.[27] Among them was Emile Vandervelde of the Belgian Labour Party. The Second International was active in proposing labour legislation and was the first to campaign for the eight-hour day.

The onset of war did not bring a halt to union meetings. The most important meeting was the July 1916 Leeds Conference spearheaded by William Appleton, head of the British General Federation of Trade Unions,[28] and by Léon Jouhaux, the General Secretary of the French Confédération Générale du Travail (CGT). Although this took place alongside the regular annual meeting of the British federation, it attracted 'such widespread publicity' that 'the resolutions adopted by the small group of fraternal delegates … [we]re commonly believed to reflect the considered opinion of the whole labor world'.[29] The delegates to this conference made recommendations for the express purpose of being prepared for an international union congress that would be held in the same place and at the same time as the peace conference[30] attended by diplomats that would take place after the end of the war.[31] Among the improvements demanded by the Leeds conference delegates was 'freedom of association'.[32]

---

[26] J Shotwell (ed), *The Origins of the International Labor Organization* (New York, Columbia University Press, 1934) 46. These related to restrictions on night work for women in industry and one prohibiting the use of white phosphorus in matches.

[27] BE Lowe, *The International Protection of Labor* (New York, Macmillan, 1921) xvi–xxi. This publication resulted from Lowe's doctoral thesis and it is exhaustive in noting late-19th-century meetings. In this section he details meetings of socialist and social democratic unions from several countries.

[28] The Trades Union Congress (TUC), dating to the 1860s, was (and is) the main federation of trade unions in Britain. In 1899, the TUC set up the General Federation of Trade Unions (GFTU), as an organisation that would exert more centralised coordination among its members and would take a more militant approach in the pursuit of economics and social demands. To do so, the GFTU was designed to serve as source of financial support, principally during strikes when affiliated unions could draw upon the GFTU's strike fund. Some unions belonged to both the TUC and the GFTU.

[29] Shotwell (n 26 above) 64. Delevigne comments that Samuel Gompers and the AFL had not been invited to the Leeds Conference to what the British organisers deemed a private and informal meeting, but upon learning that this conference had taken place, Gompers protested to Appleton and Jouhaux. See 59–64.

[30] G Van Goethem, *The Amsterdam International: The World of the International Federation of Trade Unions (IFTU), 1913–1945* (Aldershot, Ashgate Publishing, 2006) 18. Samuel Gompers (who was not present at the Leeds Conference) strongly supported the idea of a labour conference being held at the same time and in the same place as the peace conference. Léon Jouhaux was likewise supportive, and it was he who prepared the report for the Leeds Conference and who urged that there be 'industrial clauses in the peace treaty'.

[31] Standards of Labor Legislation Suggested in Resolutions of the International Labor Conference, Leeds, July 1916. Bureau of Labor Statistics, *Monthly Labor Review*, Vol 4 (January–June 1917) 912–15.

[32] The meeting mentioned in the *Monthly Labor Review* used the term 'right of coalition'. Alcock cites a memo of 9 October 1918 from EJ Phelan re Meeting of Labour in UK where 'freedom of association' was used. Since the resolutions regarding standards that should be guaranteed were prepared in French, this may be an issue of translating a French phrase into English. See, A Alcock, *History of the International Labour Organisation* (Basingstoke, Macmillan, 1971).

The 1917 revolution in Russia was the greatest expression of discontent during the war, ousting the tsarist government and captured the attention of governments in European capitals. In 1918, with the end of the First World War imminent, it seemed to many that labour unrest and the events in Russia might inspire some to seek political change even by violent means. In several of the combatant nations there was a widespread feeling that the lower classes had been drawn into a war of mass slaughter by the upper classes with governments cognisant of the fact that the returning soldiers expected something in return for their great sacrifices. This may explain why in writings from the period there is mention of the 'labour problem' with a general recognition that once the war ended some action would need to be taken. Lloyd George, the Prime Minister of Great Britain, famously expressed this sentiment when he wrote:

> The whole of Europe is filled with the spirit of revolution. There is a deep sense not only of discontent, but of anger and revolt among the workmen against pre-war condi-
> tions. In some countries, like Germany and Russia, the unrest takes the form of open rebellion, in others, like France, Great Britain and Italy, it takes the shape of strikes and of general disinclination to settle down to work, symptoms which are just as much concerned with the desire for political and social change as with wage demands.[33]

iii. *The Labour Commission Proposal*

The Paris Peace Conference was scheduled to begin on 19 January 1919. To prepare, EJ Phelan arrived in Paris on 2 January and was joined by other members of the British delegation over the next three weeks.[34] The American delegation arrived in mid-January and Phelan ascertained that they had not prepared any proposal that they intended to present. This permitted the two groups to discuss the British proposal for an international labour organisation before the Peace Conference began. It also gave the British the opportunity to obtain US and French support for the way labour matters would be introduced at the Peace Conference. The British wanted to ensure that the labour issue would be on the agenda of the Peace Conference, and also wanted it handled in a way that would enmesh the labour discussion with the general work of the Conference. They suggested that on the first day of the Peace Conference, they would propose that the labour problem be handled by a separate committee which would report back to the Conference. The Americans agreed with this approach as did the French.

---

[33] At a critical point in the discussions on the Treaty of Versailles, Lloyd George sent a private memo-randum to the other leaders of the Allied Powers, which he titled 'Some considerations for the Peace Conference before they finally draft their terms'. It was dated 25 March 1919. This subsequently was revealed by several of those who received it. See, eg, FS Nitti, *The Wreck of Europe* (Indianapolis, IN, Bobbs-Merrill, 1922) 94; RS Baker, *Woodrow Wilson and World Settlement*, vol III, Original Docu-ments of the Peace Conference (Garden City, NY, Doubleday, Page & Co, 1922) 449–57. These words of Lloyd George often appear in commentaries of this period.

[34] See Shotwell (n 26 above) 105–26, 'British Preparations' wherein Phelan discusses the meetings and issues that arose during this period.

It was not until the third week of January 1919 that attention turned to the need for a preamble as a means of setting forth the purpose of the proposed international labour organisation. The initial draft Preamble, prepared by Harold Butler[35] of the British delegation, was short. It proclaimed that conditions of labour existed which involved such 'injustice, hardship and privation to large numbers of people as to produce unrest so great that the peace and harmony of the world are imperilled'. It then declared that 'an improvement of those conditions is urgently required'. Following this was a short list of items that urgently needed attention. Freedom of association was not included in this 'first complete draft of the British Plan' that was prepared prior to the start of the Peace Conference.[36] But by 2 February 1919, the day on which the British delegation submitted the text of their proposal to the Labour Commission, the Preamble had got longer, with a longer list of items urgently needing attention, and among them now appeared 'recognition of the principle of freedom of association'.[37]

After its plenary opening on 19 January 1919, the Peace Conference began work on 29 January. As already agreed by the British, Americans and French, the Peace Conference by resolution established a Commission on International Labour Legislation to work on a proposal regarding the labour problem. It was agreed that France, the United Kingdom, the United States, Italy and Japan be included on the basis of their being the chief Allied Powers, and that they would appoint five other members. Nine countries[38] were represented on this Labour Commission with each country having two representatives.[39] The Labour Commission began work immediately, convening on 31 January.

When the chair of the Labour Commission asked for proposals, the British submitted theirs. No other delegation submitted a proposal at that point.[40] As a result, the delegates on the Labour Commission at the Paris Peace Conference

---

[35] Harold Butler in 1920 became the Deputy Director of the ILO under its first Director, Albert Thomas, and then succeeded Thomas. He was Director of the ILO from 1932 to 1938.

[36] Shotwell (n 26 above) 372. This draft is dated 26 January 1919, three days before the Peace Conference convened. The drafts and revisions are reproduced in the appendix of Shotwell, on unnumbered pages but in chronological order.

[37] Phelan stated that the French translation of the initial British proposal was prepared in late January 1919 by a translator from the British Foreign Office before the Labour Commission convened for the first time. He then commented: 'This detail, which emphasizes the lack of any international secretariat at the Peace Conference, is of some importance, as in several instances the French and English texts as finally incorporated in the Peace Treaties do not exactly correspond'. Shotwell (n 26 above) 126.

[38] Added were Belgium, Cuba, Czechoslovakia and Poland. Belgium had two members, one representing the Flemish and one representing the Walloons.

[39] It appears that while there were two official representatives, that named substitutes or alternatives were also present during the Commission's sessions and that many of these persons were quite influential. For a listing, see *A League of Nations: Labor in the Treaty of Peace* (October 1919) II(5), available at: www.library.albany.edu/preservation/brittle_bks/LeagueNations_Treaty_of_Peace/.

[40] The French government had established a committee in 1917 to consider social policy issues, and this committee did confer with its British counterparts. But under the press of work, it had not formulated a complete proposal by the time the Commission started working. Shotwell (n 26 above) 83–97; R Tosstorff, 'The International Trade-Union Movement and the Founding of the International Labour Organization' (2005) 50 *International Review of Social History* 399, 416.

considered only one full proposal.[41] That formed the basis for all further deliberations. The version of the Labour Charter that was presented to the Peace Conference delegates contained nine principles.

The very first principle, that labour is not a commodity, directly addressed the issue of combination. The phrase itself was well known to Samuel Gompers as it was taken from an American statute, the Clayton Act, enacted only five years earlier after intense lobbying by unions persuaded President Woodrow Wilson to support a statutory exemption for unions from the Sherman Antitrust Act.[42] The Clayton Act declared that 'the labor of a human being is not a commodity' and expressly stated that union members engaged in legitimate objects of a union are not to be deemed illegal combinations or conspiracies in restraint of trade.[43]

The second principle in the Labour Charter was freedom of association. As noted, the British proposal from the first day of the Labour Commission's deliberations included 'recognition of the principle of freedom of association' in the Preamble.[44] In the Labour Charter, the phrasing changed to the 'principle that employers and workers should be allowed the right of association and combination for all purposes, subject only to such restrictions as are essential for safeguarding the national interests'.[45] Phelan stated that with regard to the principle of freedom of association,

> [t]he Commission was faced with a difficulty which has not yet been solved: namely, the difficulty of finding a formula which could guarantee the right of free association within the State without interfering with or diminishing the State's right to protect what it may conceive to be its essential interests. The discussion did not go very deep.[46]

---

[41] Wilfred Jenks commented: 'There were, however, some almost accidental circumstances which contributed to the success achieved in Paris, notably the combination of the general desire to do something about the labour question with the absence of any rival plan elaborated in anything like the same detail'. W Jenks, 'The Origins of the International Labour Organization' (1934) 30 *International Labour Review* 575, 577.

[42] Starting in 1908, when the Supreme Court held that the Sherman Act extended to unions, any union taking industrial action was placed in an impossible legal situation. Woodrow Wilson, a Democrat, became President in 1913.

[43] 'The labor of a human being is not a commodity or article of commerce. Nothing contained in the antitrust laws shall be construed to forbid the existence and operation of labor, ... or to forbid or restrain individual members of such organizations from lawfully carrying out the legitimate objects thereof; nor shall such organizations, or the members thereof, be held or construed to be illegal combinations or conspiracies in restraint of trade, under the antitrust laws' (15 October 1914, ch 323, § 6, 38 Stat 731).

[44] The draft of the British proposal introduced the first day is printed in the Appendix to Shotwell (n 26 above).

[45] Shotwell (n 26 above) 187.

[46] ibid, 195. The Shotwell book was published in 1934. Commenting on this 15 years after the Labour Commission deliberations and after the inconclusive attempt at the ILO in the 1920s to draft an instrument on freedom of association, Phelan observed that this was 'the first clash of views on a question which in one form or another has arisen at almost every meeting of the International Labour Conference since'.

The Labour Commission met 18 times between 1 February and 28 February, during which time it completed the first reading of the British draft. The Commission then adjourned until 11 March, in part to give the delegations the opportunity to consult with their governments. The second reading occurred in 17 sessions between 11 March and 24 March. During this period changes were proposed, but as Phelan noted 'few changes were made in the Preamble' with only one being of importance: namely the inclusion of 'social justice' as an object of the new international labour organisation with the explicit recognition that 'such peace can be established only if it is based upon social justice'.[47] Recognition of the principle of freedom of association was apparently never discussed in any detail and it did not provoke any disagreement.[48]

The final version that became Part XIII of the Treaty contains a preamble. It is almost exactly the same as the Labour Commission's final draft. It contains the phrase 'recognition of the principle of freedom of association' which is exactly the same as the phrase that appeared in the British proposal on the first day the Labour Commission met. The final version contains the Labour Charter in Article 427, which states General Principles regarding the regulation of labour. In the relevant part, it states:

> Among these methods and principles, the following seem to the High Contracting Parties to be of special and urgent importance:
>
> First. – The guiding principle above enunciated that labour should not be regarded merely as a commodity or article of commerce.
>
> Second. – The right of association for all lawful purposes by the employed as well as by the employers.

Whether there is any difference in the scope of the right of freedom of association between this phrasing and the phrasing of the Labour Commission cannot be definitely determined. It is known that the key members of the British, American and French delegations on the Labour Commission saw no major difference. All agreed that violent or revolutionary insurrectionist industrial action (which was occurring at the very time the Peace Conference was meeting) was not included within the notion of a protected right of association and thus permissible for a State to outlaw.

---

[47] Shotwell (n 26 above)132.

[48] Phelan later observed that '[i]t is no means easy to give a clear account of the work of the Commission' noting that there was no international secretariat at the time, and that no official published minutes of the Commission's deliberations were kept. Several of those present kept their own notes. Those present relied on their own delegation's translators who mainly were drawn from the military and even at the time there was some question as to the accuracy of these translations in light of the differences between French and English regarding labour relations concepts. Shotwell (n 26 above) 127–28 and 130. In 1934, Jenks noted that although 'the British were the sponsors of the plan and the Americans the chief critics of its key article, with the natural result that many of the most important speeches were originally made in English', no English stenographic record survived. He deemed this 'a grave misfortune' especially because the surviving record of these speeches was made by the French stenographers based on simultaneous oral interpreters which is often more of a summary than a strict translation. Jenks (n 41 above) 576.

As such, there would have been no objection to including this in the statement on freedom of association to allay the fears of some delegates to the Peace Conference.

iv. *The Meaning of Freedom of Association*

Coming from different countries with different histories, the delegates often saw different issues as pressing and displayed different attitudes regarding the role of trade unions, the meaning of the collective bargaining process, and the utility of industrial action compared with political action. To determine what the Labour Commission meant by 'recognition of the principle of freedom of association' requires some consideration of these differences.

a. The US Perspective

President Woodrow Wilson personally participated in the Paris Peace Conference and was committed to the idea of international organisations, and in particular to the League of Nations. Shortly after being elected President of the United States in 1912, he supported the work of the new Commission on Industrial Relations to study the labour problem.[49] Professor John R Commons, who was active in the work of the Commission on Industrial Relations, deemed the possibility of a strike as 'integral to the process of collective bargaining' such that a 'strike may in a sense be a step in that process'.[50] Wilson also supported the passage of the Clayton Act in 1914 which stated that unions should not be deemed to be illegal combinations of workers engaging in anti-competitive practices or conspiracies in restraint of trade. Moreover, Wilson was aware that unions typically went on strike and/or engaged in picketing and boycotts in support of their demands. As a result, it is reasonable to assume that Woodrow Wilson supported the principle of freedom of association and was aware that this term encompassed a wide range of actions, including the possibility of such collective action such as strikes.

Wilson seemingly was content for the two delegates he sent to the Paris Peace Conference, Samuel Gompers (labour) and Edward Hurley (management), to express the viewpoint of the United States at the Labour Commission. Wilson certainly was well acquainted with Gompers, with his views, and with the fact that he was most outspoken, but nonetheless strongly supported Gompers.[51] Wilson

---

[49] Responding to instances of severe industrial violence, the US President, William Howard Taft, appointed a Commission on Industrial Relations in 1912. It held hearings between during the presidency of Woodrow Wilson. These hearings documented the dire and oppressive conditions under which many persons and children worked. John R Commons, the noted labour economist at the University of Wisconsin, was a key member of the Commission's staff.

[50] J Commons and J Andrews, *Principles of Labor Legislation*, 4th rev edn (New York, Harpers & Brothers, 1936) 373.

[51] See E McKillen, 'Beyond Gompers: The American Federation of Labor, the Creation of the ILO, and US Labor Dissent' in J Van Daele, G Rodriguez, G Van Goethem and M van der Linden (eds), *Essays on the International Labour Organization and Its Impact on the World During the Twentieth Century* (Bern, Peter Berg, 2010) 43.

appointed a person from the employers' side who was not known to be anti-union or even to have strong views about unions. Hurley left Paris in February soon after the first sitting of the Labour Commission.[52] Neither he, nor his successor (Henry Robinson, also of the US Shipping Board) are mentioned in the writings of other participants at the Labour Conference. It appears that the other delegates perceived that Samuel Gompers was presenting the position of the United States.

Gompers' position as chairman of the Labour Commission gave him the opportunity to ensure that his views were heard. Samuel Gompers' views on freedom of association, strikes and other forms of industrial action are crucial in any consideration of what the term 'recognition of the principle of freedom of association' in the Preamble of Part XIII of the Treaty of Versailles means. Gompers, President of the American Federation of Labor since 1886, believed in workers organising themselves, on occupational lines, to pursue improvement in their working conditions through the process of collective bargaining. Compared with many European trade unions, which viewed political action (leading to legislation or other form of regulation) as important as collective bargaining, the American trade union movement by 1919 had focused almost exclusively on collective bargaining.[53] Samuel Gompers took an unyielding position regarding how workers should seek to improve their terms and conditions of employment. He believed that they should use the collective bargaining process and not pursue legislative action.[54] Gompers adhered to a theory of worker organisation based on what he termed 'pure and simple' trade unionism which meant 'economic power organized in an effective association of persons with similar needs and goals, directed for an objective, immediate and practical'.[55] Rather than the class consciousness of European unions, American unions focused on 'job consciousness' as the basis of a cohesive labour movement.[56]

Gompers viewed a strike as an economic weapon used to increase the workers' bargaining power when the collective bargaining process had not produced the desired result. In 1910 he said:

> Let a man have the right to decide when he is to work or is not to work, and let that decision be backed by his power to keep himself from being obliged by immediate

---

[52] In memoirs written by Hurley, his account of the Peace Conference focuses almost entirely on shipping matters, with no mention of the Labour Commission. See: www.gwpda.org/wwi-www/Hurley/bridge7.htm#ch36.

[53] H Millis and R Montgomery, *Organized Labor* (New York, McGraw-Hill, 1945) 123–25.

[54] This caused some tension between Gompers and the British delegation who supported the use of both collective bargaining and legislative action.

[55] FC Thorne, *Samuel Gompers - American Statesman* (New York, Philosophical Library, 1957) 36.

[56] S Perlman, *A Theory of the Labor Movement* (New York, Macmillan, 1949). In ch 2, 'Labor and Capitalism in America', he discusses why the American experience differed from that of Britain, Germany and Russia, highlighting the stronger emphasis on private property rights in the United States, the relative lack of class consciousness, and the particularly harsh reaction to revolutionary syndicalism and the 'ferocious self-defence' of the capitalist class to 'any real or fancied industrial rebellion': see 159–60. In his classic study, Perlman takes the view that the 'pure and simple' trade unions advocated by Samuel Gompers and the AFL which focused on gains workers could achieve was the more effective way of engaging American workers in trade union activity.

necessity to offer his labor to an employer, and the consequence must be that he will not sell his labor-power until the terms offered him are the best that the industry can warrant.[57]

Besides this pragmatic view of the utility of a strike, Gompers also took the philosophical position that the right to strike was an aspect of freedom. In testimony before a US Senate Committee in 1916, he asked rhetorically whether 'it is the course of right for any period of time to compel the workman to give involuntary servitude so that the companies may operate their railroad and perform their obligation to society?'[58] Gompers was totally opposed to government restrictions on striking, although he did take the view that during national emergencies workers should voluntarily forego the use of the right to strike.[59] He adhered to this view even in wartime. In May 1918 he said:

> Workers, decide every industrial question fully mindful of those men ... who are on the battle line ... needing munitions of war to fight the battle ... No strike ought to be inaugurated that cannot be justified to the men facing momentary death. A strike during the war is not justified unless principles are involved equally fundamental as those of which fellow citizens have offered their lives.[60]

In light of his firm views regarding workers' right to strike, Gompers' views on other forms of industrial action were predictable. He fervently believed in freedom of speech, and to him, peaceful picketing on the public highway was a form of communication and persuasion. He viewed boycotts in the same way, as a form of speech whereby those who supported the union cause communicated with others. His position was adamant, as he explained to a government committee:

> Workmen have a right to say that they will not patronize those who are unfriendly to them and those who support their adversaries. This is all that boycotting implies. There is no aggression here, no criminal purpose, and no criminal way of accomplishing a proper purpose.[61]

b. The British Perspective

On the British delegation, the members worked as a team. The government's spokesman was George Barnes, a minister in the War Cabinet. Barnes, a member of the Labour Party from its founding, had been a union leader. By 1919, trade

---

[57] Thorne (n 55 above) 69, quoting from the President's report published in the Proceedings of the 1910 AFL Annual Convention.

[58] ibid, 67, quoting Gompers' testimony before the Senate's Interstate Commerce Commission, on 31 August 1916.

[59] ibid, 68.

[60] ibid, 69, quoting Gompers' statement in an article in the AFL's monthly publication, the *American Federationist*, in May 1918.

[61] ibid, 71, quoting Gompers' testimony to the Industrial Commission, Washington, DC, 18 April 1899.

unions in Britain had been able to secure legislation permitting trade union action. Thus, the British delegation's views of unions and their sphere of action was based on their own experience. Their views were also influenced by the generally accepted writings of prominent intellectuals. In London, the Bloomsbury Set, a loose collection of intellectuals hailing mainly from upper-middle-class professional backgrounds, was known for its left-liberal political views which were favourable to trade unions. Some in the Bloomsbury circle were active in political groups that promoted trade union rights, such as the Socialist society, among whom were Sidney and Beatrice Webb.

The Webbs were the most influential scholars of the trade union movement in Britain. For them, 'The strike was regarded, not as a distinct method of Trade Union action, but merely as the culminating incident of a breakdown of the Method of Collective Bargaining'.[62] Further emphasising this point that a strike is part of the collective bargaining process, the Webbs recalled the statement they made in their 1897 book, *Industrial Democracy*:

> It is impossible to deny that the perpetual liability to end in a strike or a lock-out is a grave drawback to the Method of Collective Bargaining. So long as the parties to a bargain are free to agree or not to agree, it is inevitable that, human nature being what it is, there should now and again come a deadlock, leading to that trial of strength and endurance which lies behind all bargaining. We know of no device for avoiding this trial of strength except a deliberate decision of the community expressed in legislative enactment.[63]

The Webbs' stance was common at the time. Within the Fabian socialist group, there were those who were even more stridently supportive of allowing workers to resort to strikes. Writing at the time of the First World War, GDH Cole observed that 'collective bargaining ... may and usually does amount merely to a trial of strength, or of estimated strength, between the parties involved' but cautioned that although 'the avoidance of conflict ... may be highly desirable, ... the abandonment of the method of collective bargaining involved in arbitration and in a good deal of conciliation is certainly not so'.[64] Cole pointed out that conciliation had a 'very useful function' but only when '*backed up by the threat of a strike*'.[65]

The British team who wrote the draft proposal that became Part XIII of the Treaty of Versailles would have been familiar with this line of reasoning. In addition, they would have been aware that their Prime Minister, Lloyd George, personally had been involved in settling strikes in the decade before the war and had been in favour of social reform. Most notable was that Lloyd George was a member of the Cabinet that supported the Trade Disputes Act 1906 that gave immunity to

---

[62] S Webb and B Webb, *The History of Trade Unionism 1666–1920* (London self-published, 1920) 664.
[63] ibid, fn 1 quotation from 'Industrial Democracy' 221.
[64] GDH Cole, *The World of Labour*, rev edn (London, G Bell and Sons, 1917) 287.
[65] ibid, emphasis supplied.

those acting in combination for actions taken pursuant to a trade dispute.[66] As such, the drafters would have had no doubt that Lloyd George deemed freedom of association to mean the right to join together (combine) to seek better terms and conditions of employment through the collective bargaining method which might lead workers to engage in industrial action, including strikes.

c. The Labour Perspective

Commentaries on the Paris Peace Conference written in the decade after were nearly always written by those who had represented governments. These accounts by politicians and social-reformist intellectuals typically overlooked the importance of other actors, notably unions. But with regard to the Commission on International Labour Legislation it is evident that certain persons from different countries had communicated before 1919 and had had discussions regarding desired outcomes of the Peace Conference. For the most part, this occurred on the part of those supportive of labour. The importance of this network of reform-minded individuals is difficult to gauge but its impact on the work of the Labour Commission should not be underestimated.[67]

Recent scholarship has revealed that the network of trade unionists, especially socialist and social democratic trade unionists, was of critical importance in proposing an international labour organisation, in having trade union leaders on the Labour Commission, and in putting forward specific elements of the labour charter.[68] Although there were significant divisions among trade unions at the time, due to views on effective organisational structures and political orientation,[69] there were certain issues on which there was widespread agreement, such as a mandated shorter working day. Some scholars have credited the trade union movement as primarily responsible for the substantive principles that were included in Part XIII, and in particular in Article 427 because of the demands that the trade union movement had made at the 1916 Leeds Conference and the

---

[66] The relevant section states: 'An act done in pursuance of an agreement or combination by two or more persons shall, if done in contemplation or furtherance of a trade dispute, not be actionable unless the act, if done without any such agreement or combination, would be actionable'.

[67] R Holton, *Global Networks* (Basingstoke, Palgrave Macmillan, 2008) 186.

[68] Tosstorff (n 40 above) 400. Tosstorf takes the position that while Shotwell 'presented government as the main protagonists' in the formation of the ILO, the 'trade-union federations were the real driving force that pressured government to include social-policy programmes in the peace treaty'.

[69] Scholarly works on labour history focus on craft, industrial and general workers' unions as different approaches to organisation of a trade union. Political goals or views distinctions are less precisely labelled. Scholars mention centrist, social democratic, socialist, Bolshevik and anarcho-syndicalist unions. Even among socialist unions, there were those who saw political matters as purely in the realm of the party versus those who saw the union as having a political role. Writing just before and during the First World War, Professor GDH Cole in discussing how to categorise or label unions expressly notes the differing views of what the term 'socialist' meant and that it took 'more than half a century to get its definite connotation' but highlights the fact that 'there is something new in the air needing a name' which has led to a 'vagueness in terminology' but which some call 'syndicalism' although he admits that what that means is 'ill understood'. See Cole (n 64 above) 55–57.

1919 Berne Conference, demands which were well known to those in government ministries responsible for labour matters.[70]

When the war ended and Paris was announced as the site of the Peace Conference, Gompers and others, following up on the Leeds Conference resolution, attempted to arrange an international trade union conference in Paris but the French authorities would not grant the necessary visas to delegates from Germany and Austria.[71] The unions held their conference in Berne during the first week of February 1919. The delegates at the Berne Conference passed resolutions, including several dealing with 'International Labour Legislation' in which they called for an 'international labour charter'.[72] In so doing, they were reiterating what rights they wanted established. Most of the Berne Conference resolutions related to specific working conditions. One however stated a matter of principle. Resolution 8 stated:

> Workers shall have the right of combination and association in all countries. Laws and decrees (domestic service laws, prohibition of combination, etc) which place certain classes of workers in an exceptional position ... which deprive them of their right of combination and association, and of the representation of their economic interests, shall be repealed.

As these were trade unionists, it is likely that many, like Jouhaux, would personally have taken part in organising unions and in industrial action, and would be well aware that a positive statement of the right of association was needed, and how any law granting freedom of association could be undercut by carving out exceptions. It may be that the Berne delegates were prescient or simply that they anticipated an issue that would be controversial at the Peace Conference: namely, the equal treatment of foreign workers. At a time when empires were collapsing and country boundaries were being redrawn, the Berne Conference delegates must have been sensitive to the fact that workers from one country might be going into another country to work. Moreover, persons like Jouhaux, who had been fired for going on strike, realised the difficulty of organising a union and demanding recognition by the employer, and of maintaining solidarity while threatening a strike if demands were not met. They knew a strike would collapse if a part of the workforce was excluded from this effort because of some exception in the law guaranteeing freedom of association. Significantly, the delegates identified the most controversial aspect of freedom of association and emphasised that it applied to all workers by stating in the next paragraph of Resolution 8 that 'Immigrant workers shall enjoy the same rights as native workers as regards joining and taking part in the work of trade unions, including the right to strike'.

---

[70] FG Wilson, *Labor in the League System: A Study of the International Labor Organization in Relation to International Administration* (Palo Alto, CA, Stanford University Press, 1934) 30–31.

[71] D Ligou, *Histoire du Socialisme en France 1871–1961* (Paris, Presses Universitaires de France, 1962) 305.

[72] *International Socialism and World Peace.* Resolutions of the Berne Conference, February 1919, 9 (edition printed by the Independent Labour Party, London, 1919), available at: www.archive.org/stream/InternationalSocialismAndWorldPeaceResolutionsOfTheBerneConference/BerneConference#page/n3/mode/2up.

The delegates at the Berne Conference were alert to the need to act quickly if they were going to have any impact on the work of the Commission on International Labour Legislation meeting at the same time in Paris. In Berne, they appointed four persons to 'watch over the work' of the Peace Conference.[73] They also decided to send a delegation to Paris to present the Berne resolution to Georges Clemenceau, the President of the Peace Conference.[74] The timing of the events is critical to understanding the impact of the Berne Conference. It concluded on 10 February 1919. The Labour Commission had begun meeting on 1 February and continued until Friday, 28 February. It then recessed for a week until Tuesday 11 March. As noted above, the original British proposal had contained a preamble listing items urgently needing attention, but nothing more. Sometime after 10 February and before 28 February, several delegations insisted that guiding principles in the form of a labour charter be inserted into the proposal that would be recommended to the Peace Conference. Léon Jouhaux of France and Angiolo Cabrini of Italy took the position that the labour clauses in the Treaty should be 'a start toward the realization of the Berne trade union and social conference.'[75] A sub-committee, appointed to examine the question of what guiding principles should be included, made its report on 15 March. By 24 March, the Commission had drafted its report to the Peace Conference, a report which included the guiding principles. This inclusion of a section on 'guiding principles', referred to as the Labour Charter, was viewed by some as 'revolutionary' because it represented a 'statement of the demands of Labour *for itself* and since the Charter was adopted by the Commission and later by the Conference, it represented an acceptance of general principles regarding social justice.[76]

B. Freedom of Association in the Aftermath of Versailles

With the Treaty of Versailles having established an international organisation to deal with labour matters and in light of substantial industrial and political unrest in several European countries, many of the delegates who took part in the Labour Commission's work were determined to have the new International Labour Organization begin its work without delay. With the United States willing to provide support,[77] the first International Labour Conference (ILC) convened

[73] *Resolutions*, ibid, 15, fn 101. One of the delegates sent to present the resolution was Albert Thomas of France, who would become the first Director of the new ILO.

[74] It appears that they did achieve this aim. See Ligou (n 71 above) 305.

[75] Wilson (n 70 above) 47.

[76] Solano and Barnes (n 25 above) 45–46. Article 427 at the beginning of Section II is the Labour Charter.

[77] In discussing this first Conference, Harold Butler stated that US President Wilson was 'particularly anxious' that it should meet in Washington and took a 'keen personal interest' in the Conference but since the United States had not ratified the Peace Treaty, this made its role awkward as it had no official voting delegates at the Conference. Thus, Gompers could not play a role. However, George Barnes and Léon Jouhaux, both of whom had been very influential in the discussions of the Labour Commission, were elected Vice Presidents of the Conference: ibid, 198–99 and 203.

only six months later, in Washington, DC on 29 October 1919 even before the League of Nations came into being.[78]

At its 1919 International Labour Conference, delegates to the Conference considered items listed in the Preamble to Part XIII as 'urgently' needing attention and adopted six conventions on topics such as the eight-hour day, night work for women, minimum age in industry and maternity protection. Four conventions were adopted at the 1920 Conference, mostly dealing with maritime and seamen's matters. In 1921, however, the proposed Convention 11, Right of Association (Agriculture), covered a matter that had been highlighted in one of the resolutions of the Berne Conference of 1919: namely, that certain categories of workers were denied the right of association that other workers were accorded. The Berne Conference resolution had mentioned, as an example, workers in domestic service, who at the time were often not free to leave their employ and who often worked long hours and received non-wage compensation. Agricultural workers in some countries were in an analogous position in that they might be tied to the land, and their compensation might be based on a share-cropping arrangement. Convention 11 and two other conventions[79] expressly extending rights to workers in agriculture were adopted in the face of French government objections.[80]

The language of Article 1 of Convention 11 tracks the language of the Berne resolution, in particular its requirement that legislation limiting the right of association be repealed. Article 1 states:

> Each Member of the International Labour Organisation which ratifies this Convention undertakes to secure to all those engaged in agriculture the same rights of association and combination as to industrial workers, and to repeal any statutory or other provisions restricting such rights in the case of those engaged in agriculture.

This is the sole substantive article in Convention 11. It presupposes that industrial workers do have rights of association and combination, otherwise it would make no sense.

---

[78] The League of Nations came into being on 10 January 1920. Its first session took place on 26 January 1920.

[79] Convention 10 covered the issue of minimum age for agricultural workers, and Convention 12 addressed workers' compensation for personal injuries.

[80] It appears that some governments that were in favour of the labour rights expressed in Part XIII of the Treaty assumed that these rights only applied to those working in industry, such as in a factory or a mine, and in a conventional employment relationship. There is, however, nothing in Part XIII that mentions any exclusion or limiting criterion. Similarly, during the 1920s some Member States, such as Great Britain, which had ratified Convention 4, Night Work (Women) 1919, asserted that it did not include within its scope female managers whereas others, such as France, believed it did. The continuing controversy caused the Governing Body to refer the matter to the Permanent International Court of Justice for an interpretation of the Convention. The Court held that the Convention covered all female workers as there was no exclusion or limiting criterion in the Convention. 26th Session, 15 November 1932), available at: www.ilo.org/public/libdoc/igo/P/01327/01327(1932)Avis_du_15_novembre_1932.pdf.

Even if the delegates did believe that workers had a right of association and combination, that did not mean they agreed on the exact scope of this right. This led the Governing Body to direct the International Labour Office to collect information with regard to the position in all Member States on the application of the principle of freedom of association.[81] In response to such a request, the Office usually would have drafted a questionnaire or survey and sent it to the Member States. But many worker representatives were opposed to this as they feared that the mere formulation of questions might be the basis for a restriction on the right of freedom of association, and in particular, that a question might imply that an individual worker had a right not to join a union.[82] Some employers and governments also were hostile to the idea of a questionnaire as they feared it might lead to the expanded notion of freedom of association, one more encompassing than recognized by the courts in their countries. Others, such as Ernest Mahaim and Léon Jouhaux, feared that the phrasing of certain questions about freedom of association implied possible limitations.[83] Jouhaux was adamant that freedom of association must be viewed in light of what it meant in the Treaty. He flatly stated that 'the question of individual liberty has nothing to do with this' and asserted that it was 'now intended indirectly to deny rights which have been admitted and to deny the principles on which the whole Organisation is founded' and declared that the Workers group would 'resume the struggle' outside the ILO if the ILO failed 'to perform its essential task' to protect the 'rights and the needs of the workers to associate themselves freely for the defence of their common interests'.[84] In the face of this opposition from the tripartite constituents, no questionnaire was approved, and the idea of drafting an instrument on freedom of association was dropped,[85] not to resurface for 20 years.

---

[81] ILO, 1927, vi.

[82] The report being debated was the proposed questionnaire on freedom of association. One of the proposed amendments would have included 'provided that the right not to combine is safeguarded'. Tenth International Labour Conference, Final Record, 349. The record of the sittings on 11 and 14 June 1927 reveals the heated and polarised debate: 264–84 and 339–63. The debate was so controversial that one of the British delegates complained that he could not hear the translation (from French into English) because of the number of persons near him discussing the matter, and the chair noted that he had called for silence 'on many occasions': 283 See: www.ilo.org/public/libdoc/ilo/P/09616/09616(1927-10).pdf.

[83] One question asked about the right to engage in industrial action 'by all such means as are not contrary to the community'. Mahaim proposed deleting those words and asked 'But what is the right of combined action for trade union purposes which would not affect the interests of the community?': ibid, 274.

[84] ibid, 281.

[85] The tripartite Committee on Freedom of Association at the ILC (not the same committee as the CFA, a committee of the GB, of later years) produced its report on the draft questionnaire, which indicates the differences between the Workers' and Employers' representatives (638–55). Tenth Session, ILC, 1927, Vol I, available at: www.ilo.org/public/libdoc/ilo/P/09616/09616%281927-10%29.pdf.

C. The Preparatory Work of Convention 87 and the Circumstances of its Conclusion Confirm the Existence of a Right to Strike

It is without doubt from the early history that among the founders of the ILO, the concept of freedom of association contemplated the right to strike, as derivative of the right and/or necessary to give it effect. Early efforts to codify the right in a convention were rebuffed, not because there was any doubt on this point, but out of concern that some parties involved in negotiating such a convention might attempt to impose unwanted restrictions. Following the Second World War, and the devastation that it wrought on workers and industry, the constituents eventually negotiated such a convention. This effort was given a push from the fact that the UN, formed in 1945, was busily drafting the Universal Declaration on Human Rights, which was to cover matters including freedom of association. Both the World Federation of Trade Unions and the AFL–CIO had requested that the newly established Economic and Social Council (ECOSOC) of the United Nations take up the matter of the exercise of trade union rights.[86] ECOSOC referred the matter to the ILO in March 1947 and requested a report back by July of that year. In order that ECOSOC would not regulate in matters so core to the ILO, the ILO Governing Body decided in June 1947 to commence drafting a standard on freedom of association as quickly as possible before ECOSOC moved forward on its own.[87]

By May, the Office had drafted the preparatory paper and by June, an item on freedom of association was on the agenda of the ILC. By early July, general principles on freedom of association had been agreed, with the proposed convention to be placed on the agenda for the ILC in 1948.[88] The preparatory paper surveyed labour legislation at the time. While there was no explicit mention of the right to strike, it observed that at times trade unions 'are obliged to resort to economic pressure' followed by a discussion of the process used in various countries to deal with labour conflict.[89] The preparatory paper suggested two possible ways to guarantee freedom of association. The first envisaged a list of detailed regulations and the second the essential principles.[90] The Office preferred the latter, which was the approach adopted by the Conference committee charged with the issue – the Committee on Freedom of Association and Industrial Relations.[91]

There were only two major points of contention. One proposal, raised by the employers, was to include text providing for the right to not join a union. The other proposal was to limit the right to associate to workers only, not employers.

[86] J Bellace, 'The ILO and the Right to Strike' (2014) 153 *International Labour Review* 29, 40.
[87] ibid, 41.
[88] ibid.
[89] ibid, citing, Freedom of Association and Industrial Relations, Report VII, ILC, 30th Session, 1947, Geneva, 55.
[90] ibid, citing, Freedom of Association and Industrial Relations, Report VII, 17.
[91] ibid, 42.

Both proposals were rejected. The 1947 draft produced by the Committee essentially became the text of Convention 87, which was adopted by the ILC the following year.[92]

The right to strike is not explicitly mentioned in Convention 87. However, during the Conference discussions in 1947 and 1948, no one proposed limitations on its exercise and indeed the issue was not discussed.[93] This was not because the parties thought it not to be germane. The preparatory paper contained excerpts of the submissions from both the World Federation of Trade Unions and the American Federation of Labor (AFL) submissions to ECOSOC, both of which mentioned the right to strike. More compelling, some government representatives proposed a qualifier in the Convention that employers' and workers' associations could act but only in a lawful manner. This proposal was rejected, as it was known that the laws in some countries banned forms of industrial action that the Convention was designed to permit.[94] Indeed, the desire on the part of some governments to maintain the right to regulate such matters at the national level is largely responsible for the failure to arrive at a convention from 1927 to 1948. The Conference delegates in 1948 must have appreciated the implications of the right of trade unions to organise their activities.[95]

In light of the time pressure under which the Committee on Freedom of Association and Industrial Relations operated, its tripartite members indicated that they were united in a strong desire to agree on a text to meet the deadline of the ILC, and acknowledged that what was produced did not, in all respects, meet their notion of a perfect statement on freedom of association.[96] It appears that the tripartite members of the Committee took the pragmatic view that a right to strike was implied in the right of freedom of association but wished to avoid the quagmire of delineating the exact contours of the right to strike.

---

[92] ibid.
[93] ibid.
[94] ibid, 42–43.
[95] ibid.
[96] ibid, 43.

11

The Right to Strike is Recognised as Customary International Law[1]

In light of the foregoing, it is reasonable to conclude that the right to strike is a customary international law norm.[2] State practice reflected in most countries' constitutions, laws and decisions of national courts confirm the right to strike. It is also reflected in the negotiation and ratification of international and regional human rights instruments. State practice is also reflected in the economic arrangements, including trade agreements, that have been negotiated over the past 20 years which also recognise the right to strike. While limits on the right to strike may vary from country to country, there is an international consensus that the right exists, and that any limits must be reasonable. Indeed, the International Court of Justice (ICJ) has never required absolute uniformity in practice to establish a custom and has permitted some degree of variation. As the ICJ ruled in *Military and Paramilitary Activities in and Against Nicaragua*:

> The Court does not consider that, for a rule to be established as customary, the corresponding practice must be in absolutely rigorous conformity with the rule. In order to deduce the existence of customary rules, the Court deems it sufficient that the conduct of States should, in general, be consistent with such rules.[3]

It is also clear that States respect this right out of a sense of legal obligation, not merely a moral one.

---

[1] Customary international law refers to international legal obligations binding on all states which arise from (1) established state practice and (2) *opinio juris* – meaning that states view the custom as obligatory, not as a mere courtesy or moral obligation. See *Military and Paramilitary Activities in and Against Nicaragua* (*Nicaragua v United States of America*) ICJ Rep 1986, 87–88, paras 183–87. See also 'Continental Shelf' (*Libyan Arab Jarnahiriyu v Malta*) ICJ Rep 1985, 29–30, para 27.

[2] There is academic support for the argument that fundamental ILO principles have become part of customary international law. See, eg, CW Jenks, *The International Protection of Trade Union Freedom* (London, Stevens, 1957) 561–62; P O'Higgins, 'International Standards and British Labour Law' in R Lewis (ed), *Labour Law in Britain* (Oxford, Blackwell, 1986) 577; B Creighton, 'The ILO and Protection of Freedom of Association in the UK' in KD Ewing, CA Gearty and BA Hepple (eds), *Human Rights and Labour Law* (London, Mansell, 1994); and see ILO, *International Labour Standards*, 3rd edn (Geneva, ILO, 1990) 106. The logic adopted by the ECtHR in resting on international law standards is consistent with the common law principle of legality explained by Lord Hoffman in *R v Secretary of State for the Home Dept, ex p Simms* [2000] 2 AC 115, 131; followed by Gleeson CJ in *Electrolux etc v Australian Workers Union* [2004] 221 CLR 309, 329.

[3] *Military and Paramilitary Activities (Nicaragua/United States of America)* Merits, Judgment, ICJ Rep 1986, 14.

I. The United Nations

No lesser authority than the United Nations (UN) specifically held that the right to strike has become customary international law. In his report to the Seventy-first Session of the UN General Assembly in 2016, the UN Special Rapporteur on the rights to freedom of peaceful assembly and of association, Maina Kiai, explained:

> The right to strike has been established in international law for decades, in global and regional instruments, and is also enshrined in the constitutions of at least 90 countries. The right to strike has, in fact, become customary international law.[4]

In March 2018, in response to questions in a press briefing concerning a strike by UN employees following announced pay cuts, Farhan Haq, Deputy Spokesman for the UN Secretary-General, reiterated the view of the UN that the right to strike is customary international law:

> Question: I guess I just … I'm now looking more closely at the letter. It says, 'It is frankly astonishing to see the UN so clearly undermine the fundamental rights which the labour movement fought for a century to achieve. With this in mind, we implore you to publicly affirm the right of UN workers to take part in industrial action'. Does the Secretary-General believe that UN staff have a right to take part in industrial action?
>
> Deputy Spokesman: We believe that the right to strike is part of customary international law.[5]

In addition to these recent affirmations is the near universal ratifications of the UN human rights covenants giving binding effect to the Universal Declaration of Human Rights. Both of these covenants, as discussed previously, have been interpreted by the relevant treaty bodies to include a right to strike.

II. The ILO

Similarly, ILO Convention 87 is nearly universally ratified, and the right to freedom of association, by means of the 1998 Declaration on Fundamental Principles and Rights at Work, applies to all Member States regardless of ratification. One need only recall the Fact-Finding Conciliation Commission on Freedom of Association conclusions in the Chile case, discussed previously, where it noted that that there are 'a certain number of general rules which have been established for the common good of the peoples of the twentieth century. Among these principles, freedom of

---

[4] UN General Assembly, 'Report of the Special Rapporteur on the Rights to Freedom of Peaceful Assembly and of Association', A/71/385, 14 September 2016, para 56, available at: www.undocs.org/A/71/385.

[5] Daily Press Briefing by the Office of the Spokesperson for the Secretary-General, 16 March 2018, available at: www.un.org/press/en/2018/db180316.doc.htm.

association has become a customary rule above the Conventions'.[6] The unanimity and consistency in the supervisory system on the question of the right to strike for nearly 70 years is further evidence. The recent and opportunistic rejection by one constituent of a well-settled right does not make it any less so.

III. National Constitutions

In the 2012 *General Survey*, the ILO found that:

> Although the exercise of the right to strike is in most countries fairly commonly subject to certain conditions or restrictions, the principle of this right as a means of action of workers' organizations is almost universally accepted. In a very large number of countries, the right to strike is now explicitly recognized, including at the constitutional level.[7]

The ILO cited 89 countries from all regions of the world (Asia, Africa, the Americas, Europe and the Middle East) whose constitutions incorporate the right to strike. A complete list of States, now 97, with the relevant text of the Constitution, is attached as Annex III.

IV. Legislation

In practically every country in the world, with or without a constitutional provision, the right to strike is nevertheless recognised in legislation. Space considerations preclude recounting them all here. Two examples at polar opposites in political and economic terms are perhaps sufficient:

- In the United States, section 13 of the National Labor Relations Act states, 'Nothing in this Act, except as specifically provided for herein, shall be construed so as either to interfere with or impede or diminish in any way the right to strike or to affect the limitations or qualifications on that right'.[8]

---

[6] ILO, *Report of The Fact-Finding and Conciliation Commission on Freedom of Association Concerning the Trade Union Situation in Chile*, GB 196/4/9, 196th session (May 1975).

[7] International Labour Conference, 101st Session, 2012 (*General Survey* 2012) 50, para 123.

[8] National Labor Relations Act of 1935 § 13, 29 USC § 163 (2006). In *National Labor Relations Board v Washington Aluminum Co* 370 US 9 (1962), a landmark decision upholding a National Labor Relations Board order to reinstate workers dismissed by their employer when they struck against intolerable conditions, the US Supreme Court held: '[S]uch conduct is protected under the provision of § 7 of the National Labor Relations Act, which guarantees that "Employees shall have the right … to engage in … concerted activities for the purpose of collective bargaining or other mutual aid or protection" … the discharge of these workers by the company amounted to an unfair labor practice under §8(a)(1) of the Act, which forbids employers "to interfere with, restrain, or coerce employees in the exercise of the rights guaranteed in section 7"'.

- In Vietnam, Article 5 of the Labour Code adopted in 2012 states, 'The employees are entitled to ... be on strike'. Article 209 states, 'The strike is the temporary, voluntary and organizational stopping of work of the labour collective in order to meet the requirements in the process of settlement of labour disputes'.[9]

Both countries' laws and regulations set out various procedural requirements for engaging in strikes such as a time frame for bargaining, mandatory use of mediation, advance notice of strikes, maintaining minimum services and so on. To a greater or lesser degree, such requirements are common to the laws of all countries, but always rest on the foundational premise that workers have a right to strike.

V. Judicial Opinion

Judicial opinion in support of the right to strike based on Convention 87 has been cited throughout this book and is not repeated here. We would note that the ILO's *Compendium of Court Decisions* cites to numerous other examples of tribunals invoking Conventions 87 and 98 to give effect to their own laws.[10] Examples from a diversity of geography and legal tradition include:

- In 1995, Russia's Constitutional Court found that a law prohibiting strikes in the civil aviation sector was unconstitutional. The Court acknowledged that 'proceeding from the regulations of the International Covenant on Economic, Social and Cultural Rights, the prohibition of the right to strike is admissible with regard to persons who are the complement of the armed forces, police and administration of the state ... In addition, the international legal acts on human rights ascribe the regulation of the right to strike to the sphere of internal legislation. But this legislation must not go beyond restrictions permitted by these acts'. The Constitutional High Court concluded that any restriction of the flight personnel's right to strike was illegal.[11]

- In 2006, a Burkina Faso appeals court found that private sector workers who went on strike in support of a general labour protest movement were unlawfully dismissed and ordered their reinstatement. The court considered that the strike, which was a general strike based on professional and economic interests aiming to find solutions to issues of social policy, was legitimate and lawful in accordance with the statements of the Committee on Freedom of Association of the Governing Body of the ILO as expressed in its *Digest of Decisions*.

---

[9] Labour Code of Vietnam, Law No 10/2012/QH13 (2012).

[10] See: www.compendium.itcilo.org/en/decisions-by-subject.

[11] Constitutional Court of the Russian Federation, On the case concerning the verification of constitutionality of Article 12 of the Law of the USSR of 9 October 1989 'On the Order of Settlement of Collective Labour Disputes (Conflicts)', 17 May 1995.

Interpreting the provisions of national law relating to strikes in the light of ILO Convention 87 and the *Digest of Decisions*, the Appeal Court ruled that the strike was legitimate and legal and declared that each of the appellants had been wrongfully dismissed.[12]

- In 2006, the Fiji Arbitration Tribunal, in *Fiji Electricity & Allied Workers Union v Fiji Electricity Authority*, found that a constitutional provision guaranteeing the right to freedom of association and collective bargaining must also include a qualified right to strike, relying on the ILO Committee of Experts.[13]

- In a 2008 decision, Colombia's Constitutional Court upheld restrictions on strikes of a political nature, but in so doing reaffirmed the right to strike. The Court said 'In light of the pronouncements of the ILO Commission of Experts and the ILO Committee on Freedom of Association, the Court concluded that the articles subject of the proceedings, when interpreted in strict terms, do not violate the text of the Constitution. Thus, the Court decided to declare the provisions constitutional, although it placed conditions on their interpretation, with the understanding that the purposes of strike action (economic and professional) do not exclude strike action taken to express positions related to social, economic or sectorial policy that directly affect the exercise of the relevant activity, occupation, trade or profession'.[14]

- In 2012, Botswana's High Court recognised the right to strike finding that the government's list of 'essential services' in which strike were prohibited violated the Constitution. The Court said, 'it is incumbent upon this court … to interpret the said section in a manner that is consistent with international law' and it noted that '[t]he right to freedom of association in international law includes the right to strike'. Moreover, 'international law does not accept the prohibition of strike action to safeguard economic interests as a limitation that is reasonably justifiable in a democratic society', which was the alleged justification for most of the added categories of essential services, and 'the ILO Committee of Experts … seems to accept that it is reasonably justifiable in a democratic society to restrict the right to strike only to the extent that meets its definition of 'essential services'.[15]

Many other high national courts have also recognised the right without necessarily invoking ILO conventions. In Spain, the Constitutional Court affirmed the right to strike in a landmark 1981 decision, finding that the strike is,

---

[12] Bobo – Dioulasso Appeal Court, Social Chamber, *Messrs Karama and Bakouan v Société Industrielle du Faso* (SIFA), 5 July 2006, No 035.

[13] *Fiji Electricity & Allied Workers Union v Fiji Electricity Authority* 9 May 2006, [2006] FJAT 62; FJAT Award 24 of 2006.

[14] Constitutional Court, 3 September 2008, Decision No C-858/08.

[15] High Court of Lobatse, Botswana Public Employees' Union and others v Minister of Labour and Home Affairs and others, MAHLB-000674-11, 9 August 2012.

an instrument of pressure that secular experience has shown to be necessary for the affirmation of workers' interests in socio-economic conflicts, conflicts that the social State cannot exclude, but which it can and must provide with adequate institutional channels; this is also the case with the right recognized to trade unions in art 7 of the Constitution, since a trade union without the right to strike would be, in a democratic society, practically devoid of content; and it is, in short, with the promotion of the conditions so that the freedom and equality of individuals and social groups are real and effective (art 9.2 of the Constitution). No constitutional right, however, is an unlimited right. Like everyone else, the right to strike must have its own, which derive, as stated above, not only from its possible connection with other constitutional rights, but also with other constitutionally protected goods. The legislator may introduce limitations or conditions for the exercise of the right, provided that this does not exceed its essential content.[16]

The Federal Supreme Court of Brazil similarly declared in a 2007 decision:

Strikes, in fact, are the most effective weapon available to workers to achieve better living conditions. Its self-applicability is unquestionable; it is a fundamental right of an instrumental nature. The Constitution, available to workers in general, does not provide for any limitation of the right to strike: it is up to them to decide on the opportunity to exercise it and on the interests that they should defend through it. For this reason, the law cannot restrict it, but protect it, and all types of strike are constitutionally admissible.[17]

In a 2012 decision involving non-union workers who had been dismissed for joining a strike without identifying themselves individually with 48 hours' advance notice, South Africa's Constitutional Court ruled:

[W]e should not restrict the right to strike more than is expressly required by the language of the provision [requiring advance notice], unless the purposes of the Act and the section on 'a proper interpretation of the statute ... imports them'. The relevance of a restrictive approach is to raise a cautionary flag against restricting the right more than is expressly provided for. Intrusion into the right should only be as much as is necessary to achieve the purpose of the provision and this requires sensitivity to the constraints of the language used ... to hold otherwise would place a greater restriction on the right to strike of non-unionised employees and minority union employees than on majority union employees.[18]

---

[16] Tribunal Constitucional de España, Sentencia 11/1981, 8 April 1981, available at: www.hj.tribunalconstitucional.es/HJ/es/Resolucion/Show/11 (authors' translation from Spanish).

[17] Supremo Tribunal Federal, MI 712/PA-PARÁ, Mandado de Injunção, Relator(a) Min Eros Grau, Julgamento 25/10/2007, Órgão Julgador: Tribunal Pleno, available at: www.stf.jus.br/portal/jurisprudencia/listarJurisprudencia.asp?s1=%28greve%2C+conquista%29&base=baseAcordaos&url=http://tinyurl.com/pf4f2rk (authors' translation from the Portuguese).

[18] *South African Transport and Allied Workers Union (SATAWU) and Others v Moloto NO and Another* (CCT128/11) [2012] ZACC 19; 2012 (6) SA 249 (CC); 2012 (11) BCLR 1177 (CC); [2012] 12 BLLR 1193 (CC); (2012) 33 ILJ 2549 (CC) (21 September 2012).

VI. Conclusion

Together, the national constitutions, laws and judicial decisions, the aforementioned UN covenants and instruments and opinions of regional human rights tribunals, as well as the voluminous jurisprudence of the ILO, lend further support to the claim of a customary norm. We do not maintain that these and other indications of international consensus on the right to strike create an absolute right under customary international law. Between an unconditional right to strike and an absolute prohibition, the international community has converged on a general principle of the right to strike within reasonable limits. These limits are precisely those which have been articulated by the ILO Committee of Experts and the Committee on Freedom of Association, which are *the* competent bodies, per their respective mandates, to set the parameters of the customary law norm on the right to strike. Recall again that Article 9 of Convention 87, concerning the police and the armed forces, is the only article of that Convention that explicitly delegates to national governments the regulation of the scope of the right to freedom of association, and by extension the right to strike.

The most recent, thorough examination of the scope of the right to strike and its permissible limits is found in the Committee of Experts' 2012 *General Survey*. As the Committee then explained:

> Over and above the armed forces and the police, the members of which may be excluded from the scope of the Convention in general, other restrictions on the right to strike may relate to: (i) certain categories of public servants; (ii) essential services in the strict sense of the term; and (iii) situations of acute national or local crisis, although only for a limited period and solely to the extent necessary to meet the requirements of the situation. In these cases, compensatory guarantees should be provided for the workers who are thus deprived of the right to strike.[19]

The Committee of Experts and the Committee on Freedom of Association have determined that national law may restrict the right to strike for public servants 'exercising authority in the name of the State'. This is a limited concept, however, and does not embrace public sector workers generally, such as teachers.[20] Similarly, the right to strike may be restricted or prohibited in essential services. This too is a limited concept and has been defined to include only those 'the interruption of which would endanger the life, personal safety or health of the whole of part of the population'. Extensive jurisprudence by the ILO supervisory system has indicated which sectors are generally speaking deemed essential services and which are not. Even here, the Committee has promoted the possibility of a strike with a negotiated minimum service as an alternative to a total prohibition of the right in essential services.[21] In both cases, those workers who are denied the right to strike

---

[19] 2012 *General Survey* (n 7 above) para 127.
[20] ibid, paras 129–30.
[21] ibid, paras 131–35.

have a right to 'compensatory guarantees' such as 'conciliation and eventually arbitration procedures which have the confidence of the parties'.[22] The Committee has also recognised that the prohibition of strikes during an emergency 'constitutes a major restriction on one of the essential means available to workers' as has thus considered such limitations justified only during an 'acute crisis' and only for a 'limited period and to the extent necessary to meet the requirements of the situation'.[23] Here, the Committee contemplates examples such as war or natural or humanitarian disasters.

Beyond these categories, the Committee of Experts has recognised some broadly permissible prerequisites (though such prerequisites are by no means required). For example, the Committee has determined that national law may require conciliation or voluntary arbitration prior to undertaking a strike, so long as these procedures 'have the sole purpose of facilitating bargaining and should not be so complex or slow that a lawful strike becomes impossible in practice or loses its effectiveness'.[24] Similarly, short cooling-off periods have been deemed permissible, but again it must be to encourage the parties to engage in final negotiations before resorting to strike action, not to create obstacles to its exercise.[25] To the extent that national law requires a vote to undertake a strike, the Committee has held that such a vote should 'ensure that account is taken only of the votes cast, and that the required quorum and majority are fixed at a reasonable level'.[26]

Again, as the Committee of Experts and Committee on Freedom of Association define the international consensus on the right to strike, any limits beyond these would not, by definition, be reasonable.

---

[22] ibid, para 141.
[23] ibid, para 140.
[24] ibid, para 144.
[25] ibid, para 145.
[26] ibid, para 147.

PART IV

Where to from Here?

12

Settling the Dispute: The International Court of Justice?

The ILO may request an advisory opinion of the International Court of Justice (ICJ) on the basis of its own Constitution and the agreement between the UN and the ILO. Article 37(1) of the ILO Constitution provides:

> Any question or dispute relating to the interpretation of this Constitution or of any subsequent Convention concluded by the Members in pursuance of the provisions of this Constitution shall be referred for decision to the International Court of Justice.

Article 9 of the Agreement between the UN and the ILO provides at subsection 2:

> The General Assembly authorises the International Labour Organisation to request advisory opinions of the International Court of Justice on legal questions arising within the scope of its activities other than questions concerning the mutual relationships of the Organisation and the United Nations or other specialised agencies.[1]

It further specifies that a request may originate with 'the Conference or by the Governing Body acting in pursuance of an authorisation by the Conference'.[2]

The dispute over the interpretation of the Constitution and Convention 87 as to the existence of the right to strike clearly meets the technical requirements for a reference to the ICJ – it concerns a question of interpretation of the Constitution or a convention, the ILO is authorised to request such an opinion, and it arises out of the scope of the ILO's activities. Thus, a referral can be made by the Governing Body to the ICJ on the basis of a simple majority vote. The Governing Body would need to settle on an exact question or questions and send them in writing to the ICJ for its Advisory Opinion.[3]

---

[1] See: Agreement between the United Nations and the International Labour Organization, 20 December 1946, available at: www.ilo.org/wcmsp5/groups/public/---dgreports/---jur/documents/genericdocument/wcms_433792.pdf.

[2] In 1949, the ILC authorised the Governing Body to request advisory opinions from the ICJ on behalf of the International Labour Conference (ILC). See ILC, Record of Proceedings, 32nd Session, Geneva, 1949, Part II, 244–45 and 394–95, available at: www.ilo.org/public/libdoc/ilo/P/09616/09616(1949-32).pdf.

[3] One ambiguity concerns the ability of the Workers' Group or Employers' Group to participate in the process once the question has been referred by the ILO to the ICJ. Under Article 66 of the ICJ Statute, only states and international organisations can participate in advisory proceedings. In the past, NGOs have presented Amicus Curiae briefs, though these are not considered as part of the official record of the case, though they are available to the justices for their review. Of course, the ILO as the organisation requesting opinion would present relevant information and could most likely send additionally the views of the three constituent bodies to the ICJ.

There is some dispute as to whether this opinion would be legally binding. Advisory opinions typically are just that, and thus do not have the force of law as would an opinion rendered under the contentious jurisdiction of the ICJ.[4] However, organisations seeking an advisory opinion may determine beforehand that such an opinion is nevertheless binding. The fact that the ILO Constitution refers to a 'decision', and that there is no further forum to appeal would lead to the conclusion that the ILO intended to treat the ICJ's Advisory Opinion as binding on it. In any case, the effect would be to put an end to this dispute since the highest possible court would have rendered an opinion.[5]

As the ILO explained in 2014:

> It should also be noted that the rationale underlying article 37 of the ILO Constitution is to recognize the referral to the International Court of Justice as the ultimate recourse in matters of interpretation disputes and to accept the Court's 'decision' as final settlement of any such dispute. It is clear, therefore, that according to the letter and the spirit of the ILO Constitution, advisory opinions obtained from the International Court of Justice enjoy extra legitimacy and authority for all members of the Organisation.[6]

As mentioned previously, the initiative to refer the dispute to the ICJ failed. Though not foreclosed, it is unlikely that the dispute will be referred to the ICJ. Since 2014, the Employers' Group position regarding referral has not changed. Further, with a political shift to the right in many countries around the world, especially in Europe and Latin America, where support for referral of the dispute to the ICJ was once strong, the chance of doing so any time soon would appear remote.

Should the matter come before the ICJ, in our view it would find that the right to strike is protected by the ILO Constitution and Convention 87. In previous decisions, the ICJ has established a standard of deference to the interpretation of independent international bodies which have been given a mandate to supervise the application of a treaty. For example, in the case of *Ahmadou Sadio Diallo (Republic of Guinea v Democratic Republic of the Congo)* Judgment of 30 November 2010, the ICJ articulated a clear statement concerning the degree of deference it affords such supervisory bodies. In referring to the interpretive case law of the Human Rights Committee with regard to the International Covenant on Civil and Political Rights, the Court held:

> Although the Court is in no way obliged, in the exercise of its judicial functions, to model its own interpretation of the Covenant on that of the Committee, it believes that it should ascribe *great weight* to the interpretation adopted by this independent body

---

[4] See ICJ Statute Articles 59 and 63 (explicitly providing that decisions in contentious cases are binding on the parties and any interveners).

[5] See E Osieke, *Constitutional Law and Practice in the International Labour Organisation* (Leiden, Martinus Nijhoff Publishers 1985) 203.

[6] ILO, 'The standards initiative: Follow-up to the 2012 ILC Committee on the Application of Standards, GB.322/INS/5', 16 October 2014, para 27, available at: www.ilo.org/wcmsp5/groups/public/---ed_norm/---relconf/documents/ meetingdocument/wcms_315494.pdf.

that was established specifically to supervise the application of that treaty. The point here is to achieve the necessary clarity and the essential consistency of international law, as well as legal security, to which both the individuals with guaranteed rights and the States obliged to comply with treaty obligations are entitled.[7]

The jurisprudence of the ILO supervisory system and in particular that of the Committee of Experts, would undoubtedly be afforded the *great weight* described in *Diallo*. The Committee of Experts was set up by the Governing Body, in accordance with the resolution adopted by the International Labour Conference in 1926 (and as subsequently amended), for the purpose of examining government reports on the application of ILO conventions and other obligations relating to international labour standards set out in the ILO Constitution. The Committee of Experts' task consists of pointing out the extent to which the law and practice in each State appear to be in conformity with the terms of ratified conventions and the obligations which the State has undertaken by virtue of the ILO Constitution.

Indeed:

> Its function is to determine whether the requirements of a given Convention are being met, whatever the economic and social conditions existing in a given country. In carrying out this work, the Committee is guided by the standards laid down in the Convention alone, mindful, however, of the fact that the modes of their implementation may be different in different States.[8]

As the Committee of Experts is set up to supervise the application of labour standards reflected in conventions such as ILO Convention 87, it falls into the category of independent bodies monitoring the application of an international standard, the observations, recommendations and considerations of which should, according to the ICJ, be ascribed 'great weight'. As also discussed herein, these views went fundamentally unchallenged by the ILO constituents for several decades. Since similar factors apply in relation to the creation, constitutional position and function of the Committee on Freedom of Association, its views too should be given 'great weight'.

In addition to the legal reasoning, the ICJ should also support the observations of the ILO for policy reasons. A finding contrary to the decades-long uncontested jurisprudence of the supervisory system would throw it into complete disarray and dispel any legal certainty or coherence upon which the tripartite constituents rely. The Committee of Experts in particular would emerge as a severely weakened body whose observations would be perpetually open to question. It would also

---

[7] *Ahmadou Sadio Diallo* (*Republic of Guniea v Democratic Republic of the Congo*) Judgment of 30 November 2010, 664, para 66 (emphasis added), available at: www.icj-cij.org/docket/files/103/16244. pdf#view=FitH&pagemode= none&search=%22Ahmadou%22.

[8] Report of the Committee of Experts on the Application of Conventions and Recommendations, Report III (Part 4A), ILC, 73rd Session, 1987, para 24.

serve to undermine the instruments and jurisprudence of other intergovernmental institutions as well as regional and national courts that have relied on the ILO for guidance. Further, an opinion in the negative would up-end industrial relations worldwide, opening a door for governments to (further) restrict or limit the right to strike – as the matter would be perceived to be one for national law only. Employers would have an enormous and unforeseen advantage over labour, as collective bargaining would become a dead letter.

13

The Aftermath

The 2012 conflict set off a series of formal and informal bipartite and tripartite meetings as well as debate in the Governing Body on the question of the mandate of the Committee of Experts and the right to strike. We do not here attempt to recount this process. However, despite the considerable research and debate put into the matter, the positions of the social partners remained unchanged. The Employers' Group still refuses to recognise the existence of a right to strike protected by Convention 87, though as explained previously they assented to an agreement with the International Trade Union Confederation (ITUC) which supported the notion of 'industrial action'. The Employers' Group also remains critical of the Committee of Experts' methods and have rejected well-settled interpretations on numerous other issues. While the supervisory system as a whole, including the Committee of Experts and the Committee on Freedom of Association (CFA), continue to assert the existence of the right to strike and the legitimacy of its methods in so doing, the impact on the supervisory system is noticeable and has created a 'new normal' for the organisation.[1] This was no doubt the intended consequence of the 2012 challenge.

I. Impact on ILO Supervisory System

A. Committee of Experts

With regard to the Committee of Experts, the ILO made a concession to the Employers' Group by restating what had been a well-settled understanding of its mandate. In the 2012 *Annual Report*, the Committee of Experts described its mandate in the Reader's Note as:

> The task of the Committee of Experts is to indicate the extent to which each member State's legislation and practice are in conformity with ratified Conventions and the extent to which member States have fulfilled their obligations under the ILO Constitution in relation to standards. In carrying out this task, the Committee adheres to its principles

---

[1] Closing Speech of Guy Ryder, Secretary-General, ILO, Provisional Record No 18, Closing Statements, ILC, 106th Session, Geneva, 11 July 2017, 29 ('That takes me on to the Committee on the Application of Standards. Entering into the spirit of that Committee, I am going to take the risk of describing it as "a case of progress". Once again, the Committee's work was completed successfully, and I now dare to believe that this is, as it should be, the "new normal" for this key Conference activity').

of independence, objectivity and impartiality. The comments of the Committee of Experts on the fulfilment by member States of their standards-related obligations take the form of either observations or direct requests. Observations contain comments on fundamental questions raised by the application of a particular Convention by a member State. These observations are reproduced in the annual report of the Committee of Experts, which is then submitted to the Conference Committee on the Application of Standards in June every year. Direct requests usually relate to questions of a more technical nature or of lesser importance. They are not published in the report of the Committee of Experts but are communicated directly to the government concerned. In addition, the Committee of Experts examines, in the context of the General Survey, the state of the legislation and practice concerning a specific area covered by a given number of Conventions and Recommendations chosen by the Governing Body. The General Survey is based on the reports submitted in accordance with articles 19 and 22 of the Constitution, and it covers all member States regardless of whether or not they have ratified the concerned Conventions.

The introduction of the 2013 *Annual Report* contained an extensive summary of the history of the mandate of the Committee of Experts and the existence of the right to strike as well as a summary of the arguments of both the Employers' and Workers' Groups on these points.[2] While the Committee of Experts acknowledged the complaints raised by the Employers' Group, it nevertheless reasserted the existence of the right to strike[3] and pointed out, as noted earlier, that the Employers' Group had previously expressed repeated support for the Committee's mandate and indeed the need for it to engage in some degree of interpretation.[4] The Committee explained again its mandate:

28. The Committee further stressed that its mandate derived from three main principles. First, assessment and evaluation of textual meaning was logically integral to the application of ratified Conventions. In this regard, the Committee noted that it needed to bring to the Conference Committee's attention: (i) any national laws or practices not in conformity with the Conventions, which inevitably required the evaluation and thus, a certain degree of interpretation, of the national legislation and the text of the Convention; and (ii) in conformity with its working methods, the cases of progress in the application of standards, which also required a degree of interpretation. Second, the equal treatment and uniformity of the application of Conventions assured predictability. The Committee highlighted in this regard that its approach to examining the meaning of Conventions also prioritized achieving equal treatment for States and uniformity in practical application. This emphasis was essential to maintaining principles of legality, which encouraged governments to accept its views on the application of a Convention and, in this manner, promoted a level of certainty needed for the proper functioning of the ILO system. Third, the Committee stressed that its composition, ie, independent persons with distinguished backgrounds in the law and direct

---

[2] ILO, Report of the Committee of Experts on the Application of Conventions and Recommendations, Application of International Labour Standards 2013, Report III (Part 1A), International Labour Conference, 102nd Session, 2013 (*Annual Report* 2013) paras 14–36.
[3] ibid, para 31.
[4] ibid, paras 27, 34.

experience of the different national legal systems to which Conventions were applied, helped to ensure a broad acceptance within the ILO community of its views on the meaning of Conventions.[5]

The Committee specifically rejected the idea of including a disclaimer or caveat, as proposed by the Employers' Group, which would have indicated that 'Committee interpretations are not authoritative and hence not legally binding for ratifying countries', arguing that the non-binding nature of the observations was never in question and that such a caveat 'would interfere in important respects with [the Committee's] independence'.[6]

However, in 2014, in addition to the Reader's Note, the following paragraph was added in the Introduction by the Committee of Experts (bold in original):

31. The Committee of Experts on the Application of Conventions and Recommendations is an independent body established by the International Labour Conference and its members are appointed by the ILO Governing Body. It is composed of legal experts charged with examining the application of ILO Conventions and Recommendations by ILO member States. The Committee of Experts undertakes an impartial and technical analysis of how the Conventions are applied in law and practice by member States, while cognizant of different national realities and legal systems. In doing so, it must determine the legal scope, content and meaning of the provisions of the Conventions. Its opinions and recommendations are non-binding, being intended to guide the actions of national authorities. They derive their persuasive value from the legitimacy and rationality of the Committee's work based on its impartiality, experience and expertise. The Committee's technical role and moral authority is well recognized, particularly as it has been engaged in its supervisory task for over 85 years, by virtue of its composition, independence and its working methods built on continuing dialogue with governments taking into account information provided by employers' and workers' organizations. This has been reflected in the incorporation of the Committee's opinions and recommendations in national legislation, international instruments and court decisions.[7]

The new statement of the mandate contains subtle differences from previous versions. For example, whereas the central task of the Committee was described to be 'to indicate the extent to which each member State's legislation and practice are in conformity with ratified Conventions' the new text states that the task is to undertake an 'analysis of how the Convention is applied in law and practice ... while cognizant of different national realities and legal systems'. The latter de-emphasises the affirmative act of judgement being made by the Committee as to whether a State has complied with a convention and instead shifts towards an analysis of how the convention is given effect at the national level and emphasised a certain margin of appreciation that States have in applying the convention.

---

[5] ibid, para 28.

[6] ibid, para 36.

[7] ILO, Report of the Committee of Experts on the Application of Conventions and Recommendations, Application of International Labour Standards 2014, Report III (Part 1A), International Labour Conference, 103rd Session, 2014, para 31.

While the difference may appear minor, it appears to be a meaningful shift. Importantly, the text also stresses the non-binding nature of the Committee's observations, and that such observations are not meant to be taken as a statement of the scope of the convention and therefore indication as to how to comply with it but rather merely 'guidance' for national authorities. While not a disclaimer per se, the text, bolded in the Introduction, is certainly a step towards one. This statement appears in all subsequent reports.

In addition to the reformulation of the mandate, the Workers' Group pointed out (rightly in our view) changes to the Committee's practice which were to the detriment of the supervisory system. One reaction of the ILO to the Employers' challenge was to set up a committee to streamline ILO reports. Between 2013 and 2014, the *Annual Report* shed nearly a third of its length (appoximately 300 pages) and lost nearly another 75 pages the following year. Some of the streamlining was accomplished by preparing shorter, more circumspect observations, while some was done by shifting away from observations to direct requests. Direct requests are typically used by the Committee of Experts to seek further additional information from Member States when necessary before making an observation. Direct requests, which are not published in the *Annual Report*, do not generally serve as the basis for discussion in the Committee on the Application of Standards (CAS).

In his opening comments to the CAS in 2014, the Workers' Spokesperson explained:

> Regarding the report of the Committee of Experts, it was regrettable to note that the Committee seemed to be limiting itself in its dialogue with governments. There had been an increase in the number of direct requests, which were far less visible and accessible than the observations. In the case of certain Conventions, the observations were very short. Any attempt to reduce the volume of the report of the Committee of Experts should not be made at the expense of the substance of its comments. This cut in the length of comments contradicted what the experts considered to be the core of their mandate, i.e. their supervisory and advisory functions. Similarly, deferring certain cases to the following report cycle would be liable to undermine the implementation of instruments and create a sense of impunity among governments. The considerable number of comments that received no reply from the governments would only continue to increase if the experts continued on this path of self-censorship.[8]

The following year, the Workers' Spokesperson also indicated that the report of the Committee of Experts had failed to consider the numerous observations submitted by the ITUC and other unions, or that their observations had been so shortened in the report as to be unusable.[9]

---

[8] ILO, Provisional Record No 13, Part 1, Report of the Committee on the Application of Standards, 103rd Session, 2014, para 67, available at: www.ilo.org/wcmsp5/groups/public/---ed_norm/---relconf/ documents/ meetingdocument/wcms_246781.pdf.

[9] ILO, Provisional Record No 14Rev, Part 1, Report of the Committee on the Application of Standards, 104th Session, 2015, para 43, available at: www.ilo.org/wcmsp5/groups/public/---ed_norm/---relconf/ documents/meeting document/wcms_375763.pdf.

B. Committee on the Application of Standards

As noted above, the shortening of the *Annual Report* and the shift to direct requests meant that the compliance of States with regard to certain conventions could not be reviewed adequately or at all. While robust debate on the right to strike continues in the CAS, there have been no conclusions which directly refer to the right to strike since 2012, meaning that the matter has been removed as a subject for direction or follow-up.[10] As mentioned previously, in 2013, the constituents were only able to agree to conclusions when the Workers' Group agreed to the Employers' Group demand for a disclaimer to be included in the record for each case concerning Convention 87 and where the right to strike was included in the Committee of Experts' observations. In 2014, when the Workers' Group refused to agree again to the disclaimer, the process again collapsed without conclusions in all but six cases. It was only after the 2015 'ceasefire' agreement that the CAS has been able to reach conclusions; however, the agreement is based on the obligation to adopt conclusions on matters for which there is consensus, which explains the absence of the right to strike in the CAS conclusions.

Further, with the Employers' Group no longer taking the Committee of Experts' observations as the accepted interpretation of the conventions, and thus the accepted evaluation of compliance with those conventions, the Employers' Group has challenged the interpretation of other well-settled precedents. Indeed, in 2013, the year after rejecting the existence of a right to strike, the Employers' Group rejected the settled principle that parties to collective bargaining have an obligation under the relevant conventions to bargain in 'good faith':

> With reference to good faith, representativeness and the recognition of organizations, the Employer members, while agreeing that good faith by the parties to collective negotiation was important in achieving a meaningful outcome, did not accept that there was an obligation to bargain in good faith which implicitly presupposed an obligation to bargain.[11]

This statement was seen as a particularly ominous sign by members of the Workers' Group. The idea that there is no obligation to engage in social dialogue (in this case in the form of collective bargaining) would threaten the modus operandi of the ILO.

---

[10] The right to strike is referred to indirectly in some recent CAS conclusions, though framed in the context of, eg, 'peaceful trade union activities'. In 2016, the CAS conclusions on Indonesia urged the government to 'ensure that workers are able to engage freely in peaceful actions in law and practice without sanctions'. That same year, the CAS conclusions urged the government of Swaziland to 'continue to conduct investigations into interference and intimidation of trade unionists during legitimate and peaceful trade union activities and hold those responsible for violations accountable'. The summary of the tripartite discussions in these cases make clear that the 'activities' referred to are strikes.

[11] ILO, Provisional Record No 16Rev, Part 1, Report of the Committee on the Application of Standards, 102nd Session, 2013, para 122, available at: www.ilo.org/wcmsp5/groups/public/---ed_norm/---relconf/documents/ meetingdocument/wcms_216379.pdf.

C. Committee on Freedom of Association

Given the attack on the right to strike in the CAS, it was only a matter of time before the CFA also fell victim. For example, the publication of the *Digest of Decisions and Principles of the Freedom of Association Committee of the Governing Body of the ILO* was delayed for nearly two years. Every decade, the *Digest of Decisions* is published which highlights the key conclusions of the CFA, including those from the previous 10-year period. The last *Digest* had been published in 2006 and a new *Digest* was due in 2016. However, the Employers' Group opposed the inclusion in the *Digest* of section 10, which has included the findings of the CFA with regard to the right to strike. The Employers' Group's intransigence blocked the publication of the *Digest of Decisions*, now called the *Compilation of Decisions of the Committee on Freedom of Association* (at the Employers' Group's insistence), until mid-2018. The *Compilation of Decisions* does include the conclusions on the right to strike in almost identical terms to the 2006 edition of the *Digest*, but with further additions drawing on recent findings.

The Employers' Group has attempted to argue that the new title marks an agreed shift in the jurisprudential value of the text, in particular the removal of the word 'principles' from the original title. In their view, the text becomes no more than a report on cases from which no generalisable principles may be identified. This is a considerable reach given the consistency of the views of the CFA over time, and that the change to the title of the document was made under duress, as it was the only way for the Employers' Group to lift their hold on its publication.

II. The Impact Outside the ILO

The consequences of this dispute did not remain within Geneva. Indeed, it took a deadly turn in Cambodia.[12] On 2–3 January 2014, the government of Cambodia mobilised the police and armed forces to quash strikes and demonstrations which erupted among garment workers after the government announced a new minimum wage rate far below what even government-supported research had indicated was an adequate wage. Several workers were shot and killed, and 25 workers were jailed in inhumane conditions for six months. The workers were tried in a legal process rife with serious procedural irregularities and sentenced to between four and five years' imprisonment. However, due to international pressure, the sentences were suspended and all the workers were freed.[13]

---

[12] See J Bellace, 'Back to the Future: Freedom of Association, the Right to Strike and National Law' (2016) 27 *King's Law Journal* 24.

[13] See Media Statement, OHCHR-ILO joint statement on the release of the 25 persons arrested in November 2013 and in January 2014, 30 May 30 2104 (stating '[we] are concerned about the criminal conviction of all 25 individuals, in view of the apparent procedural shortcomings in all three trials and the lack of evidence establishing direct responsibility of the individuals for the actions of which

The Cambodian Federation of Employers and Business Associations (CAMFEBA) and the Garment Manufacturers Association of Cambodia, which had been actively supporting the Employers' Group's position at the ILO on the right to strike, responded to the desperate protest of the garment workers by running a full-page advertisement in the local media denying the existence of the right to strike:

> The right to strike is not provided for in … [the ILO' s Convention 87 on Freedom of Association] and was not intended to be … Is the right to strike therefore a fundamental right? NO. The right to strike is NOT a fundamental right.[14]

The ILO responded stating:

> The claims that the right to strike is not a fundamental right and that C 87 does not establish a right to strike are not consistent with the position taken by the International Labour Organization and its tripartite constituency as a whole (ie governments, employers and workers) over a period of at least the last 60 + years.[15]

CAMFEBA demanded that the ILO retract its factually correct statement, arguing that there was no consensus on the existence of a right to strike.

While the Employers' Group's arguments have been rejected by most tribunals, they did find an audience in the Kingdom of Swaziland (now eSwatini), a country well known for egregious labour rights violations[16] – so much so that the country's trade benefits were suspended in January 2015 due to repression of workers' freedom of association.[17] On 31 October 2017, the Industrial Court of Appeal of Swaziland, in *NEDBANK Swaziland v Swaziland Union of Financial Institutions and Allied Workers*, overturned the court of first instance and decided that the Industrial Relations Act (IRA) permitted the use of replacement workers during a strike – a reversal of prior interpretation of the IRA (which was silent on the question). In its legally dubious holding, the Court of Appeal found that the respondent had not introduced facts showing that the use of replacement workers infringed on the right to strike, though the purpose of using striker replacements has no other purpose.[18] The Union argued that the Constitution and IRA had to be read

---

they were nevertheless found guilty. Furthermore, in a number of cases, the evidence indicates that individuals were arrested when simply exercising their fundamental rights to freedom of expression and peaceful assembly, while defending workers' socio-economic interests'). See: www.ilo.org/wcmsp5/groups/public/---asia/---ro-bangkok/---sro-bangkok/documents/pressrelease/wcms_245233.pdf.

[14] See Shane Worrell, 'Groups Tell ILO to Retract 'Right to Strike' Claim' *The Phnom Phenh Post* (6 February 2014), available at: www.phnompenhpost.com/national/groups-tell-ilo-retract-%E2%80%98right-strike%E2%80 %99-claim.

[15] ibid.

[16] See ITUC, Global Rights Index 2018, available at: www.ituc-csi.org/IMG/pdf/ituc-global-rights-index-2018-en-final-2.pdf.

[17] Press Release, USTR, 'President Obama removes Swaziland, reinstates Madagascar for AGOA Benefits', June 2014, available at: www.ustr.gov/about-us/policy-offices/press-office/press-releases/2014/June/President-Obama-removes-Swaziland-reinstates-Madagascar-for-AGOA-Benefits. The trade preferences were reinstated on 23 December 2017.

[18] *Nedbank Swaziland (Limited) v Swaziland Union of Financial Institutions and Allied Workers and Others* (12/2017) [SZICA 2017] 05/2017, paras 50–58.

consistently with Convention 87, which Swaziland had ratified; the Committee of Experts and the CFA have both found that the hiring of workers to replace those on strike (except in essential services where strikes may be banned) constitutes a serious violation of Convention 87.[19] The Court accepted the Bank's arguments that the right to strike is not contained within Convention 87 and thus Swaziland had no obligation to respect that right.[20] Further, it found that the ILO supervisory system created no legal jurisprudence, citing a 2015 International Organisation of Employers (IOE) paper construing the mandate of the Committee of Experts, and thus discarded these views from consideration.[21]

---

[19] See ILO Committee on Freedom of Association, *Compilation of Decisions*, paras 917–19.

[20] *NEDBANK* (n 18 above) para 61.

[21] International Organisation of Employers (IOE), Paper on International Labour Standards in the Contemporary Global Economy (2015) para 2.15, available at: www.ibanet.org/Document/Default. aspx?DocumentUid=051FADEB-8CA5-480E-8D43-A04D20890CAA.

14

Conclusion

With or without a legal right, workers have and will continue to engage in strikes when pushed too far. This is not to say, however, that regulation of the right to strike is not consequential, as indeed it is. That is why employers and governments have sought to constrain the collective power of workers through regressive labour reforms, including penal sanctions. As explained in this book, this is the very reason why employers globally have claimed that the right to strike is not protected in international law, and in particular ILO conventions, leaving national governments free to limit or abolish this right at the national level. Fortunately, they are wrong.

Nearly every State recognises the right to strike 'within reasonable limits'. Further, the ILO is the appropriate forum for articulating the scope of the right as it is the specialised UN agency and the entity charged by the international community with promoting 'recognition of the principle of freedom of association'.[1] The right to strike is unquestionably protected by ILO Convention 87, as well as within the broader international legal framework. Indeed, it can be said convincingly that the right to strike is customary international law. Employers' arguments to the contrary notwithstanding, the supervisory system of the ILO was correct in observing that the right to strike exists and acted within their constitutional mandate and in conformity with the rules of treaty interpretation in so holding. Were the matter to be considered by the International Court of Justice, it would certainly defer to the well-reasoned views of the ILO supervisory system, and in particular the Committee of Experts, and find that Convention 87 protects the right to strike.

I. The Return of the Strike

The debate at the ILO notwithstanding, the exercise of the right to strike has experienced a resurgence worldwide.[2] In the years immediately following the 2008 financial crisis, strikes erupted in Europe.[3] In debt-laden Greece, workers

---

[1] ILO Constitution, Preamble.

[2] A useful resource, the European Trade Union Institute (ETUI) maintains a strike map, including strike days per country. See: www.etui.org/Services/Strikes-Map-of-Europe/.

[3] N Bruun, K Lörcher and I Schömann (eds), *Economic and Financial Crisis and Collective Labour Law in Europe* (Oxford, Hart Publishing, 2014).

facing soaring unemployment, plummeting wages, and a social protection system in tatters had no option but to call a series of general strikes starting in 2010 in the hope that the government would reject the austerity measures imposed by the 'Troika' (the IMF, the European Central Bank and the European Commission).[4] These strikes are in fact ongoing.[5] A similar story played out in Spain in response to austerity measures imposed there. In France, proposals to change labour law were pushed through by President Macron against massive (but short) strikes. The legacy of discontent has led to the resistance by the '*gilets jaunes*'.

In the United States, the strike resurgence arrived later, in 2018.[6] According to Bureau of Labor Statistics data, there were 20 major work stoppages in 2018 involving 485,000 workers. The last time as many workers were involved in strike activity in a year was 1986. While the US economy had picked up, it continued to leave many workers far behind, including teachers in some of the country's poorest school systems, such as West Virginia, Oklahoma and Arizona.[7] Teachers in these and many other states took to the streets to protest not only against low wages, but more importantly the dilapidated facilities, the lack of updated textbooks, and high student to teacher ratios which affected not only teachers but also students.[8] At the same time, workers went on strike at Marriott hotels across the country, demanding higher wages in the face of record company profits, as well as an end to sexual violence and harassment on the job.

In New Zealand, over 30,000 nurses went on strike for the first time in 29 years in order to reverse over a decade of funding cuts and wage restraints,[9] while 29,000 teachers went on strike for the first time in 24 years over class sizes, a shortage of teachers, and low pay.[10] In Ireland, nearly 40,000 nurses and midwives went on strike over pay and staffing levels, as did hospital doctors in the United Kingdom, both with broad public support.[11] And in Poland, in one of the largest strikes in

---

[4] Helena Smith, 'Striking Greeks fight back against austerity plan' *The Guardian* (24 February 2010), available at: www.theguardian.com/world/2010/feb/24/greece-strikes-protest-euro.

[5] Patrick Strickland, 'Greece at a standstill as thousands strike against austerity' *Aljazeera* (30 May 2018), available at: www.aljazeera.com/news/2018/05/180530123446169.html.

[6] See US Department of Labor, Bureau of Labor Statistics, Work Stoppages Summary, 8 February 2019, available at: www.bls.gov/news.release/wkstp.nr0.htm.

[7] Stephen Greenhouse, 'The Return of the Strike' *American Prospect* (3 January 2019), available at: www.prospect.org/article/return-strike.

[8] ibid.

[9] Tracy Withers, 'Workers in New Zealand Strike Over Decade of Stagnant Wages' (*Bloomberg*, 31 July 2018), available at: www.bloomberg.com/news/articles/2018-07-31/workers-in-new-zealand-strike-over-decade-of-stagnating-wages; see also Ross Webb, 'The Strike Returns to New Zealand' *Jacobin Magazine* (February 2019), available at: www.jacobinmag.com/2019/02/new-zealand-strikes-unions-labour-party-austerity.

[10] Eleanor Ainge Roy, '"Crisis point": New Zealand hit by primary school teacher strike' *The Guardian* (15 August 2018), available at: www.theguardian.com/world/2018/aug/15/crisis-point-new-zealand-hit-by-primary-school-teacher-strike.

[11] '"This campaign has to succeed, it is our time": Tens of thousands march in support of nurses and midwives' *The Journal* (9 February 2019), available at: www.thejournal.ie/nurses-strike-protest-dublin-4485386-Feb2019/.

decades, tens of thousands of teachers walked out to protest against low wages and public austerity more generally.[12]

The strike resurgence is by no means a phenomenon limited to the 'Global North'. In Brazil, trade unions led a general strike on 28 April 2017, the first in two decades, in major cities across the country to protest against the Temer government's proposed austerity measures and severe labour law reforms, which subsequently caused collective bargaining coverage to plummet.[13] In India, a broad front of union confederations put an estimated 150 million workers on the street during a general strike on 8–9 January 2019 to promote a 12-point agenda, including stopping the sweeping labour law reforms proposed by President Narendra Modi.[14] Over 40,000 workers in over 48 factories in the border city of Matamoros, Mexico (successfully) went on strike for higher wages, where some workers made less than $1 an hour assembling auto components and TVs destined for the US market.[15] In Bangladesh, over 50,000 garment workers walked off the job to protest still poverty-level wages, despite a recent increase in the sectoral minimum wage.[16] In Zimbabwe, the Zimbabwe Congress of Trade Unions called a nationwide strike to pressure the government of President Emmerson Mnangagwa to rescind massive price hikes for essential goods and services after the government unilaterally imposed a 150 per cent increase in the cost of fuel.[17] And in Tunisia, 670,000 workers went on strike to demand higher pay in the face of inflation that has rapidly eroded workers' purchasing power.[18]

Importantly, transnational strikes have also brought vehemently anti-union employers, such as Ryanair, to finally recognise a union and negotiate a collective bargaining agreement. The company had for years played workers against each other from country to country. In 2018, coordinated strikes spread across the European continent, eventually forcing the carrier to capitulate.[19] The current

---

[12] Michalina Augusiak and Mikołaj Ratajczak, 'Teachers Are Striking in Poland, Too' *Jacobin Magazine* (21 April 2019), available at: www.jacobinmag.com/2019/04/poland-teachers-strike-austerity-education.

[13] Brad Brooks and Anthony Boadle, 'Brazil protesters, police clash in first general strike in decades' *Reuters* (28 April 2017), available at: www.reuters.com/article/us-brazil-politics-protests-idUSKBN17U0EX.

[14] Jamie Woodcock, 'India General Strike 2019' *Notes From Below* (10 January 2019), available at: www.notesfrombelow.org/article/india-general-strike-2019.

[15] Mark Stevenson, 'Mexican president unleashes labor unrest at border plants' *AP* (1 February 2019), available at: www.apnews.com/01e56287cf2b4e3d981544cddf62bad8.

[16] AFP, 'Bangladesh strikes: thousands of garment workers clash with police over poor pay' *The Guardian* (14 January 2019), available at: www.theguardian.com/world/2019/jan/14/bangladesh-strikes-thousands-of-garment-workers-clash-with-police-over-poor-pay.

[17] Godfrey Marawanyika, 'Zimbabweans Strike for Third Day as Crackdown Is Criticized' (*Bloomberg*, 17 January 2019), available at: www.bloomberg.com/news/articles/2019-01-16/zimbabwe-strike-enters-third-day-as-excessive-force-criticized.

[18] Tula Connell, '670,000 Public-Sector Workers Strike in Tunisia' (*Solidarity Center*, 17 January 2019), available at: www.solidaritycenter.org/670000-public-sector-workers-strike-in-tunisia/.

[19] Amie Tsang, 'Ryanair, Long Opposed to Unions, Grapples With Strikes in Europe' *New York Times* (25 July 2018), available at: www.nytimes.com/2018/07/25/business/ryanair-strike-cabin-crew.html.

wave of strikes has also not been confined to the traditionally well-organised industries. Strikes in fast food outlets like McDonald's, by Uber, Deliveroo and other platform workers, and by outsourced cleaners and security guards and others (outsourced workers now form a significant proportion of the workforce), have sprung up and continue in many countries. Such industrial action has brought new members into those unions which are structured to be active and responsive to such demands, some of them very recently formed.

Strikes have led to improvements not only in wages and working conditions but have shifted the balance of power in the workplace and society. So long as relations of oppression continue, working people will collectively withhold their labour. The actions of workers during 2018–19 are the clearest evidence of the fundamental importance of the right to strike.

Annexes

Annex I: ILO Convention 87 (Excerpted)

C087 – Freedom of Association and Protection of the Right to Organise Convention, 1948 (No 87)

Preamble

The General Conference of the International Labour Organisation,

Having been convened at San Francisco by the Governing Body of the International Labour Office, and having met in its Thirty-first Session on 17 June 1948;

Having decided to adopt, in the form of a Convention, certain proposals concerning freedom of association and protection of the right to organise, which is the seventh item on the agenda of the session;

Considering that the Preamble to the Constitution of the International Labour Organisation declares 'recognition of the principle of freedom of association' to be a means of improving conditions of labour and of establishing peace;

Considering that the Declaration of Philadelphia reaffirms that 'freedom of expression and of association are essential to sustained progress';

Considering that the International Labour Conference, at its Thirtieth Session, unanimously adopted the principles which should form the basis for international regulation;

Considering that the General Assembly of the United Nations, at its Second Session, endorsed these principles and requested the International Labour Organisation to continue every effort in order that it may be possible to adopt one or several international Conventions;

adopts this ninth day of July of the year one thousand nine hundred and forty-eight the following Convention, which may be cited as the Freedom of Association and Protection of the Right to Organise Convention, 1948:

Part I. Freedom of Association

Article 1

Each Member of the International Labour Organisation for which this Convention is in force undertakes to give effect to the following provisions.

Article 2

Workers and employers, without distinction whatsoever, shall have the right to establish and, subject only to the rules of the organisation concerned, to join organisations of their own choosing without previous authorisation.

Article 3

1.   Workers' and employers' organisations shall have the right to draw up their constitutions and rules, to elect their representatives in full freedom, to organise their administration and activities and to formulate their programmes.
2.   The public authorities shall refrain from any interference which would restrict this right or impede the lawful exercise thereof.

Article 4

Workers' and employers' organisations shall not be liable to be dissolved or suspended by administrative authority.

Article 5

Workers' and employers' organisations shall have the right to establish and join federations and confederations and any such organisation, federation or confederation shall have the right to affiliate with international organisations of workers and employers.

Article 6

The provisions of Articles 2, 3 and 4 hereof apply to federations and confederations of workers' and employers' organisations.

Article 7

The acquisition of legal personality by workers' and employers' organisations, federations and confederations shall not be made subject to conditions of such a character as to restrict the application of the provisions of Articles 2, 3 and 4 hereof.

Article 8

1.   In exercising the rights provided for in this Convention workers and employers and their respective organisations, like other persons or organised collectivities, shall respect the law of the land.
2.   The law of the land shall not be such as to impair, nor shall it be so applied as to impair, the guarantees provided for in this Convention.

Article 9

1.   The extent to which the guarantees provided for in this Convention shall apply to the armed forces and the police shall be determined by national laws or regulations.

2. In accordance with the principle set forth in paragraph 8 of Article 19 of the Constitution of the International Labour Organisation the ratification of this Convention by any Member shall not be deemed to affect any existing law, award, custom or agreement in virtue of which members of the armed forces or the police enjoy any right guaranteed by this Convention.

Article 10

In this Convention the term *organisation* means any organisation of workers or of employers for furthering and defending the interests of workers or of employers.

Part II. Protection of the Right to Organise

Article 11

Each Member of the International Labour Organisation for which this Convention is in force undertakes to take all necessary and appropriate measures to ensure that workers and employers may exercise freely the right to organise.

Annex II: Vienna Convention on the Law of Treaties (VCLT) – Relevant Sections

Article 4: Non-retroactivity of the present Convention

Without prejudice to the application of any rules set forth in the present Convention to which treaties would be subject under international law independently of the Convention, the Convention applies only to treaties which are concluded by States after the entry into force of the present Convention with regard to such States.

Article 5: Treaties constituting international organizations and treaties adopted within an international organization

The present Convention applies to any treaty which is the constituent instrument of an international organization and to any treaty adopted within an international organization without prejudice to any relevant rules of the organization.

Article 31: General rule of interpretation

1. A treaty shall be interpreted in good faith in accordance with the ordinary meaning to be given to the terms of the treaty in their context and in the light of its object and purpose.

2.   The context for the purpose of the interpretation of a treaty shall comprise, in addition to the text, including its preamble and annexes:

    (a) any agreement relating to the treaty which was made between all the parties in connection with the conclusion of the treaty;

    (b) any instrument which was made by one or more parties in connection with the conclusion of the treaty and accepted by the other parties as an instrument related to the treaty.

3.   There shall be taken into account, together with the context:

    (a) any subsequent agreement between the parties regarding the interpretation of the treaty or the application of its provisions;

    (b) any subsequent practice in the application of the treaty which establishes the agreement of the parties regarding its interpretation;

    (c) any relevant rules of international law applicable in the relations between the parties.

4.   A special meaning shall be given to a term if it is established that the parties so intended.

Article 32: Supplementary means of interpretation

Recourse may be had to supplementary means of interpretation, including the preparatory work of the treaty and the circumstances of its conclusion, in order to confirm the meaning resulting from the application of article 31, or to determine the meaning when the interpretation according to article 31:

(a)   leaves the meaning ambiguous or obscure; or

(b)   leads to a result which is manifestly absurd or unreasonable.

Annex III: The Right to Strike in National Constitutions

Country	Reference to 'Right to Strike' in the Constitution
Albania (1998) (rev 2016)	*Article 51* 1. The **right of an employee to strike** in connection with work relations is guaranteed. 2. Limitations on particular categories of employees may be established by law to assure essential social services.
Algeria (1989) (rev 2016)	*Article 71* The right to strike is recognized. It shall be exercised within the framework established by the law. The law may prohibit or restrict the exercise of the right to strike in the fields of national defense and security, or for services and public activities which are of vital interest to the community.

(continued)

(Continued)

Country	Reference to 'Right to Strike' in the Constitution
Angola (2010)	*Article 51* 1. Workers shall have the **right to strike.** 2. Lock-outs shall be prohibited and employers may not bring a company totally or partially to standstill by forbidding workers access to workplaces or similar as a means of influencing the outcome of labour conflicts. 3. The law shall regulate the exercise of the **right to strike** and shall establish limitations on the services and activities considered essential and urgent in terms of meeting vital social needs.
Argentina (1994)	*Article 14bis* Trade unions are hereby guaranteed: to conclude collective bargaining agreements; to resort to conciliation and arbitration; **the right to strike**. Union representatives shall enjoy the guarantees necessary for the performance of their union tasks and those relating to the permanence of their employment.
Armenia (1995) (rev 2015)	*Article 58* 1. Workers shall have the **right to strike** for the protection of their economic, social, or labor interests. The procedure of conducting a strike shall be stipulated by law. 2. The right to a strike may be restricted only by law with the aim of protecting public interests or the fundamental rights and freedoms of others.
Azerbaijan (1995) (rev 2016)	*Article 36* I. Everyone has the **right to strike**, both individually and together with others. II. Right to strike for persons working based on employment contracts may be restricted only in cases prescribed by law. Soldiers and civilians employed in the Armed Forces of the Republic of Azerbaijan have no right to go on strike. III. Individual and collective labor disputes are settled in accordance with procedure prescribed by law. IV. Except as prescribed by law, a lockout is prohibited.
Belarus (1994) (rev 2004)	*Article 41* Citizens shall have the right to protection of their economic and social interests, including the right to form trade unions and conclude collective contracts (agreements), and the **right to strike**.
Benin (1990)	*Article 31* The State shall recognize and guarantee **the right to strike**. Each worker may defend, under the conditions provided by law, his rights and interests whether individually, whether collectively, or by trade union action. The right to strike shall be exercised under conditions defined by law.

(continued)

(Continued)

Country	Reference to 'Right to Strike' in the Constitution
Plurinational State of Bolivia (2009)	*Article 53* **The right to strike** is guaranteed as the exercise of the legal power of workers to suspend work to defend their rights, in accordance with the law.
Brazil (1988) (rev 2014)	*Article 9* The **right to strike** is guaranteed, it being the competence of workers to decide on the advisability of exercising it and on the interests to defend thereby.
Bulgaria (1991) (rev 2015)	*Article 50* Workers and employees shall have the **right to strike** in defence of their collective economic and social interests. This right shall be exercised in accordance with conditions and procedures established by law.
Burkina Faso (1991) (rev 2012)	*Article 22* The **right to strike** is guaranteed. It is exercised conforming to the laws in force.
Burundi (2005)	*Article 37* The rights to establish unions and to affiliate with them, as well as the **right to strike** are recognized. The law may regulate the exercise of these rights and prohibit certain groups of people from striking. In all cases, these rights are prohibited to members of security or defense forces.
Cambodia (1993) (rev 2008)	*Article 37* The **rights to strike** and to organize peaceful demonstrations shall be implemented and exercised within the framework of law.
Cameroon (1972) (rev 2008)	Principle 16 — the freedom of communication, of expression, of the press, of assembly, of association, and of trade unionism, as well as the **right to strike** shall be guaranteed under the conditions fixed by law;
Cape Verde (1992)	*Article 66* (1) The **right to strike** shall be guaranteed; workers have the right to decide on the occasions to strike and the interests which the strike is intended to defend. (2) The law shall regulate the exercise of the right to strike. (3) Lock-outs shall be prohibited.
Central African Republic (2016)	*Article 12* Freedom of association is guaranteed and is exercised freely within the framework of the laws which regulate it. Any worker can affiliate with the union of their choice and defend their rights and interests through trade union action.

(continued)

(Continued)

Country	Reference to 'Right to Strike' in the Constitution
	The **right to strike** is guaranteed and is exercised within the framework of the laws which regulate it and may, in no case, infringe either the freedom to work, or the free exercise of the right of property.
Chad (1996) (rev 2005)	*Article 29* The **right to strike** is recognized. It is exercised within the limits of the laws regulating it.
Colombia (1991) (rev 2015)	*Article 56* The **right to strike** is guaranteed, except in the case of essential public services defined by the legislature. An Act shall regulate this right. A permanent commission composed of the government, the representatives of employers, and of workers shall promote sound labor relations, contribute to the settlement of collective labor disputes, and coordinate wage and labor policies. An Act shall regulate their makeup and functioning.
Congo (2015)	*Article 32* With the exception of agents of public security, the trade union freedoms and **the right to strike** within the conditions established by the law.
Democratic Republic of the Congo (2005) (rev 2011)	*Article 39* The **right to strike** is recognized and guaranteed. It is exercised under the conditions specified by the law which can forbid it or limit its exercise in the domains of national defense and of security or for any [public] activity or public service of vital interest for the Nation.
Costa Rica (1949) (rev 2015)	*Article 61* The right of employers to lock-out and of workers **to strike** is recognized, except in the public services, in accordance with the determination made of them by the law and in accordance with the regulations that it establishes, which must overrule any act of coercion or of violence.
Côte d'Ivoire (2016)	*Article 17* The right to belong to a trade union and the **right to strike** is accorded to workers in the private sector and to officials of the Public Administration. These rights are exercised within the limits determined by law.
Croatia (1991) (rev 2013)	*Article 60* The **right to strike** shall be guaranteed. The **right to strike** may be restricted in the armed forces, the police, the civil service and public services as specified by law.

(continued)

(Continued)

Country	Reference to 'Right to Strike' in the Constitution
Cyprus (1960) (rev 2013)	*Article 27* 1. The **right to strike** is recognised and its exercise may be regulated by law for the purposes only of safeguarding the security of the Republic or the constitutional order or the public order or the public safety or the maintenance of supplies and services essential to the life of the inhabitants or the protection of the rights and liberties guaranteed by this Constitution to any person. 2. The members of the armed forces, of the police and of the gendarmerie shall not have the right to strike. A law may extend such prohibition to the members of the public service.
Czech Republic (1992) (rev 2013)	*Article 27* (1) Everyone has the right to associate freely with others for the protection of his economic and social interests. (2) Trade unions shall be established independently of the state. No limits may be placed upon the number of trade union organizations, nor may any of them be given preferential treatment in a particular enterprise or sector of industry. (3) The activities of trade unions and the formation and activities of similar associations for the protection of economic and social interests may be limited by law in the case of measures necessary in a democratic society for the protection of the security of the state, public order, or the rights and freedoms of others. (4) The **right to strike** is guaranteed under the conditions provided for by law; this right does not appertain to judges, prosecutors, or members of the armed forces or security corps.
Djibouti (1992) (rev 2010)	*Article 15* All citizens have the right to constitute associations and trade unions freely, under reserve of conforming to the formalities ordered in the laws and regulations. The **right to strike** is recognized. It is exercised within the framework of the laws which govern it. It may in no case infringe the freedom to work.
Dominican Republic (2015)	*Article 62* (6) In order to resolve peaceful work conflicts, the **right of workers to strike** and of employers to lock out are recognized, only when they are exercised within the law, which shall dictate the means to guarantee the maintenance of public services or public utility.
Ecuador (2008) (rev 2015)	*Article 326* 14. The **right of workers** and their trade-union organizations **to strike** is recognized. The representatives of trade unions shall have the necessary guarantees in these cases. Employers shall have the right to lock-out pursuant to the law.

(continued)

(Continued)

Country	Reference to 'Right to Strike' in the Constitution
Egypt (2014)	Article 15: Right to strike: **Striking peacefully** is a right which is organized by law.
El Salvador (1983) (rev 2014)	*Article 48* Employers have the right to lock out and workers the **right to strike,** except in the case of indispensable public services that are established by law. To exercise these rights, no previous approval shall be necessary, after having procured the solution to the conflict which generates them through stages of peaceful solution established by law. The effects of the strike or suspension are antedated to the moment that these initiate. The law shall regulate these rights with respect to their exercise and conditions.
Equatorial Guinea (1991) (rev 2012)	*Article 10* The **right to strike** is recognized and is exercised in accordance with the conditions provided by the law.
Estonia (1992)	*Article 29* Everyone may freely belong to unions and federations of employees and employers. Unions and federations of employees and employers may uphold their rights and lawful interests by means which are not prohibited by law. The conditions and procedure for the exercise of the **right to strike** shall be provided by law.
Ethiopia (1994)	*Article 42* 1. (a) Factory and service workers, farmers, farm labourers, other rural workers and government employees whose work compatibility allows for it and who are below a certain level of responsibility, have the right to form associations to improve their conditions of employment and economic well-being. This right includes the right to form trade unions and other associations to bargain collectively with employers or other organizations that affect their interests. (b) Categories of persons referred to in paragraph (a) of this sub-Article has the right to express grievances, including the **right to strike.** (c) Government employees who enjoy the rights provided under paragraphs (a) and (b) of this sub-Article shall be determined by law.
France (1958) (rev 2008)	*Preamble to the Constitution of 1946* All men may defend their rights and interests through union action and may belong to the union of their choice. The **right to strike** shall be exercised within the framework of the laws governing it.

(continued)

(Continued)

Country	Reference to 'Right to Strike' in the Constitution
Georgia (1995) (rev 2013)	*Article 33* The **right to strike** shall be recognised. Procedure of exercising this right shall be determined by law. The law shall also establish the guarantees for the functioning of services of vital importance.
Greece (1975) (rev 2008)	*Article 23* 1. The State shall adopt due measures safeguarding the freedom to unionise and the unhindered exercise of related rights against any infringement thereon within the limits of the law. 2. **Strike constitutes a right** to be exercised by lawfully established trade unions in order to protect and promote the financial and the general labour interests of working people. Strikes of any nature whatsoever are prohibited in the case of judicial functionaries and those serving in the security corps. The **right to strike** shall be subject to the specific limitations of the law regulating this right in the case of public servants and employees of local government agencies and of public law legal persons as well as in the case of the employees of all types of enterprises of a public nature or of public benefit, the operation of which is of vital importance in serving the basic needs of the society as a whole. These limitations may not be carried to the point of abolishing the right to strike or hindering the lawful exercise thereof.
Guatemala (1985) (rev 1993)	Article 104 The **right to strike** and to lock-out exercised in accordance with the law, after all conciliation procedures have been exhausted, is recognized. These rights can be exercised solely for reasons of economic-social order. The laws shall establish the cases and situations where the strike and work stoppage will not be allowed. Article 116 The **right to strike** of the workers of the State and its decentralized and autonomous entities is recognized. This right can only be exercised in the form provided by the law of the matter and in no case may it affect the provision [atención] of the essential public services.
Guinea (2010)	*Article 20* Everyone has the right to affiliate to the union of their choice and to defend their rights through union action. Each worker has the right to participate, through their representatives, to the determination of the conditions of work The **right to strike** is recognized. It is exercised within the framework of the laws that govern it. It may not in any case infringe the freedom to work.

(continued)

(Continued)

Country	Reference to 'Right to Strike' in the Constitution
Guinea-Bissau (1984) (rev 1996)	*Article 47* 1. It is recognized that all workers have the **right to strike** in accordance with the law, and they are entitled to define the professional interest to be defended by means of the strike; the law shall establish the limitations on strikes in essential services and activities in the interests of the overriding needs of society. 2. The lock-out is forbidden.
Guyana (1980) (rev 2016)	*Article 147* (1) Except with his or her own consent, no person shall be hindered in the enjoyment of his or her freedom of assembly, association and freedom to demonstrate peacefully, that to say, his or her right to assemble freely, to demonstrate peacefully and to associate with other persons and in particular to form or belong to political parties, trade unions or other associations for the protection of his or her interests. (2) Except with his or her own consent no person shall be hindered in the enjoyment of his or her **freedom to strike**. (3) Neither an employer nor a trade union shall be deprived of the right to enter into collective agreements.
Haiti (1987) (rev 2012)	*Article 35.5* The **right to strike** is recognized under the limits set by law.
Honduras (1982)	*Article 128 (13)* Laws governing the relations between employers and workers are matters of public order. All acts, stipulations or agreements that involve the waiver, diminution or restriction or evasion of the following guarantees shall be void: The **right to strike** or to lockout is recognized. The law shall regulate its exercise and may subject it to special restrictions in specified public services.
Hungary (2011) (rev 2016)	*Article 17* (2) Employees, employers and their organisations shall have the right, as provided for by an Act, to negotiate with each other and conclude collective agreements, **and to take collective action to defend their interests, including the right of workers to discontinue work.**
Italy (1947)	*Art 40* The **right to strike** shall be exercised in compliance with the law.
Kazakhstan (1995) (rev 2017)	*Article 24* 3. The right to individual and collective labor disputes with the use of methods for resolving them, stipulated by law including the **right to strike**, shall be recognized.

(continued)

(Continued)

Country	Reference to 'Right to Strike' in the Constitution
Kenya (2010)	*Article 41* (2) Every worker has the right – (c) to form, join or participate in the activities and programmes of a trade union; and (d) **to go on strike.**
Republic of Korea (1948)	*Article 33* 1. To enhance working conditions, workers shall have the right to independent association, collective bargaining and **collective action.** 2. Only those public officials who are designated by law shall have the right to association, collective bargaining and collective action. 3. The right to **collective action** of workers employed by important defense industries may be either restricted or denied as prescribed by law.
Kyrgyzstan (2010)	*Article 43* Everyone shall have the **right to strike.**
Latvia (1922) (rev 2016)	*Article 108* Employed persons have the right to a collective labour agreement, and the **right to strike.** The State shall protect the freedom of trade unions.
Lithuania (1992)	*Article 51* While defending their economic and social interests, employees shall have the **right to strike.** The limitations of this right and the conditions and procedure for its implementation shall be established by law.
Luxembourg (1868) (rev 2009)	*Article 11* (4) The law guarantees the right to work and the State ensures to each citizen the exercise of this right. The law guarantees trade union freedoms and organizes the **right to strike.**
Republic of North Macedonia (2019)	*Article 38* The **right to strike** is guaranteed. The law may restrict the conditions for the exercise of the right to strike in the armed forces, the police and administrative bodies.
Madagascar (2010)	*Article 33* The **right to strike** is recognized without prejudice to the continuity of the public service or the fundamental interests of the Nation. The other conditions for exercising this right are set by law.

(continued)

(Continued)

Country	Reference to 'Right to Strike' in the Constitution
Malawi (1994) (rev 2017)	*Article 31* 4. The State shall take measures to ensure **the right to withdraw labour.**
Maldives (2008)	*Article 31* Every person employed in the Maldives and all other workers have the **freedom to stop work and to strike** in order to protest.
Mali (1992)	*Article 21* The **right to strike** is guaranteed. It shall be exercised within the limits of the laws and regulations then in force.
Mauritania (1991) (rev 2012)	*Article 14* The **right to strike** is recognized. It is exercised within the framework of the laws that regulate it. The strike may be forbidden by the law for all public services or activities of vital interest to the Nation. It is forbidden in the domains of Defense and of National Security.
Mexico (1917) (rev 2019)	*Article 123* XVII: The laws shall **recognize strikes** and lockouts as rights of workers and employers. XVIII: Strikes shall be legal when their purpose is to attain equilibrium between the several factors of production, harmonizing the rights of workers with those of capital. In the case of public services, the workers must notify the labor tribunals, at least ten days in advance, about the date agreed for the suspension of work. Strikes shall be considered as illegal only when the majority of strikers carry out violent acts against persons or property, or in the event of war, when the workers belong to governmental establishments or services.
Republic of Moldova (1994)	*Article 45* (1) The **right to strike** shall be acknowledged. Strikes may be unleashed only with the view of protection the employees' professional interests of economic and social nature. (2) The law shall set forth conditions governing the exercise of the right to strike, as well as the responsibility for illegal unleash of the strikes.
Montenegro (2007) (rev 2013)	*Article 66* The employed shall have the **right to strike.** The right to strike may be limited to the employed in the Army, police, state bodies and public service with the aim to protect public interest, in accordance with the law.

(continued)

(Continued)

Country	Reference to 'Right to Strike' in the Constitution
Morocco (2011)	*Article 29* The freedoms of reunion, of assembly, of peaceful demonstration, of association and of trade union and political membership [appartenance], are guaranteed. The **right to strike** is guaranteed. An organic law establishes the conditions and the modalities of its exercise.
Mozambique (2004)	*Article 87* 1. Workers shall have the **right to strike**, and the law shall regulate the exercise of this right. 2. The law shall restrict the exercise of the **right to strike** in essential services and activities, in the interest of the pressing needs of society and of national security. 3. Lock outs shall be prohibited.
Namibia (1990) (rev 2014)	*Article 21* 1. All persons shall have the right to: e. freedom of association, which shall include freedom to form and join associations or unions, including trade unions and political parties; f. **withhold their labour** without being exposed to criminal penalties;
Nicaragua (1987) (rev 2014)	*Article 83* **The right to strike** is recognized.
Niger (2010) (rev 2017)	*Article 34* The State recognizes and guarantees the right to freedom of association and the **right to strike** which are exercised within the conditions specified by the laws and regulations in force.
Panama (1972) (rev 2004)	*Article 69* The **right to strike** is recognized. The law shall regulate the exercise of this right, including special restrictions for public service it establishes.
Paraguay (1992) (rev 2011)	*Article 98* All workers in the public and private sectors have the **right to strike** in the case of conflict of interests. The employers enjoy the right to lock-out in the same conditions. The rights to strike and to lock-out do not extend to members of the Armed Forces or the police. The law will regulate the exercise of these rights, so that they do not affect public services essential to the community.

(continued)

(Continued)

Country	Reference to 'Right to Strike' in the Constitution
Peru (1993) (rev 2009)	*Article 28* The State recognizes **the right of workers** to join trade unions, to engage in collective bargaining, and **to strike**. It ensures their democratic exercise by: 1. Guaranteeing freedom to form trade unions. 2. Encouraging collective bargaining and promoting peaceful settlement to labor disputes. Collective agreements are binding in the matters concerning their terms. 3. Regulating the right to strike so that it is exercised in harmony with the social interest. It defines exceptions and limitations. *Article 42* The rights of civil servants to unionize and strike are recognized. State officials with decision-making powers, those in posts of trust or of management, as well as members of the Armed Forces and the National Police are not included herein.
Philippines (1987)	*Section 3* The State shall afford full protection to labor, local and overseas, organized and unorganized, and promote full employment and equality of employment opportunities for all. It shall guarantee the rights of all workers to self-organization, collective bargaining and negotiations, and peaceful concerted activities, including the **right to strike** in accordance with law. They shall be entitled to security of tenure, humane conditions of work, and a living wage. They shall also participate in policy and decision-making processes affecting their rights and benefits as may be provided by law.
Poland (1997) (rev 2009)	*Article 59(3)* Trade unions shall have the **right to organize strikes** or other forms of protest subject to limitations specified by statute. In the public interest, statutes may limit or prohibit the strikes by specified categories of workers or in specific sectors.
Portugal (1976) (rev 2005)	*Article 57* 1. The **right to strike** shall be guaranteed. 2. Workers shall be responsible for defining the scope of the interests that are to be defended by a strike and the law shall not limit that scope. 3. The law shall define the conditions under which such services as are needed to ensure the safety and maintenance of equipment and facilities and such minimum services as are indispensable to the fulfilment of essential social needs are provided during strikes. 4. Lock-outs shall be prohibited.

(continued)

(Continued)

Country	Reference to 'Right to Strike' in the Constitution
Romania (1991) (rev 2003)	*Article 43* (1) The employees have the **right to strike** in the defence of their professional, economic and social interests. (2) The law shall regulate the conditions and limits governing the exercise of this right, as well as the guarantees necessary to ensure the essential services for the society.
Russian Federation (1993) (rev 2014)	*Article 37* 4. The right of individual and collective labour disputes with the use of the methods for their resolution, which are provided for by federal law, including the **right to strike**, shall be recognized.
Rwanda (2003) (rev 2015)	*Article 33* The **right of workers to strike** is recognised and exercised within the limits provided for by the law. The exercise of this right shall not infringe upon the freedom at work, which is guaranteed to everyone.
San Marino (1974)	*Article 9* Work is a right and duty of all citizens. The law shall guarantee to workers a fair remuneration, annual holidays, weekly rest and the right to strike.
Sao Tome and Principe (1975) (rev 2003)	*Article 43* All the workers have rights: b) To labour-union freedom, as a means of promoting their unity, defending their legitimate rights and protecting their interests; f) **To strike**, under terms to be regulated by law, taking into account the interests of the workers and of the national economy.
Senegal (2001) (rev 2016)	*Article 25* The **right to strike** is recognized. It is exercised within the framework of the laws which govern it. It may not in any case infringe the freedom to work, or place the enterprise in peril.
Serbia (2006)	*Article 61* The employed shall have the **right to strike** in accordance with the law and collective agreement. The right to strike may be restricted only by the law in accordance with nature or type of business activity.
Seychelles (1993) (rev 2017)	*Article 35* g) subject to such restrictions as are necessary in a democratic society, and necessary for safeguarding public order, for the protection of health or morals and the rights and freedoms of others, to ensure the right of workers to organise trade unions and to guarantee the **right to strike**.

(continued)

(Continued)

Country	Reference to 'Right to Strike' in the Constitution
Slovakia (1992) (rev 2017)	*Article 37* (4) The **right to strike** is guaranteed. The conditions shall be laid down by law. Judges, prosecutors, members of the armed forces and armed corps, and members and employees of the fire and rescue brigades do not have this right.
Slovenia (1991) (rev 2016)	*Article 77* Employees have the **right to strike**. Where required by the public interest, the right to strike may be restricted by law, with due consideration given to the type and nature of activity involved.
Somalia (2012)	*Article 24* 1. Every person shall have the right to: (a) **Assemble freely** with other persons and in particular to form or belong to trade unions or other associations for the protection of his/her interests; 2. The workers of the Transitional Federal Government of Somalia shall have the right to form Trade Unions for the protection of their interests as specified by law.
South Africa (1996) (rev 2012)	*Article 23* 1. Everyone has the right to fair labour practices. 2. Every worker has the right a. to form and join a trade union; b. to participate in the activities and programmes of a trade union; and c. **to strike.**
Spain (1978) (rev 2011)	*Section 28* (2) The **right of workers to strike** in defence of their interests is recognized. The law governing the exercise of this right shall establish the safeguards necessary to ensure the maintenance of essential public services.
Suriname (1987) (rev 1992)	*Article 33* The **right to strike** is recognized subject to the limitations which stem from the law.
Sweden (2012)	*Article 14* A trade union or an employer or employers' association shall be entitled to take **industrial action** unless otherwise provided in an act of law or under an agreement.

(continued)

(Continued)

Country	Reference to 'Right to Strike' in the Constitution
Switzerland (1999) (rev 2014)	*Article 28* 1. Employees, employers and their organisations have the right to join together in order to protect their interests, to form associations and to join or not to join such associations. 2. Disputes must wherever possible be resolved through negotiation or mediation. 3. Strikes and lock outs are lawful if they relate to labor relations and if they do not contravene any requirements to preserve labor peace or to undertake conciliation. 4. The law may prohibit certain categories of person from taking strike action.
Syrian Arab Republic (2012)	*Article 44* Citizens shall have the right to assemble, **peacefully demonstrate and to strike** from work within the framework of the Constitution principles, and the law shall regulate the exercise of these rights.
Timor-Leste (2002)	*Section 51* 1. Every worker has the **right to resort to strike**, the exercise of which shall be regulated by law. 2. The law shall determine the conditions under which services are provided, during a strike, that are necessary for the safety and maintenance of equipment and facilities, as well as minimum services that are necessary to meet essential social needs.
Togo (1992) (rev 2007)	*Article 39* The **right to strike** is recognized as to workers. It is exercised within the framework of the laws that regulate it. The workers may constitute unions or affiliate with the unions of their choice. Any worker may defend, within the conditions provided for by the law, their rights and interests, either individually, collectively or by union action.
Tunisia (2014)	*Article 36* The right to join and form unions is guaranteed, **including the right to strike**. This right does not apply to the national army. The right to strike does not apply to the forces of internal security and to customs officers.

(continued)

(Continued)

Country	Reference to 'Right to Strike' in the Constitution
Turkey (1982) (rev 2017)	*Article 54* Workers have the **right to strike** if a dispute arises during the collective bargaining process. The procedures and conditions governing the exercise of this right and the employer's recourse to a lockout, the scope of both actions, and the exceptions to which they are subject shall be regulated by law. The **right to strike**, and lockout shall not be exercised in a manner contrary to the principle of goodwill to the detriment of society, and in a manner damaging national wealth. During a strike, the labour union is liable for any material damage caused in a work-place where the strike is being held, as a result of deliberately negligent behaviour by the workers and the labour union. The circumstances and places in which strikes and lockouts may be prohibited or postponed shall be regulated by law. In cases where a strike or a lockout is prohibited or postponed, the dispute shall be settled by the Supreme Arbitration Board at the end of the period of postponement. The disputing parties may apply to the Supreme Arbitration Board by mutual agreement at any stage of the dispute. The decisions of the Supreme Arbitration Board shall be final and have the force of a collective bargaining agreement. The organisation and functions of the Supreme Arbitration Board shall be regulated by law. Politically motivated strikes and lockouts, solidarity strikes and lockouts, occupation of work premises, labour go-slows, and other forms of obstruction are prohibited. Those who refuse to go on strike, shall in no way be barred from working at their work-place by strikers.
Uganda (1995) (rev 2017)	*Article 40* 3. Every worker has a right – 1. c. to **withdraw his or her labour** according to law.
Ukraine (1996) (rev 2016)	*Article 44* Those who are employed shall have the **right to strike** in order to protect their economic and social interests. A procedure for exercising the right to strike shall be established by law taking into account the necessity to ensure national security, public health protection, and rights and freedoms of others. No one shall be forced to participate or not to participate in a strike. The prohibition of a strike shall be possible only on the basis of the law.

(continued)

(Continued)

Country	Reference to 'Right to Strike' in the Constitution
Uruguay (1967) (rev 2014)	*Article 57* The law shall promote the organization of trade unions, according them charters and issuing regulations for their recognition as juridical persons. It shall likewise promote the creation of tribunals of conciliation and arbitration. It is declared that the **strike is a right of trade unions**. On that basis, regulations shall be made governing its exercise and effect.
Bolivarian Republic of Venezuela (1999) (rev 2009)	*Article 97* All workers in the public and private sector have the right to strike, subject to such conditions as may be established by law.
Zimbabwe (2017)	*Article 65* **3.** Except for members of the security services, every employee has the right to participate in collective job action, **including the right to strike**, sit in, withdraw their labour and to take other similar concerted action, but a law may restrict the exercise of this right in order to maintain essential services.

INDEX

Introductory Note

References such as '178–79' indicate (not necessarily continuous) discussion of a topic across a range of pages. Wherever possible in the case of topics with many references, these have either been divided into sub-topics or only the most significant discussions of the topic are listed. Because the entire work is about the 'right to strike', the use of this term (and certain others which occur constantly throughout the book) as an entry point has been restricted. Information will be found under the corresponding detailed topics.